Workshop on Graph-Based Methods for Natural Language Processing 2009

(TextGraphs-4)

Held at ACL-IJCNLP 2009

Singapore
7 August 2009

ISBN: 978-1-61738-454-7

Printed from e-media with permission by:

Curran Associates, Inc.
57 Morehouse Lane
Red Hook, NY 12571

Some format issues inherent in the e-media version may also appear in this print version.

Printed by Curran Associates, Inc. (2010)

Association for Computational Linguistics
209 N. Eighth Street
Stroudsburg, Pennsylvania 18360

Phone: 1-570-476-8006
Fax: 1-570-476-0860

acl@aclweb.org

Additional copies of this publication are available from:

Curran Associates, Inc.
57 Morehouse Lane
Red Hook, NY 12571 USA
Phone: 845-758-0400
Fax: 845-758-2634
Email: curran@proceedings.com
Web: www.proceedings.com

Introduction

The last few years have shown a steady increase in applying graph-theoretic models to computational linguistics. In many NLP applications, entities can be naturally represented as nodes in a graph and relations between them can be represented as edges. There have been extensive research showing that graph-based representations of linguistic units such as words, sentences and documents give rise to novel and efficient solutions in a variety of NLP tasks, ranging from part-of-speech tagging, word sense disambiguation and parsing, to information extraction, semantic role labeling, summarization, and sentiment analysis.

More recently, complex network theory, a popular modeling paradigm in statistical mechanics and physics of complex systems, was proven to be a promising tool in understanding the structure and dynamics of languages. Complex network based models have been applied to areas as diverse as language evolution, acquisition, historical linguistics, mining and analyzing the social networks of blogs and emails, link analysis and information retrieval, information extraction, and representation of the mental lexicon. In order to make this field of research more visible, this time the workshop incorporated a special theme on *Cognitive and Social Dynamics of Languages in the framework of Complex Networks*. Cognitive dynamics of languages include topics focused primarily on language acquisition, which can be extended to language change (historical linguistics) and language evolution as well. Since the latter phenomena are also governed by social factors, we can further classify them under social dynamics of languages. In addition, social dynamics of languages also include topics such as mining the social networks of blogs and emails. A collection of articles pertaining to this special theme will be compiled in a special issue of the *Computer Speech and Language* journal.

This volume contains papers accepted for presentation at the TextGraphs-4 2009 Workshop on Graph-Based Methods for Natural Language Processing. The event took place on August 7, 2009, in Suntec, Singapore, immediately following ACL/IJCNLP 2009, the Joint conference of the 47th Annual Meeting of the Association for Computational Linguistics and the 4th International Joint Conference on Natural Language Processing of the Asian Federation of Natural Language Processing. Being the fourth workshop on this topic, we were able to build on the success of the previous TextGraphs workshops, held as part of HLT-NAACL 2006, HLT-NAACL 2007 and Coling 2008. It aimed at bringing together researchers working on problems related to the use of graph-based algorithms for NLP and on pure graph-theoretic methods, as well as those applying complex networks for explaining language dynamics. Like last year, TextGraphs-4 has also been endorsed by SIGLEX.

We issued calls for both regular and short papers. Nine regular and three short papers were accepted for presentation, based on the careful reviews of our program committee. Our sincere thanks to all the program committee members for their thoughtful, high quality and elaborate reviews, especially considering our extremely tight time frame for reviewing. The papers appearing in this volume have surely benefited from their expert feedback. This year's workshop attracted papers employing graphs in a wide range of settings and we are therefore proud to present a very diverse program. We received quite a few papers on discovering semantic similarity through random walks. Daniel Ramage et al. explore random walk based methods to discover semantic similarity in texts, while Eric Yeh et al. attempt to discover semantic relatedness through random walks on the Wikipedia. Ameç Herdağdelen et al. describes a method for measuring semantic relatedness with vector space models and random walks.

Another set of papers were focused on popular graph-based machine learning techniques including classification and clustering. Swapna Somasundaran et al. employ opinion graphs for the purpose of polarity and discourse classification. Delip Rao and David Yarowsky propose a semi-supervised classification method on large scale graphs using map reduce. Yoshimi Suzuki and Fumiyo Fukumoto classify Japanese polysemous verbs using fuzzy C-means clustering method. Linlin Li and Caroline Sporleder discuss a cohesion graph based approach for unsupervised recognition of literal and nonliteral use of multiword expressions. Zheng Chen and Heng Ji propose a graph-based method for event coreference resolution. Scott Martens presents a quantitative analysis of treebanks using frequent subtree mining methods.

In the special theme category, we could select three papers. Sitabhra Sinha et al. present a paper pertaining to a topic that has recently been quite controversial. They show that a thorough network analysis reveals a structure indicative of syntax in the corpus of undeciphered Indus civilization inscriptions. Martijn Wieling and John Nerbonne discuss a bipartite spectral graph partitioning method to co-cluster varieties and sound correspondences in dialectology. David Ellis discusses social (distributed) language modeling, clustering and dialectometry.

Finally, we would like to thank Vittorio Loreto from University of Rome "La Sapienza" for his invited speech on "Collective dynamics of social annotation." The talk was highly interesting and very pertinent to the special theme of the workshop. We are also grateful to Microsoft Research India for sponsoring the travel and accommodations for the invited speaker.

Monojit Choudhury, Samer Hassan, Animesh Mukherjee and Smaranda Muresan
August 2009

Organizers:

Monojit Choudhury, Microsoft Research (India)
Samer Hassan, University of North Texas (USA)
Animesh Mukherjee, Indian Institute of Technology (India)
Smaranda Muresan, Rutgers University (USA)

Program Committee:

Eneko Agirre, Basque Country University (Spain)
Edo Airoldi, Harvard University (USA)
Alain Barrat, C.N.R.S. (France)
Pushpak Bhattacharyya, IIT Bombay (India)
Chris Biemann, Powerset (USA)
Andras Csomai, Google Inc. (USA)
Hang Cui, Yahoo Inc (USA)
Hal Daume III, University of Utah (USA)
Mona Diab, Columbia University (USA)
Santo Fortunato, ISI Foundation (Italy)
Michael Gammon, Microsoft Research Redmond (USA)
Niloy Ganguly, IIT Kharagpur (India)
Lise Getoor, University of Maryland (USA)
Simon Kirby, University of Edinburgh (UK)
Ben Leong, University of Delaware (USA)
Vittorio Loreto, University of Rome "La Sapienza" (Italy)
Irina Matveeva, Accenture Technology Labs (USA)
Alexander Mehler, Universitt Bielefeld (Germany)
Rada Mihalcea, University of North Texas (USA)
Roberto Navigli, University of Rome "La Sapienza" (Italy)
John Nerbonne, University of Groningen (Netherlands)
Dragomir Radev, University of Michigan (USA)
Raghavendra Udupa, Microsoft Research (India)
Xiaojun Wan, Peking University (China)
Sren Wichmann, MPI for Evolutionary Anthropology (Germany)

Invited Speaker:

Vittorio Loreto, University of Rome "La Sapienza" (Italy)

Table of Contents

Conference Program

Friday, August 7, 2009

Session I: Opening

8:30–8:45 Inauguration by Chairs

8:45–9:48 Invited Talk by Prof. Vittorio Loreto

9:48–10:00 *Social (distributed) language modeling, clustering and dialectometry*
David Ellis

10:00–10:30 Coffee Break

Session II: Special Theme

10:30–10:55 *Network analysis reveals structure indicative of syntax in the corpus of undeciphered Indus civilization inscriptions*
Sitabhra Sinha, Raj Kumar Pan, Nisha Yadav, Mayank Vahia and Iravatham Mahadevan

10:55–11:20 *Bipartite spectral graph partitioning to co-cluster varieties and sound correspondences in dialectology*
Martijn Wieling and John Nerbonne

11:20–12:10 Panel Discussion

Session III: Semantics

13:50–14:15 *Random Walks for Text Semantic Similarity*
Daniel Ramage, Anna N. Rafferty and Christopher D. Manning

14:15–14:40 *Classifying Japanese Polysemous Verbs based on Fuzzy C-means Clustering*
Yoshimi Suzuki and Fumiyo Fukumoto

14:40–15:05 *WikiWalk: Random walks on Wikipedia for Semantic Relatedness*
Eric Yeh, Daniel Ramage, Christopher D. Manning, Eneko Agirre and Aitor Soroa

15:05–15:18 *Measuring semantic relatedness with vector space models and random walks*
Amaç Herdağdelen, Katrin Erk and Marco Baroni

Friday, August 7, 2009 (continued)

Invited Talk
Collective Dynamics of Social Annotation

Vittorio Loreto
Dipartimento di Fisica, "Sapienza" Università di Roma,
Piazzale Aldo Moro 5, 00185 Roma, Italy
and
Complex Networks Lagrange Laboratory,
Institute for Scientific Interchange (ISI), Torino, Italy
vittorio.loreto@roma1.infn.it

The enormous increase of popularity and use of the WWW has led in the recent years to important changes in the ways people communicate. An interesting example of this fact is provided by the now very popular social annotation systems, through which users annotate resources (such as web pages or digital photographs) with text keywords dubbed tags. Collaborative tagging has been quickly gaining ground because of its ability to recruit the activity of web users into effectively organizing and sharing vast amounts of information. Understanding the rich emerging structures resulting from the uncoordinated actions of users calls for an interdisciplinary effort. In particular concepts borrowed from statistical physics, such as random walks, and the complex networks framework, can effectively contribute to the mathematical modeling of social annotation systems. First I will introduce a stochastic model of user behavior embodying two main aspects of collaborative tagging: (i) a frequency-bias mechanism related to the idea that users are exposed to each others tagging activity; (ii) a notion of memory, or aging of resources, in the form of a heavy-tailed access to the past state of the system. Remarkably, this simple modeling is able to account quantitatively for the observed experimental features with a surprisingly high accuracy. This points in the direction of a universal behavior of users who, despite the complexity of their own cognitive processes and the uncoordinated and selfish nature of their tagging activity, appear to follow simple activity patterns. Next I will show how the process of social annotation can be seen as a collective but uncoordinated exploration of an underlying semantic space, pictured as a graph, through a series of random walks. This modeling framework reproduces several aspects, so far unexplained, of social annotation, among which the peculiar growth of the size of the vocabulary used by the community and its complex network structure that represents an externalization of semantic structures grounded in cognition and typically hard to access.

Social (distributed) language modeling, clustering and dialectometry

David Ellis
Facebook
Palo Alto, CA
dellis@facebook.com

Abstract

We present ongoing work in a scalable, distributed implementation of over 200 million individual language models, each capturing a single user's dialect in a given language (multilingual users have several models). These have a variety of practical applications, ranging from spam detection to speech recognition, and dialectometrical methods on the social graph. Users should be able to view any content in their language (even if it is spoken by a small population), and to browse our site with appropriately translated interface (automatically generated, for locales with little crowd-sourced community effort).

1 Introduction

We approach several key questions from a data-driven (statistical) perspective, drawing on large, dynamic annotated corpora:

1. What social factors affect language change (and evolution)? How?

2. How do individuals adjust their speech or writing depending on context and audience? (e.g., register, formality, humor, reference)

3. What are the minimum requirements for a language (or dialect)? (e.g., number of speakers, corpus size)

4. Is a common language necessary for communication? Can a pidgin be predicted from its speaker-population?

To this end, we describe a framework for language modeling on the social graph, which incorporates similarity clustering and lays the groundwork for personalized (and multimodal) machine translation.

2 Related Work

Research on large scale language modeling (Brants et al., 2007) has addressed sharding, smoothing and integration with a machine translation pipeline. Our work takes a similar approach, using Hadoop (Borthakur, 2007) and Hive to query and process distributed data. Social annotations enhanced smoothing for language modeling in the context of information retrieval (Xu et al., 2007), and hierarchical Bayesian networks were used (Zhou et al., 2008) to incorporate user domain interest in such models. Language models are often used to detect spam, including in social bookmarking (Bogers and van den Bosch, 2008).

Proposed scoring models for social search (Schenkel et al., 2008) use friendship strengths and an extension of term frequency[1]. These could benefit from a deeper integration with friends' language models, perhaps to approximate a user-specific inverse document frequency, rather than treat each tag by a user as equally relevant to all his friends of a given (relationship) strength. Strehl et al. (2000) found that similarity clustering perform best using weighted graph partitioning.

3 Language Model

An individual's language model is a mixture of their locale (or another language they speak) and token frequencies from the content they produce (write) and consume (read). Since we have hundreds of milliions of users, each of whose language model can depend on a variety of data sources, it is essential to distribute these counts (and other figures derived from them) in a way that optimizes the efficiency of our access patterns[2].

We also tried clustering users, and representing the language of each as deviations from its neighbors (or the norm of the cluster). However,

[1] Called "socially-enhanced tag frequency".

[2] See Section 5 for discussion of a variety of use cases.

Proceedings of the 2009 Workshop on Graph-based Methods for Natural Language Processing, ACL-IJCNLP 2009, pages 1–4,
Suntec, Singapore, 7 August 2009.

there are significantly more edges than nodes in our graph (more friendships than people), so this alternative is less efficient.

An individual's language use varies greatly depending on his interlocutor or audience[3]. Messages I send (privately) to a friend differ in style from comments I make on a public photo of my nephew, which in turn differ from my writing style as realized in an academic or industry paper or article.

An obvious optimization is to describe a minimum spanning tree (MST) on the graph, where each edge is weighted according to the similarity of dialects associated with the nodes (individuals, groups or other entities) it connects. Then, language models of nodes connected by the MST can depend on each other's counts. Singletons default to the general language model from their locale.

3.1 Detecting Deviations

People who aren't friends (and have no mutual friends or other evident connection) may yet use more similar language than siblings. This example seems highly improbable or unnatural, and in fact serves as a good heuristic for detecting compromised, spam-sending accounts (even if not organized in a botnet).

If a user sends a message with high perplexity:

1. Their account is compromised, and being used to spam (or phish) their friends.
2. They are using a different language than usual. Users are often bilingual (sometimes multi)-, so we may not yet have realized they are proficient in a given language.
3. There may be a problem with the language model:
   (a) large vocabulary (tends to inflate perplexity)
   (b) genre mix (user interface v. user communication)

3.2 Locale Induction

A regional cluster of personal language models can be combined to create a new locale. A crowd-sourced translation process (Ellis, 2009) can thus be bootstrapped by indirect community contributions.

[3]This is not novel in or of itself, but the scale of our data and experiments should lead to finer-grained understanding, both of issues peculiar to a single language or its family, and of language universals (or.patterns; priors likely intuitively encoded).

4 Machine Translation

For an English-sepaking user, in order to optimize the probability of the target (translated) sentence given its source (Foreign), we follow Och and Ney's (2004) optimization of a set of feature functions:

$$\hat{\boldsymbol{e}} = \arg\max_{\boldsymbol{e}} \sum_{m=1}^{M} \lambda_m h_m(\boldsymbol{e}, \boldsymbol{f})$$

It is thus easy for us to aggregate scores from multiple language models (e.g., from individuals comprising your network of friends or others you interact with).

Our distributed, individual language models can be a component of personalized machine translation, where the target language may be a penpal's. Either the decoder incorporates the counts from user communications by supplementing the language model used in its n-best candidate search, or it uses the locale's general language model and factors in individual variance in a rescoring step.

We plan to offer inline statistical machine translation (SMT) of user-generated content, where the translation model combines features from:

1. Our (interface) translations corpus for the language pair
2. Related langauges or dialects[4]
3. Linguistic rules (Ellis, 2009), in some combination of:
   (a) Explicitly encoded
   (b) Induced from training corpora
   (c) Borrowed from related languages (esp. for relatively minor or resource-poor)

4.1 Sparse Data

Data sparseness is clearly an issue for modeling with this degree of specificity, so we explore a range of possible smoothing techniques, as well as methods for leveraging resources from related languages (Genzel, 2005). If a user signed up for Facebook last week, (s)he may not yet have connected with many friends or shared much content (which exacerbates the problem).

[4]e.g. Spanish (Argentina, Spain), Chinese (Mandarin, Cantonese (Hong Kong, Taiwan)), or Finnish and its neighbors: inc. Estonian, Sámi, Komi

Domain adaptation is also important, since the base corpus is for a user interface: usually more formal, less varied than conversation. Ideally, we would like to capture not only language change (diversion, creolization) but an individual's linguistic evolution in a variety of contexts:

- She learns a language, practices its use, becomes increasingly accustomed to its twists and turns (syntactic, lexical, morphological, etc.)
- His mood shifts, he moves into a new apartment or city, let alone grander (potentially dynamic) features of context
- A startup company is suddently more visible (e.g., resulting from press coverage, or a tech blogger's reference), and so an image (and website design, copy) revamp is in order.
- Afflicted with post-traumatic stress, after sensory deprivation, or in cases of neurological disorders or brain damage.

5 Similarity

We use a pipeline to cluster strings (to suggest translations) and users (based on language use):

1. Preprocessing
   - normalization (lowercasing)
   - {segment,{lemmat,token}iz}ation
2. Similarity (pick one)
   - fuzzy (hash) similarity[5]
   - string edit distance
   - phonetic (or phonological) edit distance
   - language model perplexity
   - KL-divergence (btn. language models)
3. Clustering (modular: select-an-algo)
   - hierarchical (agglomerative or divisive)
   - K-means (partitioning)
   - graph-theoretic methods (cover as opposed to cluster)

This is architected for ease of experimentation and modification, testing and tuning, so any combination of the above should be functional. Some applications of similarity require high accuracy but can be processed offline, whereas others need to be computed in less than ten milliseconds in response to a live query.

[5]i.e., Jaccard coefficient (Wikipedia, 2008)

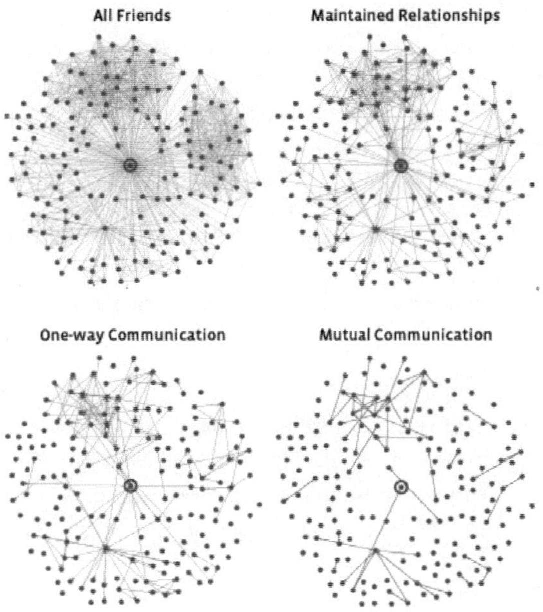

Figure 1: Visualization of a user's friends, where the extent of each type of relationship or communication is indicated by saturation (shade of blue) of the connection.

6 Evaluation

Although the components we use can be (and in most cases, have been) thoroughly evaluated in relative isolation, it is important to understand the consequences of their use in concert. Improvements to spam detection should be evident both in tests on annotated[6] data and in decreased reports or complaints from users.

User-generated metadata, in some cases a simple report of offensive content or a friend's compromised account, is a natural source of both labeled test data and training data. Our customer service processes are thus tightly integrated with machine learning efforts. See Figure 1 for communications in a small segment of the social graph.

7 Conclusion

Preliminary experiments with user-initiated machine translation of friend-generated content suggest it will soon be valuable. It is crucial to design this in a scalable way, such that it extends to arbitrarily many languages[7], both draws on and sup-

[6]Either a binary classification (spam or non-spam) or a gradient scale, possibly incorporating dimensions of phishiness, spamminess, or other types of solicitousness.

[7]Including underrepresented ones like Oshindonga.

ports our internationalization efforts, and should be useful on mobile devices (including in the spoken modality).

Our introductory questions (from Section 1) are far from fully answered, but we hope this work might help to address them.

1. The number and strength of connections, speed and frequency of communication, and diversity of languages individuals are exposed to all have strong influences on language change.

2. Stylistic variations in an individual's language are evident in that it can be more accurately captured as a mixture of models, each of which is suited to a specific situation, style, or set of interlocutors.

3. Two speakers is sufficient for a language. A small model can adequately describe a language, if each data point is a deviation from another language.

4. A common language is far from necessary for communication[8]. A set of arbitrary individuals' language models can be combined (and pruned, evolved) to derive the pidgin they might speak.

7.1 Future Work

Social natural language processing is (in a sense) in its infancy. We hope to capture aspects of its evolution, just as the field comes to better describe and understand ongoing changes in human languages. We have not yet satisfactorily answered our second question, but expect more fine-grained analyses to follow, using our framework to compare and contrast a variety of languages (from Bantu to Balinese) and phenomena (inside jokes, cross-linguistic usage of l33t and txt msg terms).

We hope to facilitate this by providing an API to allow researchers access to anonymized[9], aggregated data.

Acknowledgments

This technology is developed with support from i18n team (engineers, language managers and others) at Facebook, and all our international users. Thanks to our data scientists for the visualization of a user's friends, and the extent of communication connecting them.

[8] Photos, emoticons and tone of voice (for example) go a long way. We hope personalized (including speech-to-speech) translation will continue to bridge the language divide.

[9] Also honoring users' privacy settings.

References

Toine Bogers and Antal van den Bosch. 2008. Using language models for spam detection in social bookmarking. In *Proceedings of the ECML/PKDD Discovery Challenge*.

Dhruba Borthakur, 2007. *The Hadoop Distributed File System: Architecture and Design*. The Apache Software Foundation.

Thorsten Brants, Ashok C. Popat, Peng Xu, Franz J. Och, and Jeffrey Dean. 2007. Large language models in machine translation. In *Proceedings of the 2007 Joint Conference on Empirical Methods in Natural Language Processing and Computational Natural Language Learning (EMNLP-CoNLL)*, pages 858–867.

David Ellis. 2009. A case study in community-driven translation of a fast-changing website. In *Proceedings of the 13th International Conference on Human-Computer Interaction HCII (to appear)*, San Diego, California, USA.

Dmitriy Genzel. 2005. *Creating Algorithms for Parsers and Taggers for Resource-Poor Languages Using a Related Resource-Rich Language*. Ph.D. thesis, Brown University.

Franz Josef Och and Hermann Ney. 2004. The alignment template approach to statistical machine translation. *Comput. Linguist.*, 30(4):417–449.

Ralf Schenkel, Tom Crecelius, Mouna Kacimi, Thomas Neumann, Josiane Parreira, Marc Spaniol, and Gerhard Weikum. 2008. Social wisdom for search and recommendation, June.

Er Strehl, Joydeep Ghosh, and Raymond Mooney. 2000. Impact of similarity measures on web-page clustering. In *In Workshop on Artificial Intelligence for Web Search (AAAI 2000*, pages 58–64. AAAI.

Wikipedia. 2008. Jaccard's similarity coefficient.

Shengliang Xu, Shenghua Bao, Yunbo Cao, and Yong Yu. 2007. Using social annotations to improve language model for information retrieval. In *Proceedings of the sixteenth ACM conference on Conference on information and knowledge management*, pages 1003–1006. CIKM.

Ding Zhou, Jiang Bian, Shuyi Zheng, Hongyuan Zha, and Lee C. Giles. 2008. Exploring social annotations for information retrieval. In *WWW '08: Proceeding of the 17th international conference on World Wide Web*, pages 715–724, New York, NY, USA. ACM.

Network analysis reveals structure indicative of syntax in the corpus of undeciphered Indus civilization inscriptions

Sitabhra Sinha
Institute of Mathematical Sciences
Taramani, Chennai 600113, India
sitabhra@imsc.res.in

Raj Kumar Pan
Institute of Mathematical Sciences
Taramani, Chennai 600113
rajkp@imsc.res.in

Nisha Yadav
Tata Institute of Fundamental Research, Homi Bhabha Road, Mumbai 400005, India
Y_nisha@tifr.res.in

Mayank Vahia
Tata Institute of Fundamental Research, Homi Bhabha Road, Mumbai 40005, India
vahia@tifr.res.in

Iravatham Mahadevan
Indus Research Center,
Taramani, Chennai 600113, India
iravatham@vsnl.net

Abstract

Archaeological excavations in the sites of the Indus Valley civilization (2500-1900 BCE) in Pakistan and northwestern India have unearthed a large number of artifacts with inscriptions made up of hundreds of distinct signs. To date, there is no generally accepted decipherment of these sign sequences, and there have been suggestions that the signs could be non-linguistic. Here we apply complex network analysis techniques on the database of available Indus inscriptions, with the aim of detecting patterns indicative of syntactic structure in this sign system. Our results show the presence of regularities, e.g., in the segmentation trees of the sequences, that suggest the existence of a grammar underlying the construction of the sequences.

1 Introduction

The recent interest in complex networks among physicists over the past few years has meant that the graph theoretic paradigm has been applied to many different areas, including networks defined in corpora of textual units (Mehler, 2008), and has often revealed hitherto unsuspected patterns. While graph-based representation of texts had been used for some time in natural language processing tasks, such as, text parsing, disambiguation and clustering (Radev and Mihalcea, 2008), the approach based on the new physics of complex networks often asks questions from a different perspective that can shed new light on the organization of linguistic structure. For example, networks constructed on the basis of co-occurrence of words in sentences have been seen to exhibit the small-world effect, i.e., a small average distance between any pair of arbitrarily chosen words, and, a scale-free distribution of the number of words a given word is connected to (i.e., its degree) (Ferrer i Cancho and Sole, 2001). These properties have been proposed to reflect the evolutionary history of lexicons and the origin of their flexibility and combinatorial nature. Note that, a recent study of a lexical network of words that are phonological neighbors has found that the degree distribution might be better fit by an exponential rather than a power-law function (Vitevitch, 2008). A theoretical model for such word co-occurrence network, which treats language as a self-organizing network of interacting words, has led to the suggestion that languages may have a core (the "kernel lexicon") that does not vary as the language evolves (Dorogovtsev and Mendes, 2001). However, even though text and speech are sequential, the local correlation between immediately consecutive words may not describe natural languages well – due to the presence of non-local relations between words that occur apart from each other in a sentence. Therefore, network

Proceedings of the 2009 Workshop on Graph-based Methods for Natural Language Processing, ACL-IJCNLP 2009, pages 5–13,
Suntec, Singapore, 7 August 2009.

Fig. 1: A typical example of Indus sign sequence (having 8 distinct signs) occurring at the top of a seal, with the picture of a "unicorn" in the foreground (i.e., the field symbol), one of the common animal motifs observed in such artifacts. Note that, on seals, the conventional order in which the signs are read (right to left) is reversed.

analysis has been extended to syntactic dependency networks, where two words are connected if they have been related syntactically in a number of sentences (Ferrer i Cancho et al, 2003). The theory of complex networks has also been used to investigate the structure of meaningful concepts in the written texts of individual authors, which have been seen to have small-world as well as scale-free characteristics (Caldeira et al, 2006). The conceptual network of a language has been explored by using the semantic relatedness of words as defined by a thesaurus, and this network too is seen to have small-world nature with scale-free degree distribution (Motter et al, 2002).

In this article, we look at a corpus of inscriptions obtained through archaeological excavations carried out in the ruins of the Indus valley civilization. The sequences comprise signs, of which there are more than four hundred unique and distinct types. Since discovery in the early part of the 20th century, there have been attempts at deciphering them. However, to date there is no generally accepted method of interpreting these inscriptions. We analyze a representative database of these sequences using techniques inspired by complex network theory. Our aim is to see whether such methods can reveal the existence of patterns suggesting syntactic organization in the sign sequences. In the next section, we briefly introduce the historical context of the Indus inscriptions, while in Section 3, we discuss the dataset on which analysis has been carried out. Our results are reported in Section 4, and we finally conclude with a discussion of unresolved questions and further work that needs to be carried out.

2 The Indus inscriptions

The Indus civilization, also known as the Mature Harappan civilization (2500-1900 BCE), was geographically spread over what is now Pakistan and northwestern India, covering approximately a million square kilometers (Possehl, 2002). It was marked by urbanization centered around large planned cities, as evidenced in the ruins of Harappa and Mohenjo-daro. Craft specialization and long-distance trade with Mesopotamia and Central Asia have been well-demonstrated. This civilization came to an end early in the 2nd millennium BC. There were no historical records of its existence until archaeological excavations in the late 19th and early 20th century uncovered artifacts, and some of the ruined urban centers (Marshall, 1931).

Among the artifacts uncovered during these discoveries were a variety of objects (especially seals) that were inscribed with a variety of signs arranged in sequences (Fig. 1). Although found primarily on seals and their impressions (sealings), inscriptions with similar signs have also been discovered on miniature tablets, pottery, copper tablets, bronze implements, etc. Unsurprisingly, given the high sophistication of the civilization and the level of social complexity it implies, with the concomitant requirements of coordination and communication, these inscriptions have been interpreted as corresponding to writing. However, despite periodic claims about decipherment of this writing system, there has as yet been no generally accepted interpretation of the signs. The failure of decipherment is partly due to lack of knowledge about the language which the signs encode and the lack of any bilingual texts such as the Rosetta stone which was crucial in deciphering Egyptian hieroglyphs. While there is disagreement on the exact number of unique and distinct signs that occur in the inscriptions, there is overall agreement that they lie in the range of a few hundred. This rules out the possibility of the signs belonging either to an alphabetic system, which contains on average about 25 letters (such as English) or an ideographic (e.g., Chinese) writing system, comprising more than 50,000 characters. The brevity of the inscriptions (the longest that occurs on a single line has 14 signs) and the existence of a large number of signs that occur with very low frequency have led to some alternative suggestions regarding the meaning of the sign sequences. These include the possibilities that, e.g., (i) the signs correspond to a label specifying an individual and his belongings, in the manner of heraldic badges (Fairservis, 1971) and (ii) the signs are ritual or religious symbols which do not encode speech nor serve as mnemonic devices, much as the Vinca signs or emblems in Near Eastern artifacts (Farmer et al, 2004). The latter possibility implies the absence of any syntactic structure in the Indus inscriptions, a possibility that can be tested without making any *a priori* assumptions about the meaning of the signs.

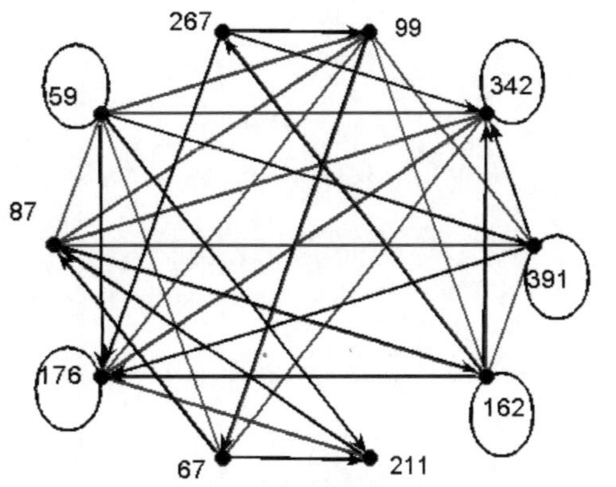

Fig. 3: The subnetwork of connections between the 10 highest frequency signs in EBUDS. Different colors are used to represent the two different orientations possible for arrows between a nodal pair (e.g., the pairs 342-162 and 162-342 are both possible and are indicated by a blue and a black arrow, respectively). Loops indicate successive occurrences of the same sign.

3 Description of dataset

The database for Indus sign sequences that we have used is based on the electronic concordance constructed by Mahadevan (1977), referred here as M77. This is based on the study of a total of 3573 sequences recorded from 2906 distinct artifacts and it identifies 417 unique signs. In the following we identify each sign in a sign sequence by its corresponding identification number (1, …, 417) in M77. Most of the inscriptions seem to have been written from right to left. However, according to the convention we use, the sequence of numbers representing each text is read from left to right (i.e., the leftmost number in the sequence is read as the first sign in the inscription). Yadav et al (2008) have constructed an Extended Basic Unique Data Set (EBUDS) by removing from M77 all sequences that are incomplete, because of the presence of signs that are damaged, lost, illegible or not unambiguously identified. Further, only sequences which are written on a single line are retained. This is to remove the ambiguity regarding the interpretation of sequences with multiple lines, namely, whether the different lines should be considered as independent sequences or whether they form one continuous sequence. Moreover, if the same sequence is found in multiple artifacts, it is represented only once in EBUDS. Following these operations, the original number of 3573 sequences in M77 is reduced to 1548 sequences in EBUDS. Moreover, 40 of the 417 unique signs in M77, which occur with relatively very low frequency, do not have any representation in EBUDS – so that latter dataset comprises 377 unique signs. However, it has been verified by Yadav et al (2008) that the frequency distributions of signs in the two datasets are qualitatively similar.

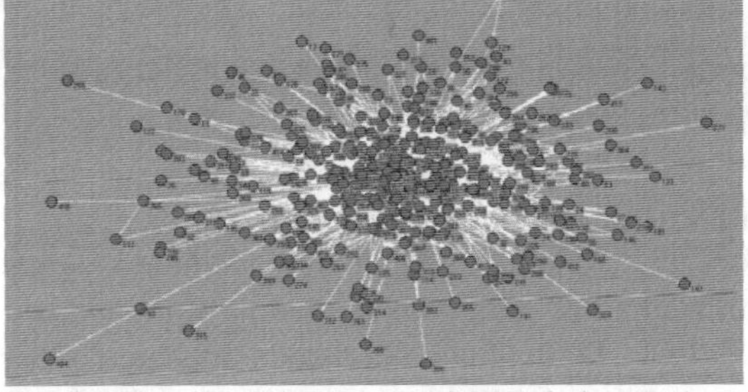

Fig. 2: The directed network of 377 distinct Indus signs in EBUDS, with arrows pointing from a preceding sign to a sign that follows it in the corpus of empirically observed sign sequences. Links are weighted by the frequency of occurrence of that particular sign pair.

4 Results

In the following sections we report the results of applying network analysis techniques to the sign sequences in EBUDS. We should note at this point that, the distributions of the in- and out- strengths of all the nodes (i.e., the sum of the weights of the incoming and outgoing links,

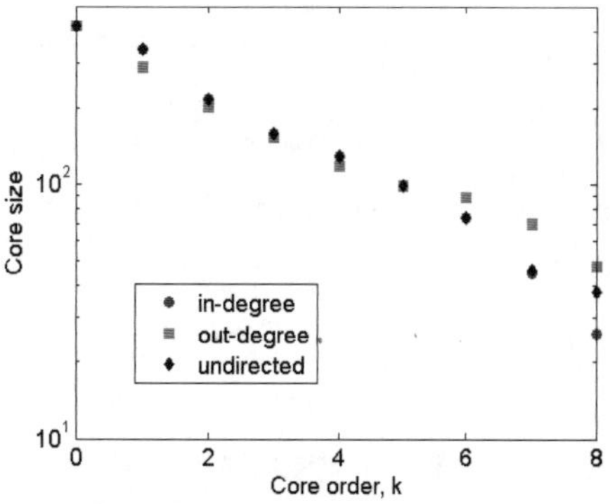

Fig. 4: Core-decomposition of the undirected and directed networks of Indus signs. For the latter, both the in-degree (circles) and out-degree (squares) cores are shown, while the undirected cores are represented with diamonds. All three core decompositions show an innermost core of order 8.

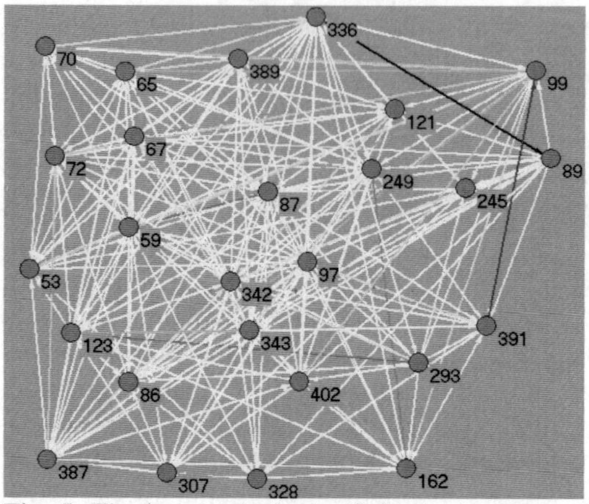

Fig. 5: The innermost (order 8) in-degree core of the Indus sign network with 26 signs. Grayscale color of each link corresponds to the frequency of occurrence of a particular pair (e.g., 391-99 and 336-89 are the commonest pairs).

respectively) do not show a scale-free distribution.

4.1 The directed network of signs

To have a graphical view of the entire sign system, we first construct the directed network of Indus signs (Fig. 2). This has 377 nodes corresponding to the distinct, uniquely identified signs. Node *i* has a directed link to node *j*, if sign *j* immediately follows sign *i* in any of the inscriptions included in EBUDS. The link between *i* and *j* is weighted by the frequency of occurrence of **ij** in the corpus ("*" is a wildcard character that may be substituted by any of the 377 signs or blank space).

We note immediately that only 1.5% (=2178) of the 377×377 possible directed pairs are seen to occur in the actual inscriptions. Furthermore, most of the signs are connected to only one or two other signs. The connectance (probability of link between any given pair) is only around 0.01, implying that the network is extremely sparse. However, if we plot the sub-network of connections between nodes corresponding to the 10 most common signs in EBUDS (i.e., the ones occurring with the highest frequency), we note that they are strongly inter-connected (Fig. 3). Therefore the adjacency matrix of the sign network is far from homogeneous, with patches of dense connectivity in certain regions.

As the above evidence indicates that there exists a core set of signs which occur very frequently as pairs, a natural question is whether the network generated from EBUDS has a core-periphery organization. This would imply the existence of a densely connected central core (central in terms of graph distance) and a larger class of sparsely connected peripheral nodes, like that seen in the case of geographically embedded transportation networks (Holme, 2005). To obtain such a decomposition of the network we use a pruning algorithm that successively peels away layers of a given core-order of the network. The *k*-core of a network is defined as the subnetwork containing all nodes that have degree *at least* equal to k. Thus, to obtain it, we have to iteratively remove all nodes having degree less than *k*. In particular, the 2-core of a network is obtained by eliminating all nodes that do not form part of a loop (i.e., a closed path through a subset of the connected nodes). For a *k*-core, there exist at least *k* paths between any pair of nodes belonging to it. It is obvious that for any network, there exists an innermost core of maximum order which cannot exceed the highest degree of the network.

In a directed network, one can define a *k*-core either in terms of the in-degree (number of connections arriving at the node) or the out-degree (number of connections sent from the node). For the EBUDS network, the innermost core turns out to have order 8, regardless of the type of network considered (Fig. 4). Fig. 5 shows the innermost core for the in-degree network. Even a casual inspection shows that many of the common sign pairs in the database belong to this subnetwork. Thus, a large part of the corpus can

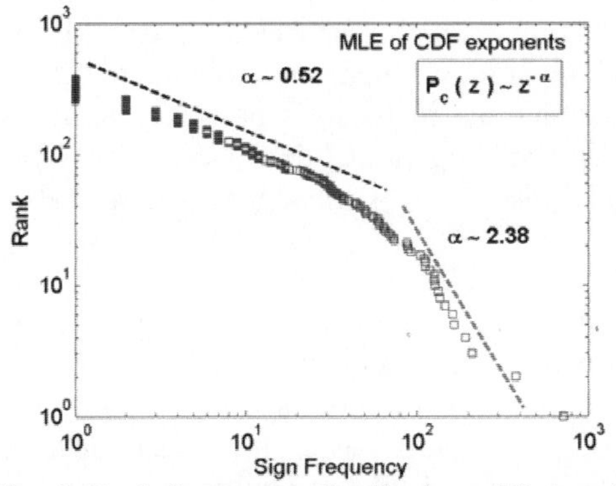

Fig. 6: Rank-frequency distribution of Indus sign occurrences, shown on a double logarithmic scale. The two lines indicate power law fits to different regions of the distribution, with distinct exponents. The latter are calculated using Maximum Likelihood Estimation (MLE). Neither equal 1, as would have been the case for a simple Zipf distribution.

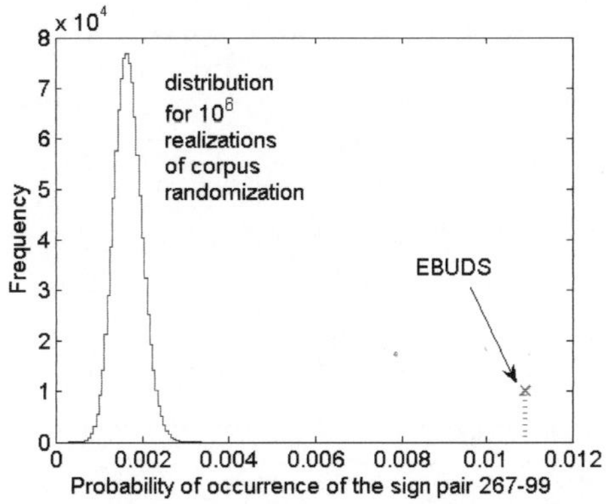

Fig. 7: The probability of occurrence of the sign pair 267-99 in EBUDS compared against the corresponding distribution for the randomized corpus (obtained by considering a million realizations). The large deviation of the empirical value of the pair occurrence probability from the randomized corpus indicates that this is a statistically significant sign pair.

be generated by using members of these "kernel lexicons".

4.2 Modularity of the network

Many networks that we see in nature are modular, i.e., they comprise several subnetworks (often called *communities*) whose members are more densely connected to each other than with the rest of the network. In several systems, such structural modules are often associated with functional modularity, with each community being identified as being responsible for certain specific functions (e.g., in the protein interaction network). In the EBUDS network, existence of modules will imply that certain sets of signs occur together far more often than would be expected had their frequencies of appearance in the corpus been statistically independent.

The unambiguous identification of communities in a network is a problem that still has not been solved to complete satisfaction. However, several near-optimal algorithms exist. The technique we use was proposed in Newman and Girvan (2004) and involves calculating the following measure of modularity of a network:

$$Q = \sum_s \left[\frac{L_s}{L} - \left(\frac{d_s}{2L} \right)^2 \right],$$

where, L is the total number of links in the network, L_s is the number of links between nodes within a module s and d_s is the sum of the degrees for nodes belonging to module s. By definition, this gives a large value when the network has an unambiguous partition into several communities. Thus, the method for finding the modules involves carrying out many trial divisions of the network into modules and calculating the corresponding Q. The partition for which Q is maximum will correspond to the true modular partition of the system. Needless to say, a brute force method for finding the best partition is impossible for modest sized networks, and we use an extremal optimization technique for this purpose. We obtain 8 communities whose sizes range from 6 to 87 nodes.

Having identified the communities in the sign network, the obvious question is whether they correspond to sign groups that occur in a particular context, e.g., commercial or religious. With this aim in view we have examined the correlation between the modules and (i) artifact types, (ii) nature of the field symbols and (iii) site of excavation. None of them show any significant correlation with the modules, implying that the signs are not simple attributes of either artifact or symbol portrayed in a seal, nor were the use of certain sign subsets confined exclusively to certain regions. The latter point underlines the surprising homogeneity of sign usage over the vast area that the Indus civilization covered. Let us stress that we are looking at correlation between *groups* of signs (that have a strong probability of co-occurrence) and specific contexts, rather than the significant frequency of occurrence of an *individual sign* in a specific context, of which there

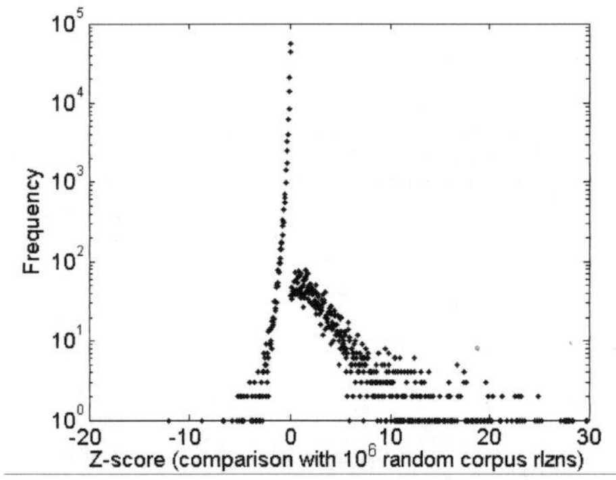

Fig. 8: Distribution of z-scores for all 377 × 377 possible sign pairs. Note that many potential sign pairs are not observed in EBUDS at all, which are responsible for the negative z-score values. The randomization is over the entire corpus, and the mean and standard deviation are calculated over a million random realizations.

are several examples. By focusing on correlation patterns at the level of groups of signs, rather than individual signs, we aim to arrive at results that are robust with respect to fluctuations in individual sign frequencies occurring as a result of further archaeological excavations.

4.3 Network of "significant" links

So far we had placed all sign pairs that occur in EBUDS on an equal footing. However, certain pairs may occur with high probability simply because the individual signs that make up the pair occur with high frequency. Fig. 6 shows that the frequency distribution of sign occurrence in EBUDS has an approximately power law distribution. This implies that the few commonest signs will occur over a very large number of cases (the most frequent sign appearing as many as 715 times, which is 10% of the total of 7000 occurrences of the 377 signs in EBUDS). By using the information about the probability of occurrence for individual signs in EBUDS we can investigate significant sign relations, i.e., sign combinations that occur far more frequently than that expected from the individual probabilities of the component signs.

Thus, if sign i occurs with a probability $p(i)$ and j with $p(j)$, then the pair ij is significant if $p(ij) >> p(i)p(j)$. To measure by how much $p(ij)$ has to be larger than the product of $p(i)$ and $p(j)$ in order to be "significant", we need to compare the empirical joint occurrence probability against the corresponding value for randomized surrogates. The randomized corpus is generated by shuffling the sign sequences in the dataset so that, while the individual sign frequencies are unchanged, all pair correlations in the original inscriptions are lost. The shuffling can be done over either (i) the entire corpus, or (ii) over each individual seal.

Fig. 7 shows a comparison between the empirical probability of a certain significant sign pair, and the corresponding probability distribution obtained upon corpus randomization. It is evident that the pair would never have been observed with the actual EBUDS frequency had the two signs been independent, i.e., had there been no dependency relation between them. This deviation can be quantified by computing the z-score, which is the difference between the empirical sign pair probability and the mean of the randomized cases, divided by the standard deviation for the randomizations. The distribution of z-scores for all 377×377 possible pairs are shown in Fig. 8. We note that there are 284 sign pairs with z-score larger than 10, while 46 pairs have z-score more than 20.

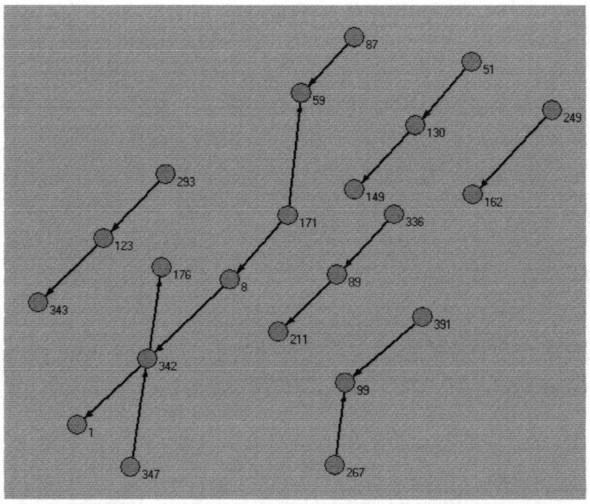

Fig. 9: The network of significant sign pairs as obtained after comparison with the randomized corpus constructed by shuffling signs in each seal.

As an example, using the individual seal shuffled randomization we obtain significant relations among 22 signs for a specified z-score threshold (Fig. 9). There are 6 isolated clusters in this sub-network, with the longest cluster containing 8 signs including sign 342 (the commonest sign in the corpus). Out of the 16 most frequently appearing signs in the database, 13 appear in this group, indicating that some of the common signs have significant relations with each other. While most pair relations are between such common signs, one exception is the cluster of signs no. 51 (35th most common sign), no. 149 (50th most

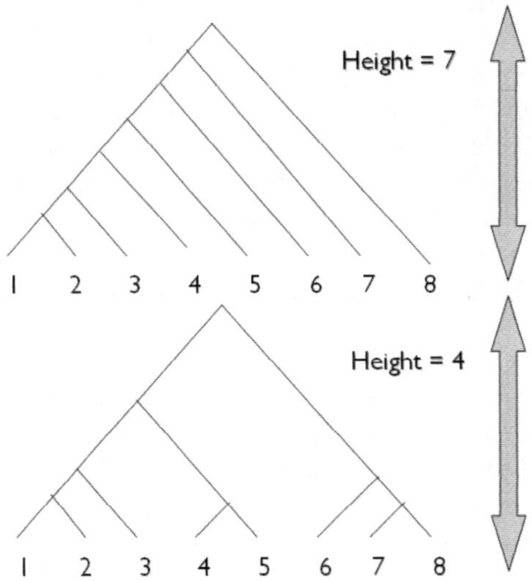

Fig. 10: Schematic segmentation trees for a sign sequence of length 8, representing two alternative possibilities. The top example is a relatively unstructured sign sequence, with the tree height being almost identical to the sequence length. The bottom example shows significant recursive structure and a corresponding lower tree height.

common sign) and no. 130 (59th most common sign). As the individual signs are themselves not very common, the observed sign relation is indeed quite intriguing and possibly has some functional significance in terms of interpreting the sign sequences.

4.4 "Syntactic" tree generation

We will finally attempt to reveal structure indicative of syntactic trees by "parsing" the longest sign sequences. We do this by generating segmentation trees of the sign sequences based on the relative frequency of sign combination occurrences. Given a inscription of length n, sign pairs are iteratively merged to form meta-signs, with the first merge being done for the sign pair with the highest z-score among all pairs in that sequence. This merged sign is then included as a meta-sign and assigned a new number. The reduced sequence of length n-1 is now again scanned for the pair of signs or meta-signs that is most "significant" and merged together. This process continues until the entire sign sequence reduces to a single meta-sign. In case of a tie between two or more pairs at any stage, one pair is randomly chosen. The resulting segmentation tree of the sign sequence is shown schematically in Fig. 10. The height of the tree is an indicator of the presence of significant recursive structure

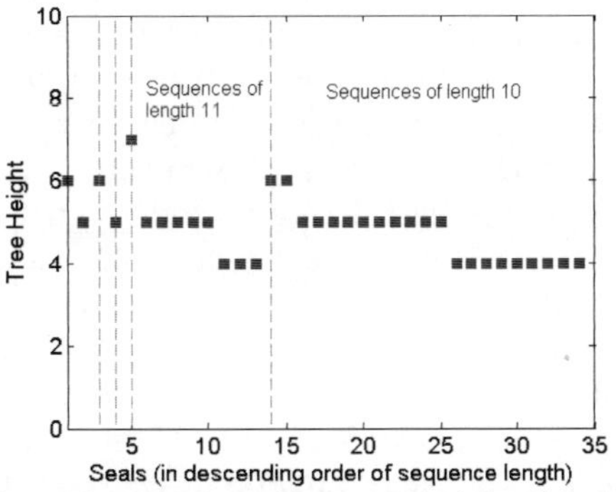

Fig. 11: Segmentation tree height for all sequences (of length 10 or more) in EBUDS arranged in descending order.

in the sign sequence. In particular, if the signs are all independent of each other, then the segmentation tree has essentially the same height as the length of the sequence (Fig. 10, top). On the other hand, if for long sequences, there exists subsequences that also appear in the corpus as separate sequences in their own right, this is indicative of recursion. The corresponding tree height is substantially reduced as compared to the sequence length (Fig. 10, bottom).

We use this criterion to seek signature of recursive, and hence syntactic, structure in the EBUDS network. For shorter length sequences, it becomes difficult to obtain subsequences that also appear as sequences in the database. We have thus confined our attention to inscriptions having 10 or more signs. Arranging the heights of the segmentation trees of these sequences in descending order (for seals of each specific length), we see that the average tree height is around 5 (Fig. 11). Such a characteristic length scale indicates that the longer sequences may actually be composed of multiple smaller sequences, each of which has a particular syntactic relation among its constituent signs.

5 Discussion

In this paper we have used complex network analysis techniques on the sign network constructed from a subset of the corpus of inscriptions obtained in Indus civilization excavations. Our results suggest that though these sign sequences are yet to be deciphered, they have a highly structured arrangement which is suggestive of the existence of syntax. The inference of a set of rules (i.e., the grammar) for arranging these signs in a particular order, so as to be able to create pseudotexts that are indistinguishable from the excavated ones is the eventual aim of the analysis described here. However, prior to this several open problems need to be addressed. One of the extensions of the present work has to do with looking beyond sign pairs to sign triplets, quadruplets, etc. Preliminary analysis of networks of meta-signs by us indicates that, combinations beyond four signs may not have statistical significance. A detailed comparison between the sign network described here and the meta-sign network may provide clues about the possible hierarchical arrangement of subsequences in the longer sequences. Evidence of this is already seen from the construction of segmentation trees of individual sequences based on relative pair frequencies.

It is also possible that there are non-local correlations between signs in a given inscription. To analyze this, we need to redefine the links in the network as being connections between all signs that occur in the same inscription. Again, preliminary analysis seems to suggest that this does not provide substantially new results from those reported here.

Based on the number of distinct signs (more than 400) there have been several suggestions that, as the number is too high to be an alphabetic system but too small to be an ideographic system, the inscriptions could well be written in a logosyllabic system. Such a writing system combines both logograms (morphemic signs) and syllabic (or phonetic) signs without inherent meaning. In future work, we plan to investigate the differences that arise in the network structure of languages belonging to these very different systems, in order to make an inference on the nature of the writing system used in the Indus inscriptions.

One of the most controversial aspects of Indus decipherment is the question of how many distinct signs are there. M77 identified 417 signs, but other researchers have come up with a wide range of different numbers. Therefore, an important open issue that needs to be settled in the future is the robustness of these results, with respect to analysis based on another sign list, e.g., that created by B. K. Wells (Wells, 2006).

Our analysis of correlations, or rather, the lack of it, between the modules of the network (i.e., groups of signs that have a high probability of co-occurrence) and contexts such as site of excavation, artifact types and field symbols, indicates that the patterns seen in the sequence organization are intrinsic to the sign usage system and not so much dependent on the context in which they arise. This supports the long-held belief that the signs encode writing, or, at least, proto-writing.

Acknowledgments
We would like to thank Bryan K. Wells for carefully reading through the manuscript and making numerous suggestions for improvement. We are grateful to the anonymous referees for several helpful suggestions. Ashraf M. Izhar helped in preparing Figures 7 and 8. We would also like to thank P. P. Divakaran for his constant encouragement.

References

S. M. G. Caldeira, T. C. Petit Lobao, R. F. S. Andrade A. Neme and J. G. V. Miranda. 2006. The network of concepts in written texts. *European Physical Journal B*, 49(4):523-529.

S. N. Dorogovtsev and J. F. Mendes. 2001. Language as an evolving word web. *Proceedings of the Royal Society of London B*, 268(1485):2603-2606.

W. A. Fairservis. 1971. *The Roots of Ancient India*, George Allen and Unwin, London.

S. Farmer, R. Sproat and M. Witzel. 2004. The collapse of the Indus-script thesis. *Electronic Journal of Vedic Studies*, 11(2):19-57.

R. Ferrer i Cancho, and R. V. Sole. 2001. The small world of human language. *Proceedings of the Royal Society of London B*, 268(1482): 2261-2265.

R. Ferrer i Cancho, R. V. Sole and R. Kohler. 2003. Patterns in syntactic dependency networks. *Physical Review E*, 69(5): 051915 (1-8).

P. Holme. 2005. Core-periphery organization of complex networks. *Physical Review E*, 72(4): 046111 (1-4).

I. Mahadevan. 1977. *The Indus Script: Texts, Concordances and Tables*, Archaeological Survey of India, New Delhi.

J. Marshall. 1931. *Mohenjo-daro and the Indus Civilization*, Arthur Probsthain, London.

A. Mehler. 2008. Large text networks as an object of corpus linguistic studies. In A. Ludeling and K. Marja (Eds) *Corpus Linguistics: An Interna-*

tional Handbook, Mouton de Gruyter, Berlin, 328-382.

A. E. Motter, A. P. S. De Moura, Y-C. Lai and P. Dasgupta. 2002. Topology of the conceptual network of language. *Physical Review E*, 65(6):065102 (1-4).

M. E. J. Newman and M. Girvan. 2004. Finding and evaluating community structure in networks. *Physical Review E*, 69(2):026113 (1-15).

A. Parpola. 1994. *Deciphering the Indus Script*, Cambridge University Press, Cambridge.

G. Possehl. 2002. *The Indus Civilization: A Contemporary Perspective*, AltaMira Press, Lanham, MD.

D. R. Radev and R. Mihalcea. 2008. Networks and natural language processing. *AI Magazine*, 29(3):16-28.

M. S. Vitevitch. 2008. What can graph theory tell us about word learning and lexical retrieval. *Journal of Speech, Language and Hearing Research*, 51(2):408-422.

B. K. Wells. 2006. *Epigraphic Approaches to Indus Writing*, PhD thesis, Harvard University, Cambridge, Mass.

N. Yadav, M. N. Vahia, I. Mahadevan and H. Jogelkar. 2008. A statistical approach for pattern search in Indus writing. *International Journal of Dravidian Linguistics*, 37(1):39-52.

Bipartite spectral graph partitioning to co-cluster varieties and sound correspondences in dialectology

Martijn Wieling
University of Groningen
The Netherlands
m.b.wieling@rug.nl

John Nerbonne
University of Groningen
The Netherlands
j.nerbonne@rug.nl

Abstract

In this study we used bipartite spectral graph partitioning to simultaneously cluster varieties and sound correspondences in Dutch dialect data. While clustering geographical varieties with respect to their pronunciation is not new, the simultaneous identification of the sound correspondences giving rise to the geographical clustering presents a novel opportunity in dialectometry. Earlier methods aggregated sound differences and clustered on the basis of aggregate differences. The determination of the significant sound correspondences which co-varied with cluster membership was carried out on a *post hoc* basis. Bipartite spectral graph clustering simultaneously seeks groups of individual sound correspondences which are associated, even while seeking groups of sites which share sound correspondences. We show that the application of this method results in clear and sensible geographical groupings and discuss the concomitant sound correspondences.

1 Introduction

Exact methods have been applied successfully to the analysis of dialect variation for over three decades (Séguy, 1973; Goebl, 1982; Nerbonne et al., 1999), but they have invariably functioned by first probing the linguistic differences between each pair of a range of varieties (sites, such as Whitby and Bristol in the UK) over a body of carefully controlled material (say the pronunciation of the vowel in the word 'put'). Second, the techniques AGGREGATE over these linguistic differences, in order, third, to seek the natural groups in the data via clustering or multidimensional scaling (MDS) (Nerbonne, 2009).

Naturally techniques have been developed to determine which linguistic variables weigh most heavily in determining affinity among varieties. But all of the following studies separate the determination of varietal relatedness from the question of its detailed linguistic basis. Kondrak (2002) adapted a machine translation technique to determine which sound correspondences occur most regularly. His focus was not on dialectology, but rather on diachronic phonology, where the regular sound correspondences are regarded as strong evidence of historical relatedness. Heeringa (2004: 268–270) calculated which words correlated best with the first, second and third dimensions of an MDS analysis of aggregate pronunciation differences. Shackleton (2004) used a database of abstract linguistic differences in trying to identify the British sources of American patterns of speech variation. He applied principal component analysis to his database to identify the common components among his variables. Nerbonne (2006) examined the distance matrices induced by each of two hundred vowel pronunciations automatically extracted from a large American collection, and subsequently applied factor analysis to the covariance matrices obtained from the collection of vowel distance matrices. Prokić (2007) analyzed Bulgarian pronunciation using an edit distance algorithm and then collected commonly aligned sounds. She developed an index to measure how characteristic a given sound correspondence is for a given site.

To study varietal relatedness and its linguistic basis in parallel, we apply bipartite spectral graph partitioning. Dhillon (2001) was the first to use spectral graph partitioning on a bipartite graph of documents and words, effectively clustering groups of documents and words simultaneously. Consequently, every document cluster has a direct connection to a word cluster; the document clustering implies a word clustering and vice versa. In

Proceedings of the 2009 Workshop on Graph-based Methods for Natural Language Processing, ACL-IJCNLP 2009, pages 14–22,
Suntec, Singapore, 7 August 2009. ©2009 ACL and AFNLP

his study, Dhillon (2001) also demonstrated that his algorithm worked well on real world examples.

The usefulness of this approach is not only limited to clustering documents and words simultaneously. For example, Kluger et al. (2003) used a somewhat adapted bipartite spectral graph partitioning approach to successfully cluster microarray data simultaneously in clusters of genes and conditions.

In summary, the contribution of this paper is to apply a graph-theoretic technique, bipartite spectral graph partitioning, to a new sort of data, namely dialect pronunciation data, in order to solve an important problem, namely how to recognize groups of varieties in this sort of data while simultaneously characterizing the linguistic basis of the group. It is worth noting that, in isolating the linguistic basis of varietal affinities, we thereby hope to contribute technically to the study of how cognitive and social dynamics interact in language variation. Although we shall not pursue this explicitly in the present paper, our idea is very simple. The geographic signal in the data is a reflection of the social dynamics, where geographic distance is the rough operationalization of social contact. In fact, dialectometry is already successful in studying this. We apply techniques to extract (social) associations among varieties and (linguistic) associations among the speech habits which the similar varieties share. The latter, linguistic associations are candidates for cognitive explanation. Although this paper cannot pursue the cognitive explanation, it will provide the material which a cognitive account might seek to explain.

The remainder of the paper is structured as follows. Section 2 presents the material we studied, a large database of contemporary Dutch pronunciations. Section 3 presents the methods, both the alignment technique used to obtain sound correspondences, as well as the bipartite spectral graph partitioning we used to simultaneously seek affinities in varieties as well as affinities in sound correspondences. Section 4 presents our results, while Section 5 concludes with a discussion and some ideas on avenues for future research.

2 Material

In this study we use the most recent broad-coverage Dutch dialect data source available: data from the Goeman-Taeldeman-Van Reenen-project (GTRP; Goeman and Taeldeman, 1996; Van den Berg, 2003). The GTRP consists of digital transcriptions for 613 dialect varieties in the Netherlands (424 varieties) and Belgium (189 varieties), gathered during the period 1980–1995. For every variety, a maximum of 1876 items was narrowly transcribed according to the International Phonetic Alphabet. The items consist of separate words and phrases, including pronominals, adjectives and nouns. A detailed overview of the data collection is given in Taeldeman and Verleyen (1999).

Because the GTRP was compiled with a view to documenting both phonological and morphological variation (De Schutter et al., 2005) and our purpose here is the analysis of sound correspondences, we ignore many items of the GTRP. We use the same 562 item subset as introduced and discussed in depth in Wieling et al. (2007). In short, the 1876 item word list was filtered by selecting only single word items, plural nouns (the singular form was preceded by an article and therefore not included), base forms of adjectives instead of comparative forms and the first-person plural verb instead of other forms. We omit words whose variation is primarily morphological as we wish to focus on sound correspondences. In all varieties the same lexeme was used for a single item.

Because the GTRP transcriptions of Belgian varieties are fundamentally different from transcriptions of Netherlandic varieties (Wieling et al., 2007), we will restrict our analysis to the 424 Netherlandic varieties. The geographic distribution of these varieties including province names is shown in Figure 1. Furthermore, note that we will not look at diacritics, but only at the 82 distinct phonetic symbols. The average length of every item in the GTRP (without diacritics) is 4.7 tokens.

3 Methods

To obtain the clearest signal of varietal differences in sound correspondences, we ideally want to compare the pronunciations of each variety with a single reference point. We might have used the pronunciations of a proto-language for this purpose, but these are not available. There are also no pronunciations in standard Dutch in the GTRP and transcribing the standard Dutch pronunciations ourselves would likely have introduced between-transcriber inconsistencies. Heeringa (2004: 274–276) identified pronunciations in the variety of Haarlem as being the closest to standard Dutch.

Figure 1: Distribution of GTRP localities including province names

Because Haarlem was not included in the GTRP varieties, we chose the transcriptions of Delft (also close to standard Dutch) as our reference transcriptions. See the discussion section for a consideration of alternatives.

3.1 Obtaining sound correspondences

To obtain the sound correspondences for every site in the GTRP with respect to the reference site Delft, we used an adapted version of the regular Levenshtein algorithm (Levenshtein, 1965).

The Levenshtein algorithm aligns two (phonetic) strings by minimizing the number of edit operations (i.e. insertions, deletions and substitutions) required to transform one string into the other. For example, the Levenshtein distance between [lɛɪkən] and [likhɵn], two Dutch variants of the word 'seem', is 4:

lɛɪkən	delete ɛ	1
lɪkən	subst. i/ɪ	1
likən	insert h	1
likhən	subst. ɵ/ə	1
likhɵn		
		4

The corresponding alignment is:

l	ɛ	ɪ	k		ə	n
l		i	k	h	ɵ	n
	1	1		1	1	

When all edit operations have the same cost, multiple alignments yield a Levenshtein distance of 4 (i.e. by aligning the [i] with the [ɛ] and/or by aligning the [ə] with the [h]). To obtain only the best alignments we used an adaptation of the Levenshtein algorithm which uses automatically generated segment substitution costs. This procedure was proposed and described in detail by Wieling et al. (2009) and resulted in significantly better individual alignments than using the regular Levenshtein algorithm.

In brief, the approach consists of obtaining initial string alignments by using the Levenshtein algorithm with a syllabicity constraint: vowels may only align with (semi-)vowels, and consonants only with consonants, except for syllabic consonants which may also be aligned with vowels. After the initial run, the substitution cost of every segment pair (a segment can also be a gap, representing insertion and deletion) is calculated according to a pointwise mutual information procedure assessing the statistical dependence between the two segments. I.e. if two segments are aligned more often than would be expected on the basis of their frequency in the dataset, the cost of substituting the two symbols is set relatively low; otherwise it is set relatively high. After the new segment substitution costs have been calculated, the strings are aligned again based on the new segment substitution costs. The previous two steps are then iterated until the string alignments remain constant. Our alignments were stable after 12 iterations.

After obtaining the final string alignments, we use a matrix to store the presence or absence of each segment substitution for every variety (with respect to the reference place). We therefore obtain an $m \times n$ matrix $\boldsymbol{A}$ of m varieties (in our case 423; Delft was excluded as it was used as our reference site) by n segment substitutions (in our case 957; not all possible segment substitutions occur). A value of 1 in $\boldsymbol{A}$ (i.e. $A_{ij} = 1$) indicates the presence of segment substitution j in variety i, while a value of 0 indicates the absence. We experimented with frequency thresholds, but decided against applying one in this paper as their application seemed to lead to poorer results. We postpone a consideration of frequency-sensitive alternatives to the discussion section.

3.2 Bipartite spectral graph partitioning

An undirected bipartite graph can be represented by $G = (R, S, E)$, where R and S are two sets of vertices and E is the set of edges connecting vertices from R to S. There are no edges between vertices in a single set. In our case R is the set of varieties, while S is the set of sound segment substitutions (i.e. sound correspondences). An edge between r_i and s_j indicates that the sound segment substitution s_j occurs in variety r_i. It is straightforward to see that matrix $\boldsymbol{A}$ is a representation of an undirected bipartite graph.

Spectral graph theory is used to find the principal properties and structure of a graph from its graph spectrum (Chung, 1997). Dhillon (2001) was the first to use spectral graph partitioning on a bipartite graph of documents and words, effectively clustering groups of documents and words simultaneously. Consequently, every document cluster has a direct connection to a word cluster. In similar fashion, we would like to obtain a clustering of varieties and corresponding segment substitutions. We therefore apply the multipartitioning algorithm introduced by Dhillon (2001) to find k clusters:

1. Given the $m \times n$ variety-by-segment-substitution matrix $\boldsymbol{A}$ as discussed previously, form

$$\boldsymbol{A_n} = \boldsymbol{D_1}^{-1/2} \boldsymbol{A} \boldsymbol{D_2}^{-1/2}$$

   with $\boldsymbol{D_1}$ and $\boldsymbol{D_2}$ diagonal matrices such that $D_1(i,i) = \Sigma_j A_{ij}$ and $D_2(j,j) = \Sigma_i A_{ij}$

2. Calculate the singular value decomposition (*SVD*) of the normalized matrix $\boldsymbol{A_n}$

$$\mathit{SVD}(\boldsymbol{A_n}) = \boldsymbol{U} * \boldsymbol{\Lambda} * \boldsymbol{V}^{\mathrm{T}}$$

   and take the $l = \lceil \log_2 k \rceil$ singular vectors, $\boldsymbol{u_2}, \ldots, \boldsymbol{u_{l+1}}$ and $\boldsymbol{v_2}, \ldots, \boldsymbol{v_{l+1}}$

3. Compute $\boldsymbol{Z} = \begin{bmatrix} \boldsymbol{D_1}^{-1/2} & \boldsymbol{U}_{[2,\ldots,l+1]} \\ \boldsymbol{D_2}^{-1/2} & \boldsymbol{V}_{[2,\ldots,l+1]} \end{bmatrix}$

4. Run the k-means algorithm on $\boldsymbol{Z}$ to obtain the k-way multipartitioning

To illustrate this procedure, we will co-cluster the following variety-by-segment-substitution matrix $\boldsymbol{A}$ in $k = 2$ groups.

	[ʌ]:[ɪ]	[d]:[w]	[-]:[ə]
Vaals (Limburg)	0	1	1
Sittard (Limburg)	0	1	1
Appelscha (Friesland)	1	0	1
Oudega (Friesland)	1	0	1

We first construct matrices $\boldsymbol{D_1}$ and $\boldsymbol{D_2}$. $\boldsymbol{D_1}$ contains the total number of edges from every variety (in the same row) on the diagonal, while $\boldsymbol{D_2}$ contains the total number of edges from every segment substitution (in the same column) on the diagonal. Both matrices are show below.

$$\boldsymbol{D_1} = \begin{bmatrix} 2 & 0 & 0 & 0 \\ 0 & 2 & 0 & 0 \\ 0 & 0 & 2 & 0 \\ 0 & 0 & 0 & 2 \end{bmatrix} \qquad \boldsymbol{D_2} = \begin{bmatrix} 2 & 0 & 0 \\ 0 & 2 & 0 \\ 0 & 0 & 4 \end{bmatrix}$$

We can now calculate $\boldsymbol{A_n}$ using the formula displayed in step 1 of the multipartitioning algorithm:

$$\boldsymbol{A_n} = \begin{bmatrix} 0 & .5 & .35 \\ 0 & .5 & .35 \\ .5 & 0 & .35 \\ .5 & 0 & .35 \end{bmatrix}$$

Applying the *SVD* to $\boldsymbol{A_n}$ yields:

$$\boldsymbol{U} = \begin{bmatrix} -.5 & .5 & .71 \\ -.5 & .5 & .71 \\ -.5 & -.5 & 0 \\ -.5 & -.5 & 0 \end{bmatrix} \qquad \boldsymbol{\Lambda} = \begin{bmatrix} 1 & 0 & 0 \\ 0 & .71 & 0 \\ 0 & 0 & 0 \end{bmatrix}$$

$$\boldsymbol{V} = \begin{bmatrix} -.5 & -.71 & -.5 \\ -.5 & .71 & -.5 \\ -.71 & 0 & .71 \end{bmatrix}$$

To cluster in two groups, we look at the second singular vectors (i.e. columns) of $\boldsymbol{U}$ and $\boldsymbol{V}$ and compute the 1-dimensional vector $\boldsymbol{Z}$:

$$\boldsymbol{Z} = \begin{bmatrix} .35 & .35 & -.35 & -.35 & -.5 & .5 & 0 \end{bmatrix}^T$$

Note that the first four values correspond with the places (Vaals, Sittard, Appelscha and Oudega) and the final three values correspond to the segment substitutions ([ʌ]:[ɪ], [d]:[w] and [-]:[ə]).

After running the k-means algorithm on $\boldsymbol{Z}$, the items are assigned to one of two clusters as follows:

$$\begin{bmatrix} 1 & 1 & 2 & 2 & 2 & 1 & 1 \end{bmatrix}^T$$

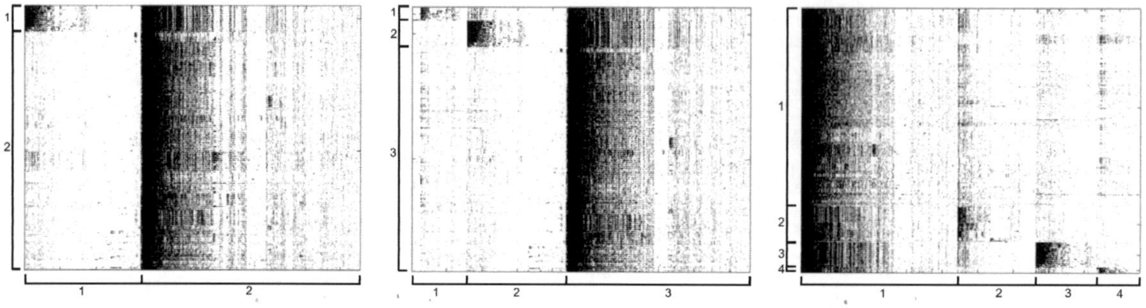

Figure 2: Visualizations of co-clustering varieties (y-axis) and segments substitutions (x-axis) in 2 (left), 3 (middle) and 4 (right) clusters

The clustering shows that Appelscha and Oudega are clustered together and linked to the clustered segment substitution of [ʌ]:[ɪ] (cluster 2). Similarly, Vaals and Sittard are clustered together and linked to the clustered segment substitutions [d]:[w] and [-]:[ə] (cluster 1). Note that the segment substitution [-]:[ə] (an insertion of [ə]) is actually not meaningful for the clustering of the varieties (as can also be observed in $\boldsymbol{A}$), because the bottom value of the second column of $\boldsymbol{V}$ corresponding to this segment substitution is 0. It could therefore just as likely be grouped in cluster 2. Nevertheless, the k-means algorithm always assigns every item to a single cluster.

In the following section we will report the results on clustering in two, three and four groups.[1]

4 Results

After running the multipartitioning algorithm[2] we obtained a two-way clustering in k clusters of varieties and segment substitutions. Figure 2 tries to visualize the simultaneous clustering in two dimensions. A black dot is drawn if the variety (y-axis) contains the segment substitution (x-axis). The varieties and segments are sorted in such a way that the clusters are clearly visible (and marked) on both axes.

To visualize the clustering of the varieties, we created geographical maps in which we indicate the cluster of each variety by a distinct pattern. The division in 2, 3 and 4 clusters is shown in Figure 3.

In the following subsections we will discuss the most important geographical clusters together with their simultaneously derived sound correspondences. For brevity, we will only focus on explaining a few derived sound correspondences for the most important geographical groups. The main point to note is that besides a sensible geographical clustering, we also obtain linguistically sensible results.

Note that the connection between a cluster of varieties and sound correspondences does not necessarily imply that those sound correspondences only occur in that particular cluster of varieties. This can also be observed in Figure 2, where sound correspondences in a particular cluster of varieties also appear in other clusters (but less dense).[3]

The Frisian area

The division into two clusters clearly separates the Frisian language area (in the province of Friesland) from the Dutch language area. This is the expected result as Heeringa (2004: 227–229) also measured Frisian as the most distant of all the language varieties spoken in the Netherlands and Flanders. It is also expected in light of the fact that Frisian even has the legal status of a different language rather than a dialect of Dutch. Note that the separate “islands” in the Frisian language area (see Figure 3) correspond to the Frisian cities which are generally found to deviate from the rest of the Frisian language area (Heeringa, 2004: 235–241).

[1] We also experimented with clustering in more than four groups, but the k-means clustering algorithm did not give stable results for these groupings. It is possible that the random initialization of the k-means algorithm caused the instability of the groupings, but since we are ignoring the majority of information contained in the alignments it is more likely that this causes a decrease in the number of clusters we can reliably detect.

[2] The implementation of the multipartitioning algorithm was obtained from `http://adios.tau.ac.il/SpectralCoClustering`

[3] In this study, we did not focus on identifying the most important sound correspondences in each cluster. See the Discussion section for a possible approach to rank the sound correspondences.

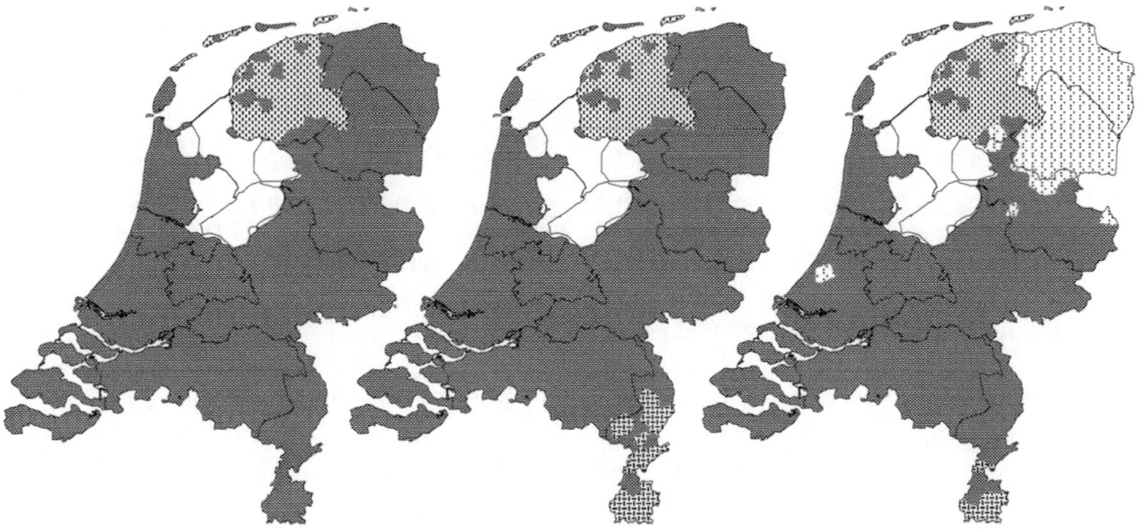

Figure 3: Clustering of varieties in 2 clusters (left), 3 clusters (middle) and 4 clusters (right)

A few interesting sound correspondences between the reference variety (Delft) and the Frisian area are displayed in the following table and discussed below.

Reference	[ʌ]	[ʌ]	[a]	[o]	[u]	[x]	[x]	[r]
Frisian	[ɪ]	[i]	[i]	[ɛ]	[ɛ]	[j]	[z]	[x]

In the table we can see that the Dutch /a/ or /ʌ/ is pronounced [i] or [ɪ] in the Frisian area. This well known sound correspondence can be found in words such as *kamers* 'rooms', Frisian [kɪməs] (pronunciation from Anjum), or *draden* 'threads' and Frisian [trɪdn] (Bakkeveen). In addition, the Dutch (long) /o/ and /u/ both tend to be realized as [ɛ] in words such as *bomen* 'trees', Frisian [bjɛmən] (Bakkeveen) or *koeien* 'cows', Frisian [kɛi] (Appelscha).

We also identify clustered correspondences of [x]:[j] where Dutch /x/ has been lenited, e.g. in *geld* (/xɛlt/) 'money', Frisian [jɪlt] (Grouw), but note that [x]:[g] as in [gɛlt] (Franeker) also occurs, illustrating that sound correspondences from another cluster (i.e. the rest of the Netherlands) can indeed also occur in the Frisian area. Another sound correspondence co-clustered with the Frisian area is the Dutch /x/ and Frisian [z] in *zeggen* (/zɛxə/) 'say' Frisian [sizə] (Appelscha).

Besides the previous results, we also note some problems. First, the accusative first-person plural pronoun *ons* 'us' lacks the nasal in Frisian, but the correspondence was not tallied in this case because the nasal consonant is also missing in Delft. Second, some apparently frequent sound correspondences result from historical accidents, e.g. [r]:[x] corresponds regularly in the Dutch:Frisian pair [dor]:[trux] 'through'. Frisian has lost the final [x], and Dutch has either lost a final [r] or experienced metathesis. These two sorts of examples might be treated more satisfactorily if we were to compare pronunciations not to a standard language, but rather to a reconstruction of a protolanguage.

The Limburg area

The division into three clusters separates the southern Limburg area from the rest of the Dutch and Frisian language area. This result is also in line with previous studies investigating Dutch dialectology; Heeringa (2004: 227–229) found the Limburg dialects to deviate most strongly from other different dialects within the Netherlands-Flanders language area once Frisian was removed from consideration.

Some important segment correspondences for Limburg are displayed in the following table and discussed below.

Reference	[r]	[r]	[k]	[n]	[n]	[w]
Limburg	[ʀ]	[ʁ]	[x]	[ʀ]	[ʁ]	[f]

Southern Limburg uses more uvular versions of /r/, i.e. the trill [ʀ], but also the voiced uvular fricative [ʁ]. These occur in words such as *over* 'over, about', but also in *breken* 'to break', i.e. both pre- and post-vocalically. The bipartite clustering likewise detected examples of the famous "second sound shift", in which Dutch /k/ is lenited to /x/, e.g. in *ook* 'also' realized as [ox] in Epen and elsewhere. Interestingly, when looking at other words there is less evidence of lenition in the words *maken* 'to make', *gebruiken* 'to use', *koken* 'to cook', and *kraken* 'to crack', where only two Limburg varieties document a [x] pronunciation of the expected stem-final [k], namely Kerkrade and Vaals. The limited linguistic application does appear to be geographically consistent, but Kerkrade pronounces /k/ as [x] where Vaals lenites further to [s] in words such as *ruiken* 'to smell', *breken* 'to break', and *steken* 'to sting'. Further, there is no evidence of lenition in words such as *vloeken* 'to curse', *spreken* 'to speak', and *zoeken* 'to seek', which are lenited in German (*fluchen, sprechen, suchen*).

Some regular correspondences merely reflected other, and sometimes more fundamental differences. For instance, we found correspondences between [n] and [ʀ] or [ʁ] for Limburg , but this turned out to be a reflection of the older plurals in -r. For example, in the word *wijf* 'woman', plural *wijven* in Dutch, *wijver* in Limburg dialect. Dutch /w/ is often realized as [f] in the word *tarwe* 'wheat', but this is due to the elision of the final schwa, which results in a pronunciation such as [taʀəf], in which the standard final devoicing rule of Dutch is applicable.

The Low Saxon area

Finally, the division in four clusters also separates the varieties from Groningen and Drenthe from the rest of the Netherlands. This result differs somewhat from the standard scholarship on Dutch dialectology (see Heeringa, 2004), according to which the Low Saxon area should include not only the provinces of Groningen and Drenthe, but also the province of Overijssel and the northern part of the province of Gelderland. It is nonetheless the case that Groningen and Drenthe normally are seen to form a separate northern subgroup within Low Saxon (Heeringa, 2004: 227–229).

A few interesting sound correspondences are displayed in the following table and discussed below.

Reference	[ə]	[ə]	[ə]	[-]	[a]
Low Saxon	[m]	[ŋ]	[ɴ]	[ʔ]	[e]

The best known characteristic of this area, the so-called "final n" (*slot n*) is instantiated strongly in words such as *strepen*, 'stripes', realized as [strepm] in the northern Low Saxon area. It would be pronounced [strepə] in standard Dutch, so the differences shows up as an unexpected correspondence of [ə] with [m], [ŋ] and [ɴ].

The pronunciation of this area is also distinctive in normally pronouncing words with initial glottal stops [ʔ] rather than initial vowels, e.g. *af* 'finished' is realized as [ʔɔf] (Schoonebeek). Furthermore, the long /a/ is often pronounced [e] as in *kaas* 'cheese', [kes] in Gasselte, Hooghalen and Norg.

5 Discussion

In this study, we have applied a novel method to dialectology in simultaneously determining groups of varieties and their linguistic basis (i.e. sound segment correspondences). We demonstrated that the bipartite spectral graph partitioning method introduced by Dhillon (2001) gave sensible clustering results in the geographical domain as well as for the concomitant linguistic basis.

As mentioned above, we did not have transcriptions of standard Dutch, but instead we used transcriptions of a variety (Delft) close to the standard langueage. While the pronunciations of most items in Delft were similar to standard Dutch, there were also items which were pronounced differently from the standard. While we do not believe that this will change our results significantly, using standard Dutch transcriptions produced by the transcribers of the GTRP corpus would make the interpretation of sound correspondences more straightforward.

We indicated in Section 4 that some sound correspondences, e.g. [r]:[x], would probably not occur if we used a reconstructed proto-language as a reference instead of the standard language. A possible way to reconstruct such a proto-language is by multiple aligning (see Prokić, 2009) all pronunciations of a single word and use the most frequent phonetic symbol at each position in the reconstructed word. It would be interesting to see if using such a reconstructed proto-language would improve the results by removing sound correspondences such as [r]:[x].

In this study we did not investigate methods to identify the most important sound correspondences. A possible option would be to create a ranking procedure based on the uniqueness of the sound correspondences in a cluster. I.e. the sound correspondence is given a high importance when it only occurs in the designated cluster, while the importance goes down when it also occurs in other clusters).

While sound segment correspondences function well as a linguistic basis, it might also be fruitful to investigate morphological distinctions present in the GTRP corpus. This would enable us to compare the similarity of the geographic distributions of pronunciation variation on the one hand and morphological variation on the other.

As this study was the first to investigate the effectiveness of a co-clustering approach in dialectometry, we focused on the original bipartite spectral graph partitioning algorithm (Dhillon, 2001). Investigating other approaches such as biclustering algorithms for biology (Madeira and Oliveira, 2004) or an information-theoretic co-clustering approach (Dhillon et al., 2003) would be highly interesting.

It would likewise be interesting to attempt to incorporate frequency, by weighting correspondences that occur frequently more heavily than those which occur only infrequently. While it stands to reason that more frequently encountered variation would signal dialectal affinity more strongly, it is also the case that inverse frequency weightings have occasionally been applied (Goebl, 1982), and have been shown to function well. We have the sense that the last word on this topic has yet to be spoken, and that empirical work would be valuable.

Our paper has not addressed the interaction between cognitive and social dynamics directly, but we feel it has improved our vantage point for understanding this interaction. In dialect geography, social dynamics are operationalized as geography, and bipartite spectral graph partitioning has proven itself capable of detecting the effects of social contact, i.e. the latent geographic signal in the data. Other dialectometric techniques have done this as well.

Linguists have rightly complained, however, that the linguistic factors have been neglected in dialectometry (Schneider, 1988:176). The current approach does not offer a theoretical framework to explain cognitive effects such as phonemes corresponding across many words, but does enumerate them clearly. This paper has shown that bipartite graph clustering can detect the linguistic basis of dialectal affinity. If deeper cognitive constraints are reflected in that basis, then we are now in an improved position to detect them.

Acknowledgments

We would like to thank Assaf Gottlieb for sharing the implementation of the bipartite spectral graph partitioning method. We also would like to thank Peter Kleiweg for supplying the L04 package which was used to generate the maps in this paper. Finally, we are grateful to Jelena Prokić and the anonymous reviewers for their helpful comments on an earlier version of this paper.

References

Fan Chung. 1997. *Spectral graph theory*. American Mathematical Society.

Georges De Schutter, Boudewijn van den Berg, Ton Goeman, and Thera de Jong. 2005. *Morfologische Atlas van de Nederlandse Dialecten (MAND) Deel 1*. Amsterdam University Press, Meertens Instituut - KNAW, Koninklijke Academie voor Nederlandse Taal- en Letterkunde, Amsterdam.

Inderjit Dhillon, Subramanyam Mallela, and Dharmendra Modha. 2003. Information-theoretic co-clustering. In *Proceedings of the ninth ACM SIGKDD international conference on Knowledge discovery and data mining*, pages 89–98. ACM New York, NY, USA.

Inderjit Dhillon. 2001. Co-clustering documents and words using bipartite spectral graph partitioning. In *Proceedings of the seventh ACM SIGKDD international conference on Knowledge discovery and data mining*, pages 269–274. ACM New York, NY, USA.

Hans Goebl. 1982. *Dialektometrie: Prinzipien und Methoden des Einsatzes der Numerischen Taxonomie im Bereich der Dialektgeographie*. Österreichische Akademie der Wissenschaften, Wien.

Ton Goeman and Johan Taeldeman. 1996. Fonologie en morfologie van de Nederlandse dialecten. Een nieuwe materiaalverzameling en twee nieuwe atlasprojecten. *Taal en Tongval*, 48:38–59.

Wilbert Heeringa. 2004. *Measuring Dialect Pronunciation Differences using Levenshtein Distance*. Ph.D. thesis, Rijksuniversiteit Groningen.

Yuval Kluger, Ronen Basri, Joseph Chang, and Mark Gerstein. 2003. Spectral biclustering of microarray data: Coclustering genes and conditions. *Genome Research*, 13(4):703–716.

Grzegorz Kondrak. 2002. Determining recurrent sound correspondences by inducing translation models. In *Proceedings of the Nineteenth International Conference on Computational Linguistics (COLING 2002)*, pages 488–494, Taipei. COLING.

Vladimir Levenshtein. 1965. Binary codes capable of correcting deletions, insertions and reversals. *Doklady Akademii Nauk SSSR*, 163:845–848.

Sara Madeira and Arlindo Oliveira. 2004. Biclustering algorithms for biological data analysis: a survey. *IEEE/ACM Transactions on Computational Biology and Bioinformatics*, 1(1):24–45.

John Nerbonne, Wilbert Heeringa, and Peter Kleiweg. 1999. Edit distance and dialect proximity. In David Sankoff and Joseph Kruskal, editors, *Time Warps, String Edits and Macromolecules: The Theory and Practice of Sequence Comparison, 2nd ed.*, pages v–xv. CSLI, Stanford, CA.

John Nerbonne. 2006. Identifying linguistic structure in aggregate comparison. *Literary and Linguistic Computing*, 21(4):463–476. Special Issue, J.Nerbonne & W.Kretzschmar (eds.), *Progress in Dialectometry: Toward Explanation.*

John Nerbonne. 2009. Data-driven dialectology. *Language and Linguistics Compass*, 3(1):175–198.

Jelena Prokić, Martijn Wieling, and John Nerbonne. 2009. Multiple sequence alignments in linguistics. In Lars Borin and Piroska Lendvai, editors, *Language Technology and Resources for Cultural Heritage, Social Sciences, Humanities, and Education*, pages 18–25.

Jelena Prokić. 2007. Identifying linguistic structure in a quantitative analysis of dialect pronunciation. In *Proceedings of the ACL 2007 Student Research Workshop*, pages 61–66, Prague, June. Association for Computational Linguistics.

Edgar Schneider. 1988. Qualitative vs. quantitative methods of area delimitation in dialectology: A comparison based on lexical data from georgia and alabama. *Journal of English Linguistics*, 21:175–212.

Jean Séguy. 1973. La dialectométrie dans l'atlas linguistique de gascogne. *Revue de Linguistique Romane*, 37(145):1–24.

Robert G. Shackleton, Jr. 2005. English-american speech relationships: A quantitative approach. *Journal of English Linguistics*, 33(2):99–160.

Johan Taeldeman and Geert Verleyen. 1999. De FAND: een kind van zijn tijd. *Taal en Tongval*, 51:217–240.

Boudewijn van den Berg. 2003. *Phonology & Morphology of Dutch & Frisian Dialects in 1.1 million transcriptions.* Goeman-Taeldeman-Van Reenen project 1980-1995, Meertens Instituut Electronic Publications in Linguistics 3. Meertens Instituut (CD-ROM), Amsterdam.

Martijn Wieling, Wilbert Heeringa, and John Nerbonne. 2007. An aggregate analysis of pronunciation in the Goeman-Taeldeman-Van Reenen-Project data. *Taal en Tongval*, 59:84–116.

Martijn Wieling, Jelena Prokić, and John Nerbonne. 2009. Evaluating the pairwise alignment of pronunciations. In Lars Borin and Piroska Lendvai, editors, *Language Technology and Resources for Cultural Heritage, Social Sciences, Humanities, and Education*, pages 26–34.

Random Walks for Text Semantic Similarity

Daniel Ramage, Anna N. Rafferty, and Christopher D. Manning
Computer Science Department
Stanford University
Stanford, CA 94305
{dramage,manning}@cs.stanford.edu
rafferty@eecs.berkeley.edu

Abstract

Many tasks in NLP stand to benefit from robust measures of semantic similarity for units above the level of individual words. Rich semantic resources such as WordNet provide local semantic information at the lexical level. However, effectively combining this information to compute scores for phrases or sentences is an open problem. Our algorithm aggregates local relatedness information via a random walk over a graph constructed from an underlying lexical resource. The stationary distribution of the graph walk forms a "semantic signature" that can be compared to another such distribution to get a relatedness score for texts. On a paraphrase recognition task, the algorithm achieves an 18.5% relative reduction in error rate over a vector-space baseline. We also show that the graph walk similarity between texts has complementary value as a feature for recognizing textual entailment, improving on a competitive baseline system.

1 Introduction

Many natural language processing applications must directly or indirectly assess the semantic similarity of text passages. Modern approaches to information retrieval, summarization, and textual entailment, among others, require robust numeric relevance judgments when a pair of texts is provided as input. Although each task demands its own scoring criteria, a simple lexical overlap measure such as cosine similarity of document vectors can often serve as a surprisingly powerful baseline. We argue that there is room to improve these general-purpose similarity measures, particularly for short text passages.

Most approaches fall under one of two categories. One set of approaches attempts to explicitly account for fine-grained structure of the two passages, e.g. by aligning trees or constructing logical forms for theorem proving. While these approaches have the potential for high precision on many examples, errors in alignment judgments or formula construction are often insurmountable. More broadly, it's not always clear that there is a correct alignment or logical form that is most appropriate for a particular sentence pair. The other approach tends to ignore structure, as canonically represented by the vector space model, where any lexical item in common between the two passages contributes to their similarity score. While these approaches often fail to capture distinctions imposed by, e.g. negation, they do correctly capture a broad notion of similarity or aboutness.

This paper presents a novel variant of the vector space model of text similarity based on a random walk algorithm. Instead of comparing two bags-of-words directly, we compare the distribution each text induces when used as the seed of a random walk over a graph derived from WordNet and corpus statistics. The walk posits the existence of a distributional particle that roams the graph, biased toward the neighborhood surrounding an input bag of words. Eventually, the walk reaches a stationary distribution over all nodes in the graph, smoothing the peaked input distribution over a much larger semantic space. Two such stationary distributions can be compared using conventional measures of vector similarity, producing a final relatedness score.

This paper makes the following contributions. We present a novel random graph walk algorithm

Proceedings of the 2009 Workshop on Graph-based Methods for Natural Language Processing, ACL-IJCNLP 2009, pages 23–31,
Suntec, Singapore, 7 August 2009.

Word	Step 1	Step 2	Step 3	Conv.
eat	3	8	9	9
corrode	10	33	53	>100
pasta	–	2	3	5
dish	–	4	5	6
food	–	–	21	12
solid	–	–	–	26

Table 1: Ranks of sample words in the distribution for *I ate a salad and spaghetti* after a given number of steps and at convergence. Words in the vector are ordered by probability at time step t; the word with the highest probability in the vector has rank 1. "–" indicates that node had not yet been reached.

for semantic similarity of texts, demonstrating its efficiency as compared to a much slower but mathematically equivalent model based on summed similarity judgments of individual words. We show that walks effectively aggregate information over multiple types of links and multiple input words on an unsupervised paraphrase recognition task. Furthermore, when used as a feature, the walk's semantic similarity score can improve the performance of an existing, competitive textual entailment system. Finally, we provide empirical results demonstrating that indeed, each step of the random walk contributes to its ability to assess paraphrase judgments.

2 A random walk example

To provide some intuition about the behavior of the random walk on text passages, consider the following example sentence: *I ate a salad and spaghetti.*

No measure based solely on lexical identity would detect overlap between this sentence and another input consisting of only the word *food*. But if each text is provided as input to the random walk, local relatedness links from one word to another allow the distributional particle to explore nearby parts of the semantic space. The number of non-zero elements in both vectors increases, eventually converging to a stationary distribution for which both vectors have many shared non-zero entries.

Table 1 ranks elements of the sentence vector based on their relative weights. Observe that at the beginning of the walk, *corrode* has a high rank due to its association with the WordNet sense of *eat* corresponding to eating away at something. However, because this concept is not closely linked with other words in the sentence, its relative rank drops as the distribution converges and other word senses more related to *food* are pushed up. The random walk allows the meanings of words to reinforce one another. If the sentence above had ended with *drank wine* rather than *spaghetti*, the final weight on the *food* node would be smaller since fewer input words would be as closely linked to *food*. This matches the intuition that the first sentence has more to do with food than does the second, although both walks should and do give some weight to this node.

3 Related work

Semantic relatedness for individual words has been thoroughly investigated in previous work. Budanitsky and Hirst (2006) provide an overview of many of the knowledge-based measures derived from WordNet, although other data sources have been used as well. Hughes and Ramage (2007) is one such measure based on random graph walks.

Prior work has considered random walks on various text graphs, with applications to query expansion (Collins-Thompson and Callan, 2005), email address resolution (Minkov and Cohen, 2007), and word-sense disambiguation (Agirre and Soroa, 2009), among others.

Measures of similarity have also been proposed for sentence or paragraph length text passages. Mihalcea et al. (2006) present an algorithm for the general problem of deciding the similarity of meaning in two text passages, coining the name "text semantic similarity" for the task. Corley and Mihalcea (2005) apply this algorithm to paraphrase recognition.

Previous work has shown that similarity measures can have some success as a measure of textual entailment. Glickman et al. (2005) showed that many entailment problems can be answered using only a bag-of-words representation and web co-occurrence statistics. Many systems integrate lexical relatedness and overlap measures with deeper semantic and syntactic features to create improved results upon relatedness alone, as in Montejo-Ráez et al. (2007).

4 Random walks on lexical graphs

In this section, we describe the mechanics of computing semantic relatedness for text passages based on the random graph walk framework. The algorithm underlying these computations is related to topic-sensitive PageRank (Haveliwala, 2002); see Berkhin (2005) for a survey of related algorithms.

To compute semantic relatedness for a pair of passages, we compare the stationary distributions of two Markov chains, each with a state space defined over all lexical items in an underlying corpus or database. Formally, we define the probability of finding the particle at a node n_i at time t as:

$$n_i^{(t)} = \sum_{n_j \in V} n_j^{(t-1)} P(n_i \mid n_j)$$

where $P(n_i \mid n_j)$ is the probability of transitioning from n_j to n_i at any time step. If those transitions bias the particle to the neighborhood around the words in a text, the particle's distribution can be used as a lexical signature.

To compute relatedness for a pair of texts, we first define the graph nodes and transition probabilities for the random walk Markov chain from an underlying lexical resource. Next, we determine an initial distribution over that state space for a particular input passage of text. Then, we simulate a random walk in the state space, biased toward the initial distribution, resulting in a passage-specific distribution over the graph. Finally, we compare the resulting stationary distributions from two such walks using a measure of distributional similarity. The remainder of this section discusses each stage in more detail.

4.1 Graph construction

We construct a graph $G = (V, E)$ with vertices V and edges E extracted from WordNet 3.0. WordNet (Fellbaum, 1998) is an annotated graph of synsets, each representing one concept, that are populated by one or more words. The set of vertices extracted from the graph is all synsets present in WordNet (e.g. *foot#n#1* meaning the part of the human leg below the ankle), all part-of-speech tagged words participating in those synsets (e.g. *foot#n* linking to *foot#n#1* and *foot#n#2* etc.), and all untagged words (e.g. *foot* linking to *foot#n* and *foot#v*). The set of edges connecting synset nodes is all inter-synset edges contained in WordNet, such as hyponymy, synonomy, antonymy, etc., except for regional and usage links. All WordNet relational edges are given uniform weight. Edges also connect each part-of-speech tagged word to all synsets it takes part in, and from each word to all its part-of-speech. These edge weights are derived from corpus counts as in Hughes and Ramage (2007). We also included a low-weight self-loop for each node.

Our graph has 420,253 nodes connected by 1,064,464 edges. Because synset nodes do not link outward to part-of-speech tagged nodes or word nodes in this graph, only the 117,659 synset nodes have non-zero probability in every random walk—i.e. the stationary distribution will always be non-zero for these 117,659 nodes, but will be non-zero for only a subset of the remainder.

4.2 Initial distribution construction

The next step is to seed the random walk with an initial distribution over lexical nodes specific to the given sentence. To do so, we first tag the input sentence with parts-of-speech and lemmatize each word based on the finite state transducer of Minnen et al. (2001). We search over consecutive words to match multi-word collocation nodes found in the graph. If the word or its lemma is part of a sequence that makes a complete collocation, that collocation is used. If not, the word or its lemma with its part of speech tag is used if it is present as a graph node. Finally, we fall back to the surface word form or underlying lemma form without part-of-speech information if necessary. For example, the input sentence: *The boy went with his dog to the store,* would result in mass being assigned to underlying graph nodes *boy#n, go_with, he, dog#n, store#n.*

Term weights are set with $tf.idf$ and then normalized. Each term's weight is proportional to the number of occurrences in the sentence times the log of the number of documents in some corpus divided by the number of documents containing that term. Our idf counts were derived from the English Gigaword corpus 1994-1999.

4.3 Computing the stationary distribution

We use the power iteration method to compute the stationary distribution for the Markov chain. Let the distribution over the N states at time step t of the random walk be denoted $\vec{v}^{(t)} \in \mathbb{R}^N$, where $\vec{v}^{(0)}$ is the initial distribution as defined above. We denote the column-normalized state-transition matrix as $M \in \mathbb{R}^{N \times N}$. We compute the stationary distribution of the Markov chain with probability β of returning to the initial distribution at each time step as the limit as $t \to \infty$ of:

$$\vec{v}^{(t)} = \beta\vec{v}^{(0)} + (1-\beta)M\vec{v}^{(t-1)}$$

In practice, we test for convergence by examining if $\sum_{i=1}^{N} \|v_i^{(t)} - v_i^{(t-1)}\| < 10^{-6}$, which in our experiments was usually after about 50 iterations.

Note that the resulting stationary distribution can be factored as the weighted sum of the stationary distributions of each word represented in the initial distribution. Because the initial distribution $\vec{v}^{(0)}$ is a normalized weighted sum, it can be re-written as $\vec{v}^{(0)} = \sum_k \gamma_k \cdot \vec{w}_k^{(0)}$ for $\vec{w}_k$ having a point mass at some underlying node in the graph and with γ_k positive such that $\sum_k \gamma_k = 1$. A simple proof by induction shows that the stationary distribution $\vec{v}^{(\infty)}$ is itself the weighted sum of the stationary distribution of each underlying word, i.e. $\vec{v}^{\infty} = \sum_k \gamma_k \cdot \vec{w}_k^{(\infty)}$.

In practice, the stationary distribution for a passage of text can be computed from a single specially-constructed Markov chain. The process is equivalent to taking the weighted sum of every word type in the passage computed independently. Because the time needed to compute the stationary distribution is dominated by the sparsity pattern of the walk's transition matrix, the computation of the stationary distribution for the passage takes a fraction of the time needed if the stationary distribution for each word were computed independently.

4.4 Comparing stationary distributions

In order to get a final relatedness score for a pair of texts, we must compare the stationary distribution from the first walk with the distribution from the second walk. There exist many measures for computing a final similarity (or divergence) measure from a pair of distributions, including geometric measures, information theoretic measures, and probabilistic measures. See, for instance, the overview of measures provided in Lee (2001).

In system development on training data, we found that most measures were reasonably effective. For the rest of this paper, we report numbers using cosine similarity, a standard measure in information retrieval; Jensen-Shannon divergence, a commonly used symmetric measure based on KL-divergence; and the dice measure extended to weighted features (Curran, 2004). A summary of these measures is shown in Table 2. Justification for the choice of these three measures is discussed in Section 6.

Cosine	$\frac{\vec{x}\cdot\vec{y}}{\|\vec{x}\|_2\|\vec{y}\|_2}$
Jensen-Shannon	$\frac{1}{2}D(x\|\frac{x+y}{2}) + \frac{1}{2}D(y\|\frac{x+y}{2})$
Dice	$\frac{2\sum_i \min(x_i,y_i)}{\sum_i x_i + \sum_i y_i}$

Table 2: Three measures of distributional similarity between vectors $\vec{x}$ and $\vec{y}$ used to compare the stationary distributions from passage-specific random walks. $D(p\|q)$ is KL-divergence, defined as $\sum_i p_i \log \frac{p_i}{q_i}$.

5 Evaluation

We evaluate the system on two tasks that might benefit from semantic similarity judgments: paraphrase recognition and recognizing textual entailment. A complete solution to either task will certainly require tools more tuned to linguistic structure; the paraphrase detection evaluation argues that the walk captures a useful notion of semantics at the sentence level. The entailment system evaluation demonstrates that the walk score can improve a larger system that does make use of more fine-grained linguistic knowledge.

5.1 Paraphrase recognition

The Microsoft Research (MSR) paraphrase data set (Dolan et al., 2004) is a collection of 5801 pairs of sentences automatically collected from newswire over 18 months. Each pair was hand-annotated by at least two judges with a binary yes/no judgment as to whether one sentence was a valid paraphrase of the other. Annotators were asked to judge whether the meanings of each sentence pair were reasonably equivalent. Inter-annotator agreement was 83%. However, 67% of the pairs were judged to be paraphrases, so the corpus does not reflect the rarity of paraphrases in the wild. The data set comes pre-split into 4076 training pairs and 1725 test pairs.

Because annotators were asked to judge if the meanings of two sentences were equivalent, the paraphrase corpus is a natural evaluation testbed for measures of semantic similarity. Mihalcea et al. (2006) defines a measure of text semantic similarity and evaluates it in an unsupervised paraphrase detector on this data set. We present their algorithm here as a strong reference point for semantic similarity between text passages, based on similar underlying lexical resources.

The Mihalcea et al. (2006) algorithm is a wrapper method that works with any underlying measure of lexical similarity. The similarity of a pair of texts T_1 and T_2, denoted as $sim_m(T_1, T_2)$, is computed as:

$$sim_m(T_1, T_2) = \frac{1}{2}f(T_1, T_2) + \frac{1}{2}f(T_2, T_1)$$
$$f(T_a, T_b) = \frac{\sum_{w \in T_a} maxSim(w, T_b) \cdot idf(w)}{\sum_{w \in T_a} idf(w)}$$

where the $maxSim(w, T)$ function is defined as the maximum similarity of the word w within the text T as determined by an underlying measure of lexical semantic relatedness. Here, $idf(w)$ is defined as the number of documents in a background corpus divided by the number of documents containing the term. $maxSim$ compares only within the same WordNet part-of-speech labeling in order to support evaluation with lexical relatedness measures that cannot cross part-of-speech boundaries.

Mihalcea et al. (2006) presents results for several underlying measures of lexical semantic relatedness. These are subdivided into corpus-based measures (using Latent Semantic Analysis (Landauer et al., 1998) and a pointwise-mutual information measure) and knowledge-based resources driven by WordNet. The latter include the methods of Jiang and Conrath (1997), Lesk (1986), Resnik (1999), and others.

In this unsupervised experimental setting, we consider using only a thresholded similarity value from our system and from the Mihalcea algorithm to determine the paraphrase or non-paraphrase judgment. For consistency with previous work, we threshold at 0.5. Note that this threshold could be tuned on the training data in a supervised setting. Informally, we observed that on the training data a threshold of near 0.5 was often a good choice for this task.

Table 3 shows the results of our system and a representative subset of those reported in (Mihalcea et al., 2006). All the reported measures from both systems do a reasonable job of paraphrase detection – the majority of pairs in the corpus are deemed paraphrases when the similarity measure is thresholded at 0.5, and indeed this is reasonable given the way in which the data were collected. The first three rows are the performance of the similarity judgments output by our walk under three different distributional similarity measures (cosine, dice, and Jensen-Shannon), with the walk score using the dice measure outperforming all other systems on both accuracy and macro-averaged F_1. The output of the Mihalcea system using a representative subset of underlying lexical measures is reported in the second and third segments. The fourth segment reports the results of baseline methods—the vector space similarity measure is cosine similarity among vectors using $tf.idf$ weighting, and the random baseline chooses uniformly at random, both as reported in (Mihalcea et al., 2006). We add the additional baseline of always guessing the majority class label because the data set is skewed toward "paraphrase."

System	Acc.	F_1: c_1	F_1: c_0	Macro F_1
Random Graph Walk				
Walk (Cosine)	0.687	0.787	0.413	0.617
Walk (Dice)	**0.708**	0.801	**0.453**	**0.645**
Walk (JS)	0.688	0.805	0.225	0.609
Mihalcea et. al., Corpus-based				
PMI-IR	0.699	**0.810**	0.301	0.625
LSA	0.684	0.805	0.170	0.560
Mihalcea et. al., WordNet-based				
J&C	0.693	0.790	0.433	0.629
Lesk	0.693	0.789	0.439	0.629
Resnik	0.690	0.804	0.254	0.618
Baselines				
Vector-based	0.654	0.753	0.420	0.591
Random	0.513	0.578	0.425	0.518
Majority (c_1)	0.665	0.799	—	0.399

Table 3: System performance on 1725 examples of the MSR paraphrase detection test set. Accuracy (micro-averaged F_1), F_1 for c_1 "paraphrase" and c_0 "non-paraphrase" classes, and macro-averaged F_1 are reported.

In an unbalanced data setting, it is important to consider more than just accuracy and F_1 on the majority class. We report accuracy, F_1 for each class label, and the macro-averaged F_1 on all systems. F_1: c_0 and Macro-F_1 are inferred for the system variants reported in (Mihalcea et al., 2006). Micro-averaged F_1 in this context is equivalent to accuracy (Manning et al., 2008).

Mihalcea also reports a combined classifier which thresholds on the simple average of the individual classifiers, resulting in the highest numbers reported in that work, with accuracy of 0.703, "paraphrase" class F_1: $c_1 = 0.813$, and inferred Macro $F_1 = 0.648$. We believe that the scores

Data Set	Cosine	Dice	Jensen-Shannon
RTE2_dev	55.00	51.75	**55.50**
RTE2_test	57.00	54.25	**57.50**
RTE3_dev	**59.00**	57.25	**59.00**
RTE3_test	55.75	55.75	**56.75**

Table 4: Accuracy of entailment detection when thresholding the text similarity score output by the random walk.

Data Set	Baseline	Cosine	Dice	JS
RTE2_dev	66.00	**66.75**	65.75	66.25
RTE2_test	63.62	**64.50**	63.12	63.25
RTE3_dev	70.25	70.50	**70.62**	70.38
RTE3_test	65.44	**65.82**	65.44	65.44

Table 5: Accuracy when the random walk is added as a feature of an existing RTE system (left column) under various distance metrics (right columns).

from the various walk measures might also improve performance when in a combination classifier, but without access to the individual judgments in that system we are unable to evaluate the claim directly. However, we did create an upper bound reference by combining the walk scores with easily computable simple surface statistics. We trained a support vector classifier on the MSR paraphrase training set with a feature space consisting of the walk score under each distributional similarity measure, the length of each text, the difference between those lengths, and the number of unigram, bigram, trigram, and four-gram overlaps between the two texts. The resulting classifier achieved accuracy of 0.719 with $F_1\!: c_1 = 0.807$ and $F_1\!: c_0 = 0.487$ and Macro $F_1 = 0.661$. This is a substantial improvement, roughly on the same order of magnitude as from switching to the best performing distributional similarity function.

Note that the running time of the Mihalcea et al. algorithm for comparing texts T_1 and T_2 requires $|T_1| \cdot |T_2|$ individual similarity judgments. By contrast, this work allows semantic profiles to be constructed and evaluated for each text in a single pass, independent of the number of terms in the texts.

The performance of this unsupervised application of walks to paraphrase recognition suggests that the framework captures important intuitions about similarity in text passages. In the next section, we examine the performance of the measure embedded in a larger system that seeks to make fine-grained entailment judgments.

5.2 Textual entailment

The Recognizing Textual Entailment Challenge (Dagan et al., 2005) is a task in which systems assess whether a sentence is entailed by a short passage or sentence. Participants have used a variety of strategies beyond lexical relatedness or overlap for the task, but some have also used only relatively simple similarity metrics. Many systems incorporate a number of these strategies, so we experimented with using the random walk to improve an existing RTE system. This addresses the fact that using similarity alone to detect entailment is impoverished: entailment is an asymmetric decision while similarity is necessarily symmetric. However, we also experiment with thresholding random walk scores as a measure of entailment to compare to other systems and provide a baseline for whether the walk could be useful for entailment detection.

We tested performance on the development and test sets for the Second and Third PASCAL RTE Challenges (Bar-Haim et al., 2006; Giampiccolo et al., 2007). Each of these data sets contains 800 pairs of texts for which to determine entailment. In some cases, no words from a passage appear in WordNet, leading to an empty vector. In this case, we use the Levenshtein string similarity measure between the two texts; this fallback is used in fewer than five examples in any of our data sets (Levenshtein, 1966).

Table 4 shows the results of using the similarity measure alone to determine entailment; the system's ability to recognize entailment is above chance on all data sets. Since the RTE data sets are balanced, we used the median of the random walk scores for each data set as the threshold rather than using an absolute threshold. While the measure does not outperform most RTE systems, it does outperform some systems that used only lexical overlap such as the Katrenko system from the second challenge (Bar-Haim et al., 2006). These results show that the measure is somewhat sensitive to the distance metric chosen, and that the best distance metric may vary by application.

To test the random walk's value for improving an existing RTE system, we incorporated the walk as a feature of the Stanford RTE system (Chambers et al., 2007). This system computes a weighted sum of a variety of features to make an entailment decision. We added the random walk score as one of these features and scaled it to have a magnitude comparable to the other features; other than scaling, there was no system-specific engineering to add this feature.

As shown in Table 5, adding the random walk feature improves the original RTE system. Thus, the random walk score provides meaningful evidence for detecting entailment that is not subsumed by other information, even in a system with several years of feature engineering and competitive performance. In particular, this RTE system contains features representing the alignment score between two passages; this score is composed of a combination of lexical relatedness scores between words in each text. The ability of the random walk to add value to the system even given this score, which contains many common lexical relatedness measures, suggests we are able to extract text similarity information that is distinct from other measures. To put the gain we achieve in perspective, an increase in the Stanford RTE system's score of the same magnitude would have moved the system's two challenge entries from 7th and 25th to 6th and 17th, respectively, in the second RTE Challenge. It is likely the gain from this feature could be increased by closer integration with the system and optimizing the initial distribution creation for this task.

By using the score as a feature, the system is able to take advantage of properties of the score distribution. While Table 4 shows performance when a threshold is picked a priori, experimenting with that threshold increases performance by over two percent. By lowering the threshold (classifying more passages as entailments), we increase recall of entailed pairs without losing as much precision in non-entailed pairs since many have very low scores. As a feature, this aspect of the score distribution can be incorporated by the system, but it cannot be used in a simple thresholding design.

6 Discussion

The random walk framework smoothes an initial distribution of words into a much larger lexical space. In one sense, this is similar to the technique of query expansion used in information retrieval. A traditional query expansion model extends a bag of words (usually a query) with additional related words. In the case of pseudo-relevance feedback,

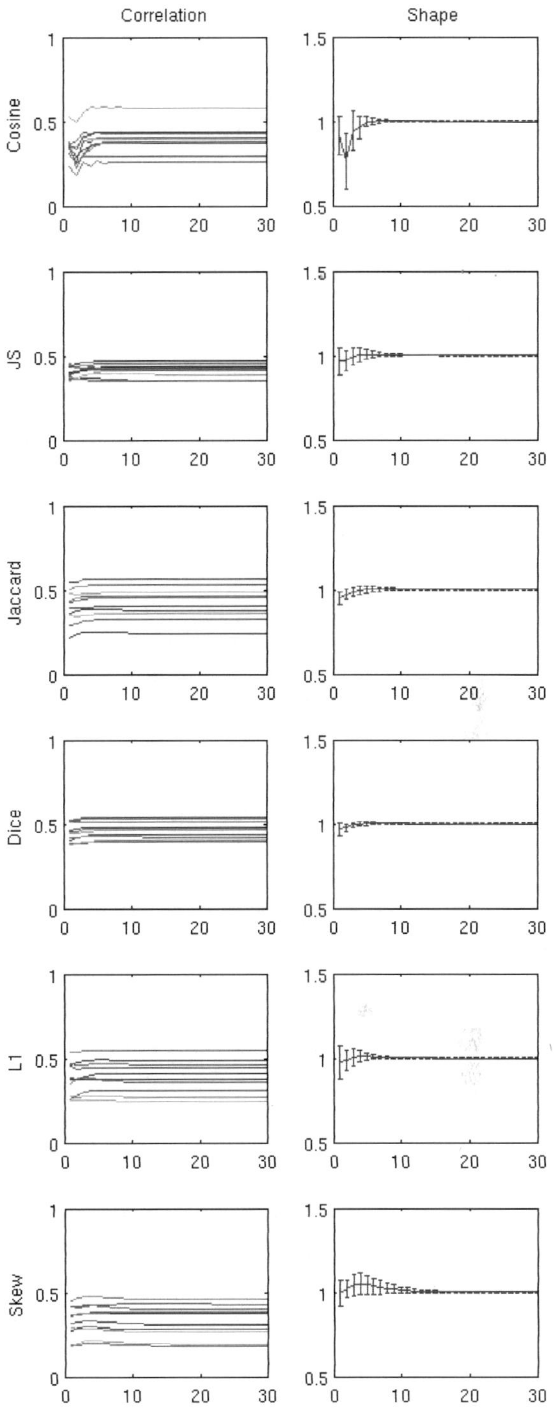

Figure 1: Impact of number of walk steps on correlation with MSR paraphrase judgments. The left column shows absolute correlation across ten resampled runs (y-axis) versus number of steps taken (x-axis). The right column plots the mean ratio of performance at step t (x-axis) versus performance at convergence.

these words come from the first documents returned by the search engine, but other modes of selecting additional words exist. In the random walk framework, this expansion is analogous to taking only a single step of the random walk. Indeed, in the case of the translation model introduced in (Berger and Lafferty, 1999), they are mathematically equivalent. However, we have argued that the walk is an effective global aggregator of relatedness information. We can formulate the question as an empirical one—does simulating the walk until convergence really improve our representation of the text document?

To answer this question, we extracted a 200 items subset of the MSR training data and truncated the walk at each time step up until our convergence threshold was reached at around 50 iterations. We then evaluated the correlation of the walk score with the correct label from the MSR data for 10 random resamplings of 66 documents each. Figure 1 plots this result for different distributional similarity measures. We observe that as the number of steps increases, performance under most of the distributional similarity measures improves, with the exception of the asymmetric skew-divergence measure introduced in (Lee, 2001).

This plot also gives some insight into the qualitative nature of the stability of the various distributional measures for the paraphrase task. For instance, we observe that the Jensen-Shannon score and dice score tend to be the most consistent between runs, but the dice score has a slightly higher mean. This explains in part why the dice score was the best performing measure for the task. In contrast, cosine similarity was observed to perform poorly here, although it was found to be the best measure when combined with our textual entailment system. We believe this discrepancy is due in part to the feature scaling issues described in section 5.2.

7 Final remarks

Notions of similarity have many levels of granularity, from general metrics for lexical relatedness to application-specific measures between text passages. While lexical relatedness is well studied, it is not directly applicable to text passages without some surrounding environment. Because this work represents words and passages as interchangeable mathematical objects (teleport vectors), our approach holds promise as a general framework for aggregating local relatedness information between words into reliable measures between text passages.

The random walk framework can be used to evaluate changes to lexical resources because it covers the entire scope of a resource: the whole graph is leveraged to construct the final distribution, so changes to any part of the graph are reflected in each walk. This means that the meaningfulness of changes in the graph can be evaluated according to how they affect these text similarity scores; this provides a more semantically relevant evaluation of updates to a resource than, for example, counting how many new words or links between words have been added. As shown in Jarmasz and Szpakowicz (2003), an updated resource may have many more links and concepts but still have similar performance on applications as the original. Evaluations of WordNet extensions, such as those in Navigli and Velardi (2005) and Snow et al. (2006), are easily conducted within the framework of the random walk.

The presented framework for text semantic similarity with random graph walks is more general than the WordNet-based instantiation explored here. Transition matrices from alternative linguistic resources such as corpus co-occurrence statistics or larger knowledge bases such as Wikipedia may very well add value as a lexical resource underlying the walk. One might also consider tailoring the output of the walk with machine learning techniques like those presented in (Minkov and Cohen, 2007).

References

E. Agirre and A. Soroa. 2009. Personalizing pagerank for word sense disambiguation. In *EACL*, Athens, Greece.

R. Bar-Haim, I. Dagan, B. Dolan, L. Ferro, D. Giampiccolo, B. Magnini, and I. Szpektor. 2006. The 2nd PASCAL recognizing textual entailment challenge. In *PASCAL Challenges Workshop on RTE*.

A. Berger and J. Lafferty. 1999. Information retrieval as statistical translation. *SIGIR 1999*, pages 222–229.

P. Berkhin. 2005. A survey on pagerank computing. *Internet Mathematics*, 2(1):73–120.

A. Budanitsky and G. Hirst. 2006. Evaluating wordnet-based measures of lexical semantic relatedness. *Computational Linguistics*, 32(1):13–47.

N. Chambers, D. Cer, T. Grenager, D. Hall, C. Kiddon, B. MacCartney, M. de Marneffe, D. Ramage, E. Yeh, and C. D. Manning. 2007. Learning alignments and leveraging natural logic. In *ACL-PASCAL Workshop on Textual Entailment and Paraphrasing*.

K. Collins-Thompson and J. Callan. 2005. Query expansion using random walk models. In *CIKM '05*, pages 704–711, New York, NY, USA. ACM Press.

C. Corley and R. Mihalcea. 2005. Measuring the semantic similarity of texts. In *ACL Workshop on Empirical Modeling of Semantic Equivalence and Entailment*, pages 13–18, Ann Arbor, Michigan, June. ACL.

J. R. Curran. 2004. *From Distributional to Semantic Similarity*. Ph.D. thesis, University of Edinburgh.

I. Dagan, O. Glickman, and B. Magnini. 2005. The PASCAL recognizing textual entailment challenge. In Quinonero-Candela et al., editor, *MLCW 2005, LNAI Volume 3944*, pages 177–190. Springer-Verlag.

B. Dolan, C. Quirk, and C. Brockett. 2004. Unsupervised construction of large paraphrase corpora: Exploiting massively parallel news sources. In *Coling 2004*, pages 350–356, Geneva, Switzerland, Aug 23–Aug 27. COLING.

C. Fellbaum. 1998. *WordNet: An electronic lexical database.* MIT Press.

D. Giampiccolo, B. Magnini, I. Dagan, and B. Dolan. 2007. The 3rd PASCAL Recognizing Textual Entailment Challenge. In *ACL-PASCAL Workshop on Textual Entailment and Paraphrasing*, pages 1–9, Prague, June.

O. Glickman, I. Dagan, and M. Koppel. 2005. Web based probabilistic textual entailment. In *PASCAL Challenges Workshop on RTE*.

T. H. Haveliwala. 2002. Topic-sensitive pagerank. In *WWW '02*, pages 517–526, New York, NY, USA. ACM.

T. Hughes and D. Ramage. 2007. Lexical semantic relatedness with random graph walks. In *EMNLP-CoNLL*, pages 581–589.

M. Jarmasz and S. Szpakowicz. 2003. Roget's thesaurus and semantic similarity. In *Proceedings of RANLP-03*, pages 212–219.

J. J. Jiang and D. W. Conrath. 1997. Semantic similarity based on corpus statistics and lexical taxonomy. In *ROCLING X*, pages 19–33.

T.K. Landauer, P.W. Foltz, and D. Laham. 1998. An introduction to latent semantic analysis. *Discourse Processes*, 25(2-3):259–284.

L. Lee. 2001. On the effectiveness of the skew divergence for statistical language analysis. In *Artificial Intelligence and Statistics 2001*, pages 65–72.

M. Lesk. 1986. Automatic sense disambiguation using machine readable dictionaries: how to tell a pine cone from an ice cream cone. *ACM SIGDOC: Proceedings of the 5th Annual International Conference on Systems Documentation*, 1986:24–26.

V. I. Levenshtein. 1966. *Binary Codes Capable of Correcting Deletions, Insertions, and Reversals.* Ph.D. thesis, Soviet Physics Doklady.

C. Manning, P. Raghavan, and H. Schutze, 2008. *Introduction to information retrieval*, pages 258–263. Cambridge University Press.

R. Mihalcea, C. Corley, and C. Strapparava. 2006. Corpus-based and knowledge-based measures of text semantic similarity. *AAAI 2006*, 6.

E. Minkov and W. W. Cohen. 2007. Learning to rank typed graph walks: Local and global approaches. In *WebKDD and SNA-KDD joint workshop 2007*.

G. Minnen, J. Carroll, and D. Pearce. 2001. Applied morphological processing of English. *Natural Language Engineering*, 7(03):207–223.

A. Montejo-Ráez, J.M. Perea, F. Martínez-Santiago, M. A. García-Cumbreras, M. M. Valdivia, and A. Ureña López. 2007. Combining lexical-syntactic information with machine learning for recognizing textual entailment. In *ACL-PASCAL Workshop on Textual Entailment and Paraphrasing*, pages 78–82, Prague, June. ACL.

R. Navigli and P. Velardi. 2005. Structural semantic interconnections: A knowledge-based approach to word sense disambiguation. *IEEE Trans. Pattern Anal. Mach. Intell.*, 27(7):1075–1086.

P. Resnik. 1999. Semantic similarity in a taxonomy: An information-based measure and its application to problems of ambiguity in natural language. *JAIR*, (11):95–130.

R. Snow, D. Jurafsky, and A. Y. Ng. 2006. Semantic taxonomy induction from heterogenous evidence. In *ACL*, pages 801–808.

Classifying Japanese Polysemous Verbs based on Fuzzy C-means Clustering

Yoshimi Suzuki
Interdisciplinary Graduate School of Medicine and Engineering
University of Yamanashi, Japan
ysuzuki@yamanashi.ac.jp

Fumiyo Fukumoto
Interdisciplinary Graduate School of Medicine and Engineering
University of Yamanashi, Japan
fukumoto@yamanashi.ac.jp

Abstract

This paper presents a method for classifying Japanese polysemous verbs using an algorithm to identify overlapping nodes with more than one cluster. The algorithm is a graph-based unsupervised clustering algorithm, which combines a generalized modularity function, spectral mapping, and fuzzy clustering technique. The modularity function for measuring cluster structure is calculated based on the frequency distributions over verb frames with selectional preferences. Evaluations are made on two sets of verbs including polysemies.

1 Introduction

There has been quite a lot of research concerned with automatic clustering of semantically similar words or automatic retrieval of collocations among them from corpora. Most of this work is based on similarity measures derived from the distribution of words in corpora. However, the facts that a single word does have more than one sense and that the distribution of a word in a corpus is a mixture of usages of different senses of the same word often hamper such attempts. In general, restriction of the subject domain makes the problem of polysemy less problematic. However, even in texts from a restricted domain such as *economics* or *sports*, one encounters quite a large number of polysemous words. Therefore, semantic classification of polysemies has been an interest since the earliest days when a number of large scale corpora have become available.

In this paper, we focus on Japanese polysemous verbs, and present a method for polysemous verb classification. We used a graph-based unsupervised clustering algorithm (Zhang, 2007). The algorithm combines the idea of modularity function Q, spectral relaxation and fuzzy c-means clustering method to identify overlapping nodes with more than one cluster. The modularity function measures the quality of a cluster structure. Spectral mapping performs a dimensionality reduction which makes it possible to cluster in the very high dimensional spaces. The fuzzy c-means allows for the detection of nodes with more than one cluster. We applied the algorithm to cluster polysemous verbs. The modularity function for measuring the quality of a cluster structure is calculated based on the frequency distributions over verb frames with selectional preferences. We collected semantic classes from IPAL Japanese dictionary (IPAL, 1987), and used them as a gold standard data. IPAL lists about 900 Japanese basic verbs, and categorizes each verb into multiple senses. Moreover, the categorization is based on verbal syntax with respect to the choice of its arguments. Therefore, if the clustering algorithm induces a polysemous verb classification on the basis of verbal syntax, then the resulting classification should agree the IPAL classes. We used a large Japanese newspaper corpus and EDR (Electronic Dictionary Research) dictionary (EDR, 1986) to obtain verbs and their subcategorization frames with selectional preferences [1]. The results obtained using two data sets were better than the baseline, EM algorithm.

The rest of the paper is organized as follows. The next section presents related work. After describing Japanese verb with selectional preferences, we present a distributional similarity in Section 4, and a graph-based unsupervised clustering algorithm in Section 5. Results using two data sets are reported in Section 6. We give our conclusion in Section 7.

[1] We did not use IPAL, but instead EDR sense dictionary. Because IPAL did not have senses for the case filler which were used to create selectional preferences.

Proceedings of the 2009 Workshop on Graph-based Methods for Natural Language Processing, ACL-IJCNLP 2009, pages 32–40, Suntec, Singapore, 7 August 2009.

2 Related Work

Graph-based algorithms have been widely used to classify semantically similar words (Jannink, 1999; Galley, 2003; Widdows, 2002; Muller, 2006). Sinha and Mihalcea proposed a graph-based algorithm for unsupervised word sense disambiguation which combines several semantic similarity measures including Resnik's metric (Resnik, 1995), and algorithms for graph centrality (Sinha, 2007). They reported that the results using the SENSEVAL-2 and SENSEVAL-3 English all-words data sets lead to relative error rate reductions of 5 - 8% as compared to the previsous work (Mihalcea, 2005). More recently, Matsuo *et al.* (2006) presented a method of word clustering based on Web counts using a search engine. They applied $Newman$ clustering (Newman, 2004) for identifying word clusters. They reported that the results obtained by the algorithm were better than those obtained by average-link agglomerative clustering using 90 Japanese noun words. However, their method relied on hard-clustering models, and thus have largely ignored the issue of polysemy that word belongs to more than one cluster.

In contrast to hard-clustering algorithms, soft clustering allows that words to belong to more than one cluster. Much of the previous work on word classification with soft clustering is based on the EM algorithm (Pereira, 1993). Torisawa *et al.*, (2002) presented a method to detect associative relationships between verb phrases. They used the EM algorithm to calculate the likelihood of co-occurrences, and reported that the EM is effective to produce associative relationships with a certain accuracy. More recent work in this direction is that of Schulte *et al.*, (2008). They proposed a method for semantic verb classification based on verb frames with selectional preferences. They combined the EM training with the MDL principle. The MDL principle is used to induce WordNet-based selectional preferences for arguments within subcategorization frames. The results showed the effectiveness of the method. Our work is similar to their method in the use of verb frames with selectional preferences. Korhonen *et al.* (2003) used verb–frame pairs to cluster verbs into Levin-style semantic classes (Korhonen, 2003). They used the Information Bottleneck, and classified 110 test verbs into Levin-style classes. They had a focus on the interpretation of verbal polysemy as represented by the soft clusters: they interpreted polysemy as multiple-hard assignments.

In the context of Japancsc taxonomy of verbs and their classes, Utsuro *et al.* (1995) proposed a class-based method for sense classification of verbal polysemy in case frame acquisition from parallel corpora (Utsuro, 1995). A measure of bilingual class/class association is introduced and used for discovering sense clusters in the sense distribution of English predicates and Japanese case element nouns. They used the test data consisting of 10 English and Japanese verbs taken from Roget's Thesaurus and BGH (Bunrui Goi Hyo) (BGH, 1989). They reported 92.8% of the discovered clusters were correct. Tokunaga *et al.* (1997) presented a method for extending an existing thesaurus by classifying new words in terms of that thesaurus. New words are classified on the basis of relative probabilities of a word belonging to a given word class, with the probabilities calculated using noun-verb co-occurrence pairs. Experiments using the Japanese BGH thesaurus showed that new words can be classified correctly with a maximum accuracy of more than 80%, while they did not report in detail whether the clusters captured polysemies.

3 Selectional Preferences

A major approach on word clustering task is to use distribution of a word in a corpus, *i.e.*, words are classified into classes based on their distributional similarity. Similarity measures based on distributional hypothesis compare a pair of weighted feature vectors that characterize two words (Hindle, 1990; Lin, 1998; Dagan, 1999).

Like previous work on verb classification, we used subcategorization frame distributions with selectional preferences to calculate similarity between verbs (Schulte, 2008). We used the EDR dictionary of selectional preferences consisting of 5,269 basic Japanese verbs and the EDR concept dictionary (EDR, 1986). For selectional preferences, the dictionary has each concept of a verb, the group of possible co-occurrence surface-level case particles, the types of concept relation label that correspond to the surface-level case as well as the range of possible concepts that may fill the deep-level case. Figure 1 illustrates an example of a verb "*taberu* (eat)".

In Figure 1, "Sentence pattern" refers to the co-occurrence pattern between a verb and a noun

[Sentence pattern]	<word1> *ga*	<word2> *wo*	*taberu* (eat)
[Sense relation]	agent	object	
[Case particle]	*ga* (nominative)	*wo* (accusative)	
[Sense identifier]	30f6b0 (human);30f6bf (animal)	30f6bf(animal);30f6ca(plants); 30f6e5(parts of plants); 3f9639(food and drink); 3f963a(feed)	

Figure 1: An example of a verb "*taberu* (eat)"

with a case marker. "Sense relation" expresses the deep-level case, while "Case particle" shows the surface-level case. "Sense identifier" refers to the range of possible concepts for the case filler. The subcategorization frame pattern of a sentence (1), for example consists of two arguments with selectional preferences and is given below:

(1) *Nana_ga apple_wo taberu.*
'Nana eats an apple.'

taberu	30f6b0_*ga*	3f9639_*wo*
eat	human_nom	entity_acc

In the above frame pattern, x of the argument "x_y" refers to sense identifier and y denotes case particle.

4 Distributional Similarity

Various similarity measures have been proposed and used for NLP tasks (Korhonen, 2002). In this paper, we concentrate on three distance-based, and entropy-based similarity measures. In the following formulae, x and y refer to the verb vectors, their subscripts to the verb subcategorization frame values.

1. **The Cosine measure (Cos):** The cosine measures the similarity of the two vectors x and y by calculating the cosine of the angle between vectors, where each dimension of the vector corresponds to each frame with selectional preferences patterns of verbs and each value of the dimension is the frequency of each pattern.

2. **The Cosine measure based on probability of relative frequencies (rfCos):** The differences between the cosine and the value based on relative frequencies of verb frames with selectional preferences are the values of each dimension, *i.e.*, the former are frequencies of each pattern and the latter are the fraction of the total number of verb frame patterns belonging to the verb.

3. **L_1 Norm (L_1):** The L_1 Norm is a member of a family of measures known as the Minkowski Distance, for measuring the distance between two points in space. The L_1 distance between two verbs can be written as:

$$L_1(x,y) = \sum_{i=1}^{n} \mid x_i - y_i \mid .$$

4. **Kullback-Leibler (*KL*):** Kullback-Leibler is a measure from information theory that determines the inefficiency of assuming a model probability distribution given the true distribution.

$$KL(x,y) = \sum_{i=1}^{n} P(x_i) * \log \frac{P(x_i)}{P(y_i)}.$$

where $P(x_i) = \frac{x_i}{|x|}$. *KL* is not defined in case $y_i = 0$. So, the probability distributions must be smoothed (Korhonen, 2002). We used two smoothing methods, *i.e.*, Add-one smoothing and Witten and Bell smoothing (Witten, 1991).[2] Moreover, two variants of *KL*, α-skew divergence and the Jensen-Shannon, were used to perform smoothing.

5. **α-skew divergence (α div.):** The α-skew divergence measure is a variant of *KL*, and is defined as:

$$\alpha div(x,y) = KL(y, \alpha \cdot x + (1-\alpha) \cdot y).$$

Lee (1999) reported the best results with α = 0.9. We used the same value.

6. **The Jensen-Shannon (*JS*):** The Jensen-Shannon is a measure that relies on the assumption that if x and y are similar, they are close to their average. It is defined as:

[2] We report Add-one smoothing results in the evaluation, as it was better than Witten and Bell smoothing.

$$JS(x,y) = \frac{1}{2}[KL(x, \frac{x+y}{2}) + KL(y, \frac{x+y}{2})].$$

All measures except Cos and rfCos showed that smaller values indicate a closer relation between two verbs. Thus, we used inverse of each value.

5 Clustering Method

The clustering algorithm used in this study was a graph-based unsupervised clustering reported by (Zhang, 2007). This algorithm detects overlapping nodes by the combination of a modularity function based on Newman Girvan's Q function (Newman, 2004), spectral mapping that maps input nodes into Euclidean space, and fuzzy c-means clustering which allows node to belong to more than one cluster. They evaluated their method by applying several data including the American college football team network, and found that the algorithm successfully detected overlapping nodes. We thus used the algorithm to cluster verbs.

Here are the key steps of the algorithm: Given a set of input verbs $V = \{v_1, v_2, \cdots v_n\}$, an upper bound K of the number of clusters, the adjacent matrix $A = (a_{ij})_{n \times n}$ of an input verbs and a threshold λ that can convert a soft assignment into final clustering, *i.e.*, the value of λ decreases, each verb is distributed into larger number of clusters. We calculated the adjacent matrix A by using one of the similarity measures mentioned in Section 4, *i.e.*, the value of the edge between v_i and v_j. a_{ij} refers to the similarity value between them.

1. Form a diagonal matrix $D = (d_{ii})$, where $d_{ii} = \sum_k a_{ik}$.
2. Form the eigenvector matrix $E_K = [e_1, e_2, \cdots, e_K]$ by calculating the top K eigenvectors of the generalized eigensystem $Ax = tDx$.
3. For each value of k, $2 \leq k \leq K$:
   (a) Form the matrix $E_k = [e_2, \cdots, e_k]$ where e_k refers to the top k-th eigenvector.
   (b) Normalize the rows of E_k to unit length using Euclidean distance norm.
   (c) Cluster the row vectors of E_k using fuzzy c-means to obtain a soft assignment matrix U_k. Fuzzy c-means is carried out through an iterative optimization (minimization) of the objective function J_m with the update of membership degree u_{ij} and the cluster centers c_j. J_m is defined as:

$$J_m = \sum_{i=1}^{n}\sum_{j=1}^{k} u_{ij}^m \parallel v_i - c_j \parallel^2,$$

   where u_{ij} is the membership degree of v_i in the cluster j, and $\sum_j u_{ij} = 1$. $m \in [1, \infty]$ is a weight exponent controlling the degree of fuzzification. c_j is the d-dimensional center of the cluster j.
   $\parallel v_i - c_j \parallel$ is defined as:

$$\parallel v_i - c_j \parallel^2 = (v_i - c_j)E(v_i - c_j)^T.$$

   where E denotes an unit matrix. The procedure converges to a saddle point of J_m.
4. Pick the k and the corresponding $n \times k$ soft assignment matrix U_k that maximizes the modularity function $\tilde{Q}(U_k)$. Here $U_k = [u_1, \cdots u_k]$ with $0 \leq u_{ic} \leq 1$ for each $c = 1, \cdots, k$, and $\sum_1^k u_{ic} = 1$ for each $i = 1, \cdots, n$. A modularity function of a soft assignment matrix is defined as:

$$\tilde{Q}(U_k) = \sum_{c=1}^{k}[\frac{A(\tilde{V}_c, \tilde{V}_c)}{A(V,V)} - (\frac{A(\tilde{V}_c, V)}{A(V,V)})^2],$$

   where

$$A(\tilde{V}_c, \tilde{V}_c) = \sum_{i \in \tilde{V}_c, j \in \tilde{V}_c} \{\frac{(u_{ic} + u_{jc})}{2}\} a_{ij},$$
$$A(\tilde{V}_c, V) = A(\tilde{V}_c, \tilde{V}_c) + \sum_{i \in \tilde{V}_c, j \in V \setminus \tilde{V}_c} \{\frac{(u_{ic} + (1 - u_{jc}))}{2}\} a_{ij},$$
$$A(V,V) = \sum_{i \in V, j \in V} a_{ij}.$$

   $\tilde{Q}(U_k)$ shows comparison of the actual values of internal or external edges with its respective expectation value under the assumption of equally probable links and given data sizes.

6 Experiments

6.1 Experimental setup

We created test verbs using two sets of Japanese Mainichi newspaper corpus. One is a set consisting one year (2007) newspapers (We call it a set from 2007), and another is a set of 17 years (from 1991 to 2007) Japanese Mainichi newspapers (We call it a set from 1991_2007). For each set, all Japanese documents were parsed using the syntactic analyzer Cabocha (Kudo, 2003). We selected verbs, each frequency $f(v)$ is, $500 \leq f(v) \leq 10{,}000$. As a result, we obtained 279 verbs for a set from 2007 and 1,692 verbs for a set from 1991_2007. From these verbs, we chose verbs which appeared in the machine readable dictionary, IPAL. This selection resulted in a total of 81 verbs for a set from 2007, and 170 verbs, for a set from 1991_2007. We obtained Japanese verb frames with selectional preferences using these two sets. We extracted sentence patterns with their frequencies. Noun words within each sentence were tagged sense identifier by using the EDR Japanese sense dictionary. As a result, we obtained 56,400 verb frame patterns for a set from 2007, and 300,993 patterns for a set from 1991_2007.

We created the gold standard data, verb classes, using IPAL. IPAL lists about 900 Japanese verbs and categorizes each verb into multiple senses, based on verbal syntax and semantics. It also listed *synonym* verbs. Table 1 shows a fragment of the entry associated with the Japanese verb *taberu*. The verb "*taberu*" has two senses, "eat" and "live". "pattern" refers to the case frame(s) associated with each verb sense. According to the IPAL, we obtained verb classes, each class corresponds to a sense of each verb. There are 87 classes for a set from 2007, and 152 classes for a set from 1991_2007. The examples of the test verbs and their senses are shown in Table 2.

For evaluation of verb classification, we used the precision, recall, and F-score, which were defined by (Schulte, 2000), especially to capture how many verbs does the algorithm actually detect more than just the predominant sense.

For comparison against polysemies, we utilized the EM algorithm which is widely used as a soft clustering technique (Schulte, 2008). We followed the method presented in (Rooth, 1999). We used a probability distribution over verb frames with selectional preferences. The initial probabilities were often determined randomly. We set the initial probabilities by using the result of the standard k-means. For k-means, we used 50 random replications of the initialization, each time initializing the cluster center with k randomly chosen. We used up to 20 iterations to learn the model probabilities.

Table 3: Results for a set from 2007

Method	m	λ	C	Prec	Rec	F
FCM	2.0	0.09	74	.815	.483	**.606**
FCM(none)	1.5	0.07	74	.700	.477	.567
EM	–	–	87	.308	.903	.463

Table 4: Results against each measure

Measure	m	λ	C	Prec	Rec	F
cos	3.0	0.02	74	.660	.517	.580
rfcos	2.0	0.04	74	.701	.488	.576
L_1	2.0	0.04	74	.680	.500	.576
KL	2.0	0.09	74	.815	.483	.606
α div.	2.0	0.04	74	.841	.471	.604
JS	1.5	0.03	74	.804	.483	.603
EM	–	–	87	.308	.903	.463

6.2 Basic results

The results using a set from 2007 are shown in Table 3. We used *KL* as a similarity measure in FCM. "FCM(none)" shows the result not applying a spectral mapping, *i.e.*, we applied fuzzy c-means to each vector of verb, where each dimension of the vector corresponds to each frame with selectional preferences. "m" and "λ" refer to the parameters used by Fuzzy C-means. "C" refers to the number of clusters obtained by each method. "m", "λ" and "C" in Table 3 denote the value that maximized the F-score. "C" in the EM is fixed in advance. The result of EM shows the best result among 20 iterations. As can be seen clearly from Table 3, the result obtained by fuzzy c-means was better to the result by EM algorithm. Table 3 also shows that a dimensionality reduction, *i.e.*, spectral mapping improved overall performance, especially we have obtained better precision. The result suggests that a dimensionality reduction is effective for clustering. Table 4 shows the results obtained by using each similarity measure. As we can see from Table 4, the overall results obtained by information theory based measures, *KL*, α div., and *JS* were slightly better to the results obtained by other distance based measures.

We note that the fuzzy c-means has two parameters λ and m, where λ is a threshold of the as-

Table 1: A fragment of the entry associated with the Japanese verb "*taberu*"

Sense_id	Pattern		Synonyms
1	*kare*(he)_*ga*(nominative)	*soba*(noodles)_*wo*(accusative)	*kuu* (eat)
2	*kare* (he)_*ga*(nominative)	*fukugyo*(a part-time job)_*de*(accusative)	*kurasu* (live)

Table 2: Examples of test verbs and their polysemic gold standard senses

Id	Sense	Verb Classes	Id	Sense	Verb Classes
1	treat	$\{ashirau, atsukau\}$	11	tell	$\{oshieru, shimesu, shiraseru\}$
2	prey	$\{negau, inoru\}$	12	persuade	$\{oshieru, satosu\}$
3	wish	$\{negau, nozomu\}$	13	congratulate	$\{iwau, syukufukusuru\}$
4	ask	$\{negau, tanomu\}$	14	accept	$\{uketoru, ukeru, morau, osameru\}$
5	leave	$\{saru, hanareru\}$	15	take	$\{uketoru, toru, kaisyakusuru, miru\}$
6	move	$\{saru, utsuru\}$	16	lose	$\{ushinau, nakusu\}$
7	pass	$\{saru, kieru, sugiru\}$	17	miss	$\{ushinau, torinogasu, itusuru\}$
8	go	$\{saru, sugiru, iku\}$	18	survive, lose	$\{ushinau, nakusu, shinareru\}$
9	remove	$\{saru, hanareru, toozakeru\ torinozoku\}$	19	give	$\{kubaru, watasu, wakeru\}$
10	lead	$\{oshieru, michibiku, tugeru\}$	20	arrange	$\{kubaru, haichisuru\}$

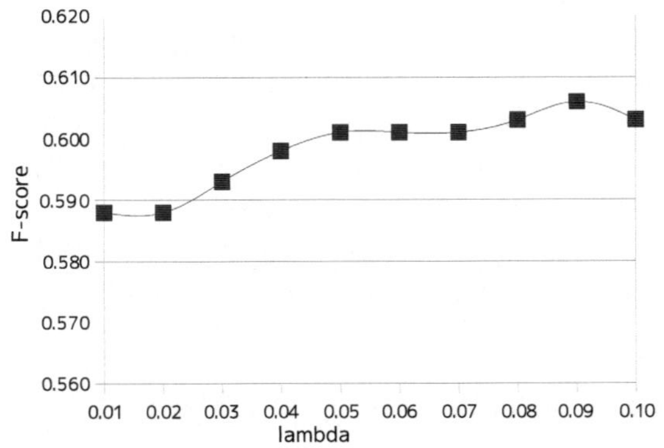

Figure 2: F-score against λ

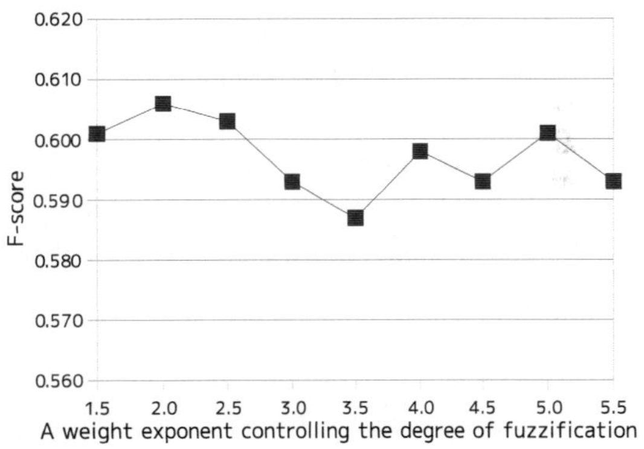

Figure 3: F-score against m

signment in the fuzzy c-means, and m is a weight controlling the degree of fuzzification. To examine how these parameters affect the overall performance of the algorithm, we performed experiments by varying these parameters. Figure 2 illustrates F-score of polysemies against the value of λ. We used *KL* as a similarity measure, m = 2, and C = 74.

As shown in Figure 2, the best result was obtained when the value of λ was 0.09. When λ value was larger than 0.09, the overall performance decreased, and when it exceeded 1.2, no verbs were assigned to multiple sense. Figure 3 illustrates F-score against the value of m. As illustrated in Figure 3, we could not find effects on accuracy against the value of m. It is necessary to investigate on the influence of the parameter m by performing further quantitative evaluation.

6.3 Error analysis against polysemy

We examined whether 46 polysemous verbs in a set from 2007 were correctly classified into classes. We manually analyzed clustering results obtained by running fuzzy c-means with *KL* as a similarity measure. They were classified into three types of error.

1. **Partially correct:** Some senses of a polysemous verb were correctly identified, but others were not. The first example of this pattern is that "*nigiru*" has at least two senses, "*motsu* (have)" and "*musubu* (double)". However, only one sense was identified correctly. The second example is that one of the senses of the verb "*watasu*" was classified correctly into the class "*ataeru* (give)", while it was classified incorrectly into the class "*uru* (sell)". This was the most frequent error type.

{*nigiru*, *motsu* (have)}
ϕ

{*watasu*, *ataeru* (give)}
{*watasu*, *uru* (sell)}

2. **Polysemous verbs classified into only one cluster:** "*hakobu*" has two senses "carry", and "progress". However, it was classified into one cluster including verbs "*motuteiku* (carry)", and "*susumu* (progress)". Because it often takes the same nominative subjects such as "human" and accusative object such as "abstract".

{*hakobu* (carry, progress),
motuteiku (carry), *susumu* (progress)}

3. **Polysemous verb incorrectly classified into clusters:** The polysemous verb "*hataraku*" has two senses, "work", and "operate". However, it was classified incorrectly into "*ochiru* (fall)" and "*tsukuru* (make)".

{*hataraku* (work, operate), *ochiru* (fall),
tsukuru (make)}

Apart from the above error analysis, we found that we should improve the definition and demarcation of semantic classes by using other existing thesaurus, *e.g.*, EDR or BGH (Bunrui Goi Hyo) (BGH, 1989). We recall that we created the gold standard data by using synonymous information. However, the algorithm classified some antonymous words such as "*uketoru*" (receive) and "*watasu*" (give) into one cluster. Similarly, transitive and intransitive verbs are classified into the same cluster. For example, intransitive verb of the verb "*ochiru*" (drop) is "*otosu*". They were classified into one cluster. It would provide further potential, *i.e.*, not only to improve the accuracy of classification, but also to reveal the relationship between semantic verb classes and their syntactic behaviors.

An investigation of the resulting clusters revealed another interesting direction of the method. We found that some senses of a polysemous verb which is not listed in the IPAL are correctly identified by the algorithm. For example, "*ukeireru*" and "*yurusu*" (forgive) were correctly classified into one cluster. Figure 4 illustrates a sample of verb frames with selectional preferences extracted by our method.

Table 5: Results for a set from 1991_2007

Method	m	λ	C	Prec	Rec	F
FCM	2.0	0.24	152	.792	.477	**.595**
FCM(none)	2.0	0.07	147	.687	.459	.550
EM	–	–	152	.284	.722	.408

"*ukeireru*" and "*yurusu*" in Table 4 have the same frame pattern, and the sense identifiers of the case filler "*wo*", for example, are "a human being" (0f0157) and "human" (30f6b0). However, these verbs are not classified into one class in the IPAL: "*ukeireru*" is not listed in the IPAL as a synonym verb of "*yurusu*". The example illustrates that these verbs within a cluster are semantically related, and that they share obvious verb frames with intuitively plausible selectional preferences. This indicates that we can extend the algorithm to solve this resource scarcity problem: semantic classification of words which do not appear in the resource, but appear in corpora.

6.4 Results for a set of verbs from 1991_2007 corpus

One goal of this work was to develop a clustering methodology with respect to the automatic recognition of Japanese verbal polysemies covering large-scale corpora. For this task, we tested a set of 170 verbs including 82 polysemies. The results are shown in Table 5. We used *KL* as a similarity measure in FCM. Each value of the parameter shows the value that maximized the F-score.
As shown in Table 5, the result obtained by fuzzy c-means was as good as for the smaller set, a set of 78 verbs. Moreover, we can see that the fuzzy c-means is better than the EM algorithm and the method not applying a spectral mapping, as an increase in the F-score of 18.7% compared with the EM, and 4.5% compared with a method without spectral mapping. This shows that our method is effective for a size of the input test data consisting 178 verbs.

One thing should be noted is that when the algorithm is applied to large data, it is computationally expensive. There are at least two ways to address the problem. One is to use several methods

[Sentence pattern]	<word1> *ga*	<word2> *wo*	*ukeireru* / *yurusu* (forgive)
[Concept relation]	agent	object	
[Case particle]	*ga* (nominative)	*wo* (accusative)	
[Sense identifier]	0ee0de; 0f58b4; 0f98ee	0f0157; 30f6b0	

0ee0de: the part of a something written that makes reference to a particular matter
0f58b4: a generally-held opinion
0f98ee: the people who citizens of a nation
0f0157: a human being
30f6b0: human

Figure 4: Extracted Verb frames of "*ukeireru*" and "*yurusu*" (forgive)

of fuzzy c-means acceleration. Kelen *et al.* (2002) presented an efficient implementation of the fuzzy c-means algorithm, and showed that the algorithm had the worse-case complexity of $O(nK^2)$, where n is the number of nodes, and K is the number of eigenvectors. Another approach is to parallelize the algorithm by using the Message Passing Interface (MPI) to estimate the optimal number of k ($2 \leq k \leq K$). This is definitely worth trying with our method.

7 Conclusion

We have developed an approach for classifying Japanese polysemous verbs using fuzzy c-means clustering. The results were comparable to other unsupervised techniques. Future work will assess by a comparison against other existing soft clustering algorithms such as the Clique Percolation method (Palla, 2005). Moreover, it is necessary to apply the method to other verbs for quantitative evaluation. New words including polysemies are generated daily. We believe that classifying these words into semantic classes potentially enhances many semantic-oriented NLP applications. It is necessary to apply the method to other verbs, especially low frequency of verbs to verify that claim.

Acknowledgments

This work was supported by the Grant-in-aid for the Japan Society for the Promotion of Science (JSPS).

References

E. Iwabuchi. 1989. Word List by Semantic Principles, *National Language Research Institute Publications*, Shuei Shuppan.

I. Dagan and L. Lee and F. C. N. Pereira. 1999. Similarity-based Models of Word Cooccurrence Probabilities. *Machine Learning*, 34(1-3), pages 43–69.

Japan Electronic Dictionary Research Institute, Ltd. http://www2.nict.go.jp/r/r312/EDR/index.html

M. Galley and K. McKeown. 2003. Improving Word Sense Disambiguation in Lexical Chaining, In *Proc. of 19th International Joint Conference on Artificial Intelligence*, pages 1486–1488.

D. Hindle. 1990. Noun Classification from Predicate-Argument Structures, In *Proc. of 28th Annual Meeting of the Association for Computational Linguistics*, pages 268–275.

GSK2007-D. http://www.gsk.or.jp/catalog/GSK2007-D/catalog.html

J. Jannink and G. Wiederhold. 1999. Thesaurus Entry Extraction from an On-line Dictionary, In *Proc. of Fusion'99*.

J. F. Kelen and T. Hutcheson. 2002. Reducing the Time Complexity of the Fuzzy C-means Algorithm, In *Trans. of IEEE Fuzzy Systems*, 10(2), pages 263–267.

A. Korhonen and Y. Krymolowski. 2002. On the Robustness of Entropy-based Similarity Measures in Evaluation of Subcategorization Acquisiton Systems. In *Proc. of the 6th Conference on Natural Language Learning*, pages 91–97.

A. Korhonen and Y. Krymolowski and Z. Marx. 2003. Clustering Polysemic Subcategorization Frame Distributions Semantically. In *Proc. of the 41st Annual Meeting of the Association for Computational Linguistics*, pages 64–71.

T.Kudo and Y.Matsumoto. 2003. Fast Methods for Kernel-based Text Analysis. In *Proc. of 41th ACL*, pages 24–31.

L. Lee. 1999. Measures of Distributional Similarity. In *Proc. of the 37th Annual Meeting of the Association for Computational Linguistics*, pages 25–32.

D. Lin. 1998. Automatic Retrieval and Clustering of Similar Words, In *Proc. of 36th Annual Meeting of the Association for Computational Linguistics and 17th International Conference on Computational Linguistics*, pages 768–773.

Y. Matsuo and T. Sakaki and K. Uchiyama and M. Ishizuka. 2006. Graph-based Word Clustering using a Web Search Engine, In *Proc. of 2006 Conference on Empirical Methods in Natural Language Processing (EMNLP2006)*, pages 542–550.

R. Mihalcea. 2005. Unsupervised Large Vocabulary Word Sense Disambiguation with Graph-based Algorithms for Sequence Data Labeling, In *Proc. of the Human Language Technology / Empirical Methods in Natural Language Processing Conference*, pages 411–418.

P. Muller and N. Hathout and B. Gaume. 2006. Synonym Extraction Using a Semantic Distance on a Dictionary, In *Proc. of the Workshop on TextGraphs*, pages 65–72.

M.E.J.Newman. 2004. Fast Algorithm for Detecting Community Structure in Networks, *Physical Review*, E 2004, 69, 066133.

G. Palla and I. Derényi and I. Farkas and T. Vicsek. 2005. Uncovering the Overlapping Community Structure of Complex Networks in Nature and Society, *Nature*. 435(7043), 814–8.

F. Pereira and N. Tishby and L. Lee. 1993. Distributional Clustering of English Words. In *Proc. of the 31st Annual Meeting of the Association for Computational Linguistics*, pages 183–190.

P. Resnik. 1995. Using Information Content to Evaluate Semantic Similarity in a Taxonomy. In *Proc. of 14th International Joint Conference on Artificial Intelligence*, pages 448–453.

M. Rooth et al. 1999. Inducing a Semantically Annotated Lexicon via EM-Based Clustering, In *Proc. of 37th ACL*, pages 104–111.

R. Sinha and R. Mihalcea. 2007. Unsupervised Graph-based Word Sense Disambiguation Using Measures of Word Semantic Similarity. In *Proc. of the IEEE International Conference on Semantic Computing*, pages 46–54.

S. Schulte im Walde. 2000. Clustering Verbs Semantically according to their Alternation Behaviour. In *Proc. of the 18th COLING*, pages 747–753.

S. Schulte im Walde et al. 2008. Combining EM Training and the MDL Principle for an Automatic Verb Classification Incorporating Selectional Preferences. In *Proc. of the 46th ACL*, pages 496–504.

T. Tokunaga and A. Fujii and M. Iwayama and N. Sakurai and H. Tanaka. 1997. Extending a thesaurus by classifying words. In *Proc. of the ACL-EACL Workshop on Automatic Information Extraction and Building of Lexical Semantic Resources*, pages 16–21.

K. Torisawa. 2002. An Unsupervised Learning Method for Associative Relationships between Verb Phrases, In *Proc. of 19th International Conference on Computational Linguistics (COLING2002)*, pages 1009–1015.

T. Utsuro. 1995. Class-based sense classification of verbal polysemy in case frame acquisition from parallel corpora. In *Proc. of the 3rd Natural Language Processing Pacific Rim Symposium*, pages 671–677.

D. Widdows and B. Dorow. 2002. A Graph Model for Unsupervised Lexical Acquisition. In *Proc. of 19th International conference on Computational Linguistics (COLING2002)*, pages 1093–1099.

I. H. Witten and T. C. Bell. 1991. The Zero-Frequency Problem: Estimating the Probabilities of Novel Events in Adaptive Text Compression. *IEEE Transactions on Information Theory*, 37(4), pages 1085–1094.

S. Zhang et al. 2007. Identification of Overlapping Community Structure in Complex Networks using Fuzzy C-means Clustering. *PHYSICA* A, 374, pages 483–490.

WikiWalk: Random walks on Wikipedia for Semantic Relatedness

Eric Yeh, Daniel Ramage, Christopher D. Manning
Computer Science Department,
Stanford University
Stanford, CA, USA
{yehl,dramage,manning}@cs.stanford.edu

Eneko Agirre, Aitor Soroa
Ixa Taldea
University of the Basque Country
Donostia, Basque Country
{e.agirre,a.soroa}@ehu.es

Abstract

Computing semantic relatedness of natural language texts is a key component of tasks such as information retrieval and summarization, and often depends on knowledge of a broad range of real-world concepts and relationships. We address this knowledge integration issue by computing semantic relatedness using personalized PageRank (random walks) on a graph derived from Wikipedia. This paper evaluates methods for building the graph, including link selection strategies, and two methods for representing input texts as distributions over the graph nodes: one based on a dictionary lookup, the other based on Explicit Semantic Analysis. We evaluate our techniques on standard word relatedness and text similarity datasets, finding that they capture similarity information complementary to existing Wikipedia-based relatedness measures, resulting in small improvements on a state-of-the-art measure.

1 Introduction

Many problems in NLP call for numerical measures of semantic relatedness, including document summarization, information retrieval, and textual entailment. Often, measuring the relatedness of words or text passages requires world knowledge about entities and concepts that are beyond the scope of any single word in the document. Consider, for instance, the following pair:

1. *Emancipation Proclamation*
2. *Gettysburg Address*

To correctly assess that these examples are related requires knowledge of the United States Civil War found neither in the examples themselves nor in traditional lexical resources such as WordNet (Fellbaum, 1998). Fortunately, a massive collaboratively constructed knowledge resource is available that has specific articles dedicated to both. Wikipedia is an online encyclopedia containing around one million articles on a wide variety of topics maintained by over one hundred thousand volunteer editors with quality comparable to that of traditional encyclopedias.

Recent work has shown that Wikipedia can be used as the basis of successful measures of semantic relatedness between words or text passages (Strube and Ponzetto, 2006; Gabrilovich and Markovitch, 2007; Milne and Witten, 2008). The most successful measure, Explicit Semantic Analysis (ESA) (Gabrilovich and Markovitch, 2007), treats each article as its own dimension in a vector space. Texts are compared by first projecting them into the space of Wikipedia articles and then comparing the resulting vectors.

In addition to article text, Wikipedia stores a great deal of information about the relationships between the articles in the form of hyperlinks, info boxes, and category pages. Despite a long history of research demonstrating the effectiveness of incorporating link information into relatedness measures based on the WordNet graph (Budanitsky and Hirst, 2006), previous work on Wikipedia has made limited use of this relationship information, using only category links (Bunescu and Pasca, 2006) or just the actual links in a page (Gabrilovich and Markovitch, 2007; Milne and Witten, 2008).

In this work, we combine previous approaches by converting Wikipedia into a graph, mapping input texts into the graph, and performing random walks based on Personalized PageRank (Haveliwala, 2002) to obtain stationary distributions that characterize each text. Semantic relatedness between two texts is computed by comparing their distributions. In contrast to previous work, we explore the use of all these link types when con-

Proceedings of the 2009 Workshop on Graph-based Methods for Natural Language Processing, ACL-IJCNLP 2009, pages 41–49,
Suntec, Singapore, 7 August 2009.

structing the Wikipedia graph, the intuition being these links, or some combination of them, contain additional information that would allow a gain over methods that use only just the article text. We also discuss two methods for performing the initial mapping of input texts to the graph, using techniques from previous studies that utilized WordNet graphs and Wikipedia article text.

We find that performance is signficantly affected by the strategy used to initialize the graph walk, as well as the links selected when constructing the Wikipedia graph. Our best system combines an ESA-initialized vector with random walks, improving on state-of-the-art results over the (Lee et al., 2005) dataset. An analysis of the output demonstrates that, while the gains are small, the random walk adds complementary relatedness information not present in the page text.

2 Preliminaries

A wide range of different methods, from corpus-based distributional similarity methods, such as Latent Semantic Analysis (Landauer et al., 1998), to knowledge-based ones that employ structured sources such as WordNet,[1] have been developed to score semantic relatedness and similarity. We now review two leading techniques which we use as starting points for our approach: those that perform random walks over WordNet's graph structure, and those that utilize Wikipedia as an underlying data source.

2.1 Random Graph Walks for Semantic Relatedness

Some of the best performing WordNet-based algorithms for computing semantic relatedness are based on the popular Personalized PageRank algorithm (Hughes and Ramage, 2007; Agirre and Soroa, 2009). These approaches start by taking WordNet as a graph of concepts $G = (V, E)$ with a set of vertices V derived from WordNet synsets and a set of edges E representing relations between synsets. Both algorithms can be viewed as random walk processes that postulate the existence of a particle that randomly traverses the graph, but at any time may jump, or *teleport*, to a new vertex with a given *teleport probability*. In standard PageRank (Brin and Page, 1998), this target is chosen uniformly, whereas for Personalized PageRank it is chosen from a nonuniform distribution of nodes, specified by a *teleport vector*.

The final weight of node i represents the proportion of time the random particle spends visiting it after a sufficiently long time, and corresponds to that node's structural importance in the graph. Because the resulting vector is the stationary distribution of a Markov chain, it is unique for a particular walk formulation. As the teleport vector is nonuniform, the stationary distribution will be biased towards specific parts of the graph. In the case of (Hughes and Ramage, 2007) and (Agirre and Soroa, 2009), the teleport vector is used to reflect the input texts to be compared, by biasing the stationary distribution towards the neighborhood of each word's mapping.

The computation of relatedness for a word pair can be summarized in three steps: First, each input word is mapped with to its respective synsets in the graph, creating its teleport vector. In the case words with multiple synsets (senses), the synsets are weighted uniformly. Personalized PageRank is then executed to compute the stationary distribution for each word, using their respective teleport vectors. Finally, the stationary distributions for each word pair are scored with a measure of vector similarity, such as cosine similarity. The method to compute relatedness for text pairs is analogous, with the only difference being in the first step all words are considered, and thus the stationary distribution is biased towards all synsets of the words in the text.

2.2 Wikipedia as a Semantic Resource

Recent Wikipedia-based lexical semantic relatedness approaches have been found to outperform measures based on the WordNet graph. Two such methods stand out: Wikipedia Link-based Measure (WLM) (Milne and Witten, 2008), and Explicit Semantic Analysis (ESA) (Gabrilovich and Markovitch, 2007).

WLM uses the anchors found in the body of Wikipedia articles, treating them as links to other articles. Each article is represented by a list of its incoming and outgoing links. For word relatedness, the set of articles are first identified by matching the word to the text in the anchors, and the score is derived using several weighting strategies applied to the overlap score of the articles' links. WLM does not make further use of the link graph, nor does it attempt to differentiate the links.

[1] See (Budanitsky and Hirst, 2006) for a survey.

In contrast to WLM, Explicit Semantic Analysis (ESA) is a vector space comparison algorithm that does not use the link structure, relying solely on the Wikipedia article text. Unlike Latent Semantic Analysis (LSA), the underlying concept space is not computationally derived, but is instead based on Wikipedia articles. For a candidate text, each dimension in its ESA vector corresponds to a Wikipedia article, with the score being the similarity of the text with the article text, subject to TF-IDF weighting. The relatedness of two texts is computed as the cosine similarity of their ESA vectors.

Although ESA reports the best results to date on both the WordSim-353 dataset as well as the Lee sentence similarity dataset, it does not utilize the link structure, which motivated a combined approach as follows.

2.3 A Combined Approach

In this work, we base our random walk algorithms after the ones described in (Hughes and Ramage, 2007) and (Agirre et al., 2009), but use Wikipedia-based methods to construct the graph. As in previous studies, we obtain a relatedness score between a pair of texts by performing random walks over a graph to compute a stationary distribution for each text. For our evaluations, the score is simply the cosine similarity between the distributions. In the following sections, we describe how we built graphs from Wikipedia, and how input texts are initially mapped into these structures.

3 Building a Wikipedia Graph

In order to obtain the graph structure of Wikipedia, we simply treat the articles as vertices, and the links between articles as the edges. There are several sources of pre-processed Wikipedia dumps which could be used to extract the articles and links between articles, including DBpedia (Auer et al., 2008), which provides a relational database representation of Wikipedia, and Wikipedia-Miner [2], which produces similar information from Wikipedia dumps directly. In this work we used a combination of Wikipedia-Miner and custom processing scripts. The dump used in this work is from mid 2008.

As in (Milne and Witten, 2008), anchors in Wikipedia articles are used to define links between articles. Because of different distributional properties, we explicitly distinguish three types of links, in order to explore their impact on the graph walk.

Infobox links are anchors found in the *infobox* section of Wikipedia articles. Article infoboxes, when present, often enumerate defining attributes and characteristics for that article's topic.

Categorical links reference articles whose titles belong in the Wiki namespace *"Category,"* as well as those with titles beginning with *"List of."* These pages are often just lists of anchors to other articles, which may be useful for capturing categorical information that roughly contains a mixture of hyponymy and meronymy relations between articles.

Content links are those that are not already classified as *infobox* nor *categorical*, and are intended to represent the set of miscellaneous anchors found solely in the article body. These may include links already found in the categorical and infobox categories.

Links can be further factored out according to *generality*, a concept introduced in (Gabrilovich and Markovitch, 2009). We say that one article is more general than another when the number of inlinks is larger. Although only a rough heuristic, the intuition is that articles on general topics will receive many links, whereas specific articles will receive fewer. We will use $+k$ notation for links which point to more general articles, i.e., where the difference in generality between source s and target t is $\#inlink(t)/\#inlink(s) \geq k$. We will use $-k$ for links to less general articles, i.e., $\#inlink(s)/\#inlink(t) \geq k$. Finally we use $=k$ when the generality is in the same order of magnitude, i.e., when the link is neither $+k$ nor $-k$. The original notion of generality from (Gabrilovich and Markovitch, 2009) restricts consideration to only more general articles by one order of magnitude (+10), without reference to the link types introduced above.

Given the size of the Wikipedia graph, we explored further methods inspired by (Gabrilovich and Markovitch, 2009) to make the graph smaller. We discarded articles with fewer than 2,000 non-stop words and articles with fewer than 5 outgoing and incoming links. We will refer to the complete

[2] http://wikipedia-miner.sourceforge.net

graph as *full* and to this reduced graph as *reduced*.[3]

4 Initializing a Wikipedia Graph Walk

In order to apply Personalized PageRank to a given passage of text or word, we need to construct a custom teleport vector, representing the initial distribution of mass over the article nodes. In this section we introduce two such methods, one based on constructing a direct mapping from individual words to Wikipedia articles (which we call dictionary-based initialization), and the other based directly on the results of ESA. We will see each technique in turn.

4.1 Dictionary based initialization

Given a target word, we would like to define its teleport vector using the set of articles in Wikipedia to which the word refers. This is analogous to a dictionary, where an entry lists the set of meanings pertaining to the entry.

We explored several methods for building such a dictionary. The first method constructed the dictionary using the article title directly, while also including redirection pages and disambiguation pages for additional ways to refer to the article. In addition, we can use the anchor text to refer to articles, and we turned to Wikipedia-Miner to extract this information. Anchors are indeed a rich source of information, as they help to relate similar words to Wikipedia articles. For instance, links to page `Monk` are created by using textual anchors such as *lama*, *brothers*, *monastery*, etc. As a result, the dictionary entries for those words will have a link to the `Monk` page. This information turned out to be very valuable, so all experiments have been carried out using anchors.

An additional difficulty was that any of these methods yielded dictionaries where the entries could refer to tens, even hundreds of articles. In most of the cases we could see that relevant articles were followed by a long tail of loosely related articles. We tried two methods to prune the dictionary. The first, coarse, method was to eliminate all articles whose title contains a space. The motivation was that our lexical semantic relatedness datasets (cf. Section 5) do not contain multiword entries (e.g., *United States*). In the second method, we pruned articles from the dictionary which accounted for less than 1% or 10% of the occurrences of that anchor word, as suggested by (Milne and Witten, 2008).

In short, for this method of initialization, we explored the use of the following variants: *all*, all articles are introduced in the dictionary; *noent*, articles with space characters are omitted; *1% (10%)*, anchors that account for less than 1% (10%) of the total number of anchors for that entry are omitted. We did not use stemming. If a target word has no matching Wikipedia article in the dictionary, then it is ignored.

Graphs		
Graph	# Vertices	# Edges
Full	2,483,041	49,602,752
Reduced	1,002,411	30,939,288
Dictionaries		
Dictionary	# Entries	Avg. Articles
all	6,660,315	1.31
1%	6,660,306	1.12
1% noent	1,058,471	1.04

Table 1: Graph and dictionary sizes. Avg. Articles column details the average number of articles per entry.

Table 1 shows the numbers for some graph and dictionary versions. Although the average number of articles per entry in the dictionary might seem low, it is actually quite high for the words in the datasets: for MC it's 5.92, and for wordsim353 it's 42.14. If we keep the articles accounting for 10% of all occurrences, the numbers drops drastically to 1.85 and 1.64 respectively.

As we will see in the results section, smaller graphs and dictionaries are able to attain higher results, but at the cost of losing information for some words. That is, we observed that some factored, smaller graphs contained less noise, but that meant that some articles and words are isolated in the graph, and therefore we are not able to compute relatedness for them. As a solution, we devised an alternative way to initialize the random walk. Instead of initializing it according to the articles in the dictionary, we initialized it with the vector weights returned by ESA, as explained in the next section.

[3] In order to keep category and infobox links, the 2,000 non-stop word filter was not applied to categories and lists of pages.

4.2 Initialization with ESA

In addition to the dictionary based approach, we also explored the use of ESA to construct the teleport vector. In contrast to dictionary initialization, ESA uses the text of the article body instead of anchor text or the article titles. Because ESA maps query text to a weighted vector of Wikipedia articles, it can be naturally adapted as a teleport vector for a random walk with a simple L_1 normalization. We used Apache Lucene[4] to implement both ESA's repository of Wikipedia articles, and to return vectors for queries. Each article is indexed as its own document, with page text preprocessed to strip out Wiki markup.

Although we followed the steps outlined in (Gabrilovich and Markovitch, 2007), we had to add an extension to the algorithm: for a return vector from ESA, we order the articles by score, and retain only the scores for the top-n articles, setting the scores of the remaining articles to 0. Without this modification, our performance results were will below the reported numbers, but with a cutoff at 625 (determined by a basic grid search), we obtained a correlation of 0.76 on the Lee sentence similarity dataset, over the previously published score of 0.72.

4.3 Teleport Probability

For this work, we used a value of 0.15 as the probability of returning to the teleport distribution at any given step. The walk terminates when the vector converges with an L_1 error of 0.0001 (circa 30 iterations). Some preliminary experiments on a related Word Sense Disambiguation task indicated that in this context, our algorithm is quite robust to these values, and we did not optimize them. However, we will discuss using different return parameters in Section 6.1.

5 Experiments

In this section, we compare the two methods of initialization as well as several types of edges. For a set of pairs, system performance is evaluated by how well the generated scores correlate with the gold scores. Gold scores for each pair are the average of human judgments for that pair. In order to compare against previous results obtained on the datasets, we use the Spearman correlation coefficient on the Miller Charles (MC) and WordSim-353 word-pair datasets, and the Pearson correlation coefficient on the (Lee et al., 2005) document-pair dataset.

[4] http://lucene.apache.org

Dictionary	Graph	MC
all	full	0.369
1%	full	0.610
1%, noent	full	0.565 (0.824)
1%	reduced	0.563
1%	reduced +2	0.530
1%	reduced +4	0.601
1%	reduced +8	0.512
1%	reduced +10	0.491 (0.522)
10%	full	0.604 (0.750)
10%	reduced	0.605 (0.751)
10%	reduced +2	0.491 (0.540)
10%	reduced +4	0.476 (0.519)
10%	reduced +8	0.474 (0.506)
10%	reduced +10	0.430 (0.484)
WordNet		0.90 / 0.89
WLM		0.70
ESA		0.72

Table 2: Spearman correlation on the MC dataset with dictionary-based initialization. Refer to Section 3 for explanation of dictionary and graph building methods. Between parenthesis, results excluding pairs which had a word with an empty dictionary entry.

5.1 Dictionary-based Initialization

Given the smaller size of the MC dataset, we explored the effect of the different variants to build the graph and dictionary on this dataset. Some selected results are shown in Table 2, alongside those of related work, where we used WordNet for (Hughes and Ramage, 2007) and (Agirre et al., 2009) (separated by "/" in the results), WLM for (Milne and Witten, 2008) and ESA for (Gabrilovich and Markovitch, 2007).

We can observe that using the full graph and dictionaries yields very low results. Reducing the dictionary (removing articles with less than 1% or 10% of the total occurrences) produces higher results, but reducing the graph does not provide any improvement. On a closer look, we realized that pruning the dictionary to 10% or removing multiwords (*noent*) caused some words to not get any link to articles (e.g., *magician*). If we evaluate only over pairs where both words get a Personalized PageRank vector, the results raise up to 0.751 and 0.824, respectively, placing our method close

Dictionary	Graph	WordSim-353
1%	full	0.449
1%, noent	full	0.440 (0.634)
1%	reduced	0.485
WordNet		0.55 / 0.66
WLM		0.69
ESA		0.75
WikiRelate		0.50

Table 3: Spearman correlation on the WordSim-353 dataset with dictionary-based initialization. Refer to Section 3 for explanation of dictionary and graph building methods. Between parenthesis, results excluding pairs which had a word with an empty dictionary entry.

Dictionary	Graph	(Lee et al., 2005)
1%, noent	Full	0.308
1%	Reduced +4	0.269
ESA		0.72

Table 4: Pearson correlation on (Lee et al., 2005) with dictionary-based initialization. Refer to Section 3 for explanation of dictionary and graph building methods.

to the best results on the MC dataset. This came at the cost of not being able to judge the relatedness of 3 and 5 pairs, respectively. We think that removing multiwords (noent) is probably too drastic, but the positive effect is congruent with (Milne and Witten, 2008), who suggested that the coverage of certain words in Wikipedia is not adequate.

The results in Table 3 show the Spearman correlation for some selected runs over the WordSim-353 dataset. Again we see that a restrictive dictionary allows for better results on the pairs which do get a dictionary entry, up to 0.63. WikiRelate refers to the results in (Strube and Ponzetto, 2006).

We only tested a few combinations over (Lee et al., 2005), with results given in Table 4. These are well below state-of-the-art, and show that initializing the random walk with all words in the document does not characterize the documents well, resulting in low correlation.

5.2 ESA-based initialization

While the results using a dictionary based approach were encouraging, they did not come close to the state-of-the-art results achieved by ESA. Here, we explore combining ESA and random

Method	Text Sim
ESA@625	0.766
ESA@625+Walk All	0.556
ESA@625+Walk Categories	0.410
ESA@625+Walk Content	0.536
ESA@625+Walk Infobox	0.710

Table 5: Pearson correlation on the (Lee et al., 2005) dataset when walking on various types of links. Note that walking tends to hurt performance overall, with Infobox links by far the least harmful.

walks, by using ESA to initialize the teleport vector. Following section 4.2, we used a top-n cutoff of 625.

Table 5 displays the results of our ESA implementation followed by a walk from that ESA distribution. Walking on any link type actually depresses performance below the baseline ESA value, although the Infobox links seem the least harmful.

However, as mentioned in Section 3, links between articles represent many different types of relationships beyond the few well-defined links present in lexical resources like WordNet. This also extends to where the link is found, and the article it is pointing to. As such, not all links are created equal, and we expect that some types of links at different levels of generality will perform better or worse than others. Table 6 presents a sample grid search across the category links choosing more general, less general, or similar generality at several factors of k, showing that there is a consistent pattern across multiple link types. Note that the best value indeed improves upon the score of the ESA distribution, albeit modestly.

We performed a similar analysis across all link types and found that the best link types were Category links at +6 and Infobox links at =2. Intuitively, these link types make sense: for semantic relatedness, it seem reasonable to expect more general pages within the same category to help. And for Infobox links, much rarer and much more common pages can both introduce their own kind of noise. While the improvement from each type of edge walk is small, they are additive—the best results on the sentence similarity dataset was from walking across both link types. Our final Pearson correlation coefficient of .772 is to our knowledge the highest number reported in the literature, al-

Generality of *Category* links			
	+k	-k	=k
$k = 2$	0.760	0.685	0.462
$k = 4$	0.766	0.699	0.356
$k = 6$	**0.771**	0.729	0.334
$k = 8$	0.768	0.729	0.352
$k = 10$	0.768	0.720	0.352

Table 6: Pearson correlation on the (Lee et al., 2005) with random walks over only a subset of the edges in the Category link information (scores .410 when taking all edges). Note that factoring the graph by link generality can be very helpful to the walk.

Method	Text Sim
ESA@625	0.766
ESA@625+Walk Cat@+6	0.770
ESA@625+Walk Cat@+6 Inf@=2	0.772
Bag of words (Lee et al., 2005)	0.5
LDA (Lee et al., 2005)	0.60
ESA*	0.72

Table 7: Pearson correlation on the (Lee et al., 2005) dataset for our best sytems compared to previously reported numbers. ESA* is the score for raw ESA as reported number in (Gabrilovich and Markovitch, 2007).

beit only a small improvement over our ESA@625 score.

Despite the results obtained for text similarity, the best settings found for the Lee dataset did not translate to consistent improvements over the ESA baseline for Spearman rank correlation on the lexical similarity datasets. While our scores on the MC dataset of 30 word pairs did improve with the walk in roughly the same way as in Lee, no such improvements were found on the larger WordSim-353 data. On WordSim-353, our implementation of ESA scored 0.709 (versus Gabrilovich's reported ESA score of 0.75), and our walk on Cat@+6 showing no gain or loss. In contrast to the text similarity dataset, Infobox links were no longer helpful, bringing the correlation down to .699. We believe this is because Infobox links helped the most with entities, which are very rare in the WordSim-353 data, but are more common in the Lee dataset.

6 Discussion

Our results suggest that even with a simple dictionary-based approach, the graph of Wikipedia links can act as an effective resource for computing semantic relatedness. However, the dictionary approach alone was unable to reach the results of state-of-the-art models using Wikipedia (Gabrilovich and Markovitch, 2007; Milne and Witten, 2008) or using the same technique on WordNet (Hughes and Ramage, 2007; Agirre et al., 2009). Thus, it seems that the text of Wikipedia provides a stronger signal than the link structure. However, a pruned dictionary can improve the results of the dictionary based initialization, which indicates that some links are informative for semantic relatedness while others are not. The careful pruning, disambiguation and weighting functions presented in (Milne and Witten, 2008) are directions for future work.

The use of WordNet as a graph provided excellent results (Hughes and Ramage, 2007), close to those of ESA. In contrast with our dictionary-based initialization on Wikipedia, no pruning of dictionary or graph seem necessary to obtain high results with WordNet. One straightforward explanation is that Wikipedia is a noisy source of link information. In fact, both ESA and (Milne and Witten, 2008) use ad-hoc pruning strategies in order to obtain good results.

6.1 ESA and Walk Comparison

By using ESA to generate the teleport distribution, we were able to introduce small gains using the random walk. Because these gains were small, it is plausible that the walk introduces only modest changes from the initial ESA teleport distributions. To evaluate this, we examined the differences between the vector returned by ESA and distribution over the equivalent nodes in the graph after performing a random walk starting with that ESA vector.

For this analysis, we took all of the text entries used in this study, and generated two distributions over the Wikipedia graph, one using ESA@625, the other the result of performing a random walk starting at ESA@625. We generated a list of the concept nodes for both distributions, sorted in decreasing order by their associated scores. Starting from the beginning of both lists, we then counted the number of matched nodes until they disagreed on ordering, giving a simple view of

	Walk Type	Avg	Std	Max
MC	Cat@+6	12.1	7.73	35
	Cat@+6 Inf@=2	5.39	5.81	20
WordSim	Cat@+6	12.0	10.6	70
	Cat@+6 Inf@=2	5.74	7.78	54
Lee	Cat@+6	28.3	89.7	625
	Cat@+6 Inf@=2	4.24	14.8	103

Table 8: Statistics for first concept match length, by run and walk type.

Prob	Corr (Pruned)	Corr (All)
0.01	0.772	0.246
0.10	0.773	0.500
0.15	0.772	0.556
0.30	0.771	0.682
0.45	0.769	0.737
0.60	0.767	0.758
0.90	0.766	0.766
0.99	0.766	0.766

Table 9: Return probability vs. correlation, on textual similarity data (Lee et al., 2005).

how the walk perturbed the strongest factors in the graphs. We performed this for both the best performing walk models (ESA@625+Walk Cat@+6 and ESA@625+Walk Cat@+6 Inf@=2) against ESA@625. Results are given in Table 8.

As expected, adding edges to the random walk increases the amount of change from the graph, as initialized by ESA. A cursory examination of the distributions also revealed a number of outliers with extremely high match lengths: these were likely due to the fact that the selected edge types were already extremely specialized. Thus for a number of concept nodes, it is likely they did not have any outbound edges at all.

Having established that the random walk does indeed have an impact on the ESA vectors, the next question is if changes via graph walk are consistently helpful. To answer this, we compared the performance of the walk on the (Lee et al., 2005) dataset for probabilities at selected values, using the best link pruned Wikipedia graph (ESA@625+Walk Cat@+6 Inf@=2), and using all of the available edges in the graph for comparison. Here, a lower probability means the distribution spreads out further into the graph, compared to higher values, where the distribution varies only slightly from the ESA vector. Results are given in Table 9. Performance for the pruned graph improves as the return probability decreases, with larger changes introduced by the graph walk resulting in better scores, whereas using all available links decreases performance. This reinforces the notion that Wikipedia links are indeed noisy, but that within a selected edge subset, making use of all information via the random walk indeed results in gains.

7 Conclusion

This paper has demonstrated that performing random walks with Personalized PageRank over the Wikipedia graph is a feasible and potentially fruitful means of computing semantic relatedness for words and texts. We have explored two methods of initializing the teleport vector: a dictionary-based method and a method based on ESA, the current state-of-the-art technique. Our results show the importance of pruning the dictionary, and for Wikipedia link structure, the importance of both categorizing by anchor type and comparative generality. We report small improvements over the state-of-the-art on (Lee et al., 2005) using ESA as a teleport vector and a limited set of links from Wikipedia category pages and infoboxes.

In future work, we plan to explore new ways to construct nodes, edges, and dictionary entries when constructing the Wikipedia graph and dictionary. We believe that finer grained methods of graph construction promise to improve the value of the Wikipedia link structure. We also plan to further investigate the differences between WordNet and Wikipedia and how these may be combined, from the perspective of graph and random walk techniques. A public distribution of software used for these experiments will also be made available.[5]

Acknowledgements

The authors would like to thank Michael D. Lee and Brandon Pincombe for access to their textual similarity dataset, and the reviewers for their helpful comments. Eneko Agirre performed part of the work while visiting Stanford, thanks to a grant from the Science Ministry of Spain.

[5]Please see http://nlp.stanford.edu/software and http://ixa2.si.ehu.es/ukb

References

E. Agirre and A. Soroa. 2009. Personalizing pagerank for word sense disambiguation. In *Proceedings of 14th Conference of the European Chapter of the Association for Computational Linguistics*, Athens, Greece.

E. Agirre, E. Alfonseca, K. Hall, J. Kravalova, M. Pasça, and A. Soroa. 2009. A study on similarity and relatedness using distributional and WordNet-based approaches. In *Proceedings of the North American Chapter of the Association for Computational Linguistics - Human Language Technologies*, Boulder, USA.

S Auer, C Bizer, G Kobilarov, J Lehmann, R Cyganiak, and Z Ives. 2008. Dbpedia: A nucleus for a web of open data. In *Proceedings of 6th International Semantic Web Conference, 2nd Asian Semantic Web Conference (ISWC+ASWC 2007)*, pages 722–735.

S. Brin and L. Page. 1998. The anatomy of a large-scale hypertextual web search engine. *Computer Networks and ISDN Systems*, 30(1-7).

A. Budanitsky and G. Hirst. 2006. Evaluating WordNet-based measures of lexical semantic relatedness. *Computational Linguistics*, 32(1):13–47.

R. C. Bunescu and M. Pasca. 2006. Using encyclopedic knowledge for named entity disambiguation. In *Proceedings of 11th Conference of the European Chapter of the Association for Computational Linguistics*.

C. Fellbaum. 1998. *WordNet: An electronic lexical database*. MIT Press.

E. Gabrilovich and S. Markovitch. 2007. Computing semantic relatedness using Wikipedia-based explicit semantic analysis. In *Proceedings of the 20th International Joint Conference on Artificial Intelligence (IJCAI-07)*.

E. Gabrilovich and S. Markovitch. 2009. Wikipedia-based semantic interpretation. *Journal of Artificial Intelligence Research*, 34:443–498.

T. H. Haveliwala. 2002. Topic-sensitive pagerank. In *WWW '02*, pages 517–526, New York, NY, USA. ACM.

T. Hughes and D. Ramage. 2007. Lexical semantic relatedness with random graph walks. In *Proceedings of EMNLP-CoNLL*, pages 581–589.

T. K. Landauer, P. W. Foltz, and D. Laham. 1998. An introduction to latent semantic analysis. *Discourse Processes*, 25(2-3):259–284.

M. D. Lee, B. Pincombe, and M. Welsh. 2005. An empirical evaluation of models of text document similarity. In *Proceedings of the 27th Annual Conference of the Cognitive Science Society*, pages 1254–1259, Mahwah, NJ. Erlbaum.

D. Milne and I.H. Witten. 2008. An effective, low-cost measure of semantic relatedness obtained from Wikipedia links. In *Proceedings of the first AAAI Workshop on Wikipedia and Artifical Intellegence (WIKIAI'08)*, Chicago, I.L.

M. Strube and S.P. Ponzetto. 2006. Wikirelate! computing semantic relatedness using Wikipedia. In *Proceedings of the 21st National Conference on Artificial Intelligence*, pages 1419–1424.

Measuring semantic relatedness with vector space models and random walks

Amaç Herdağdelen
Center for Mind/Brain Sciences
University of Trento
amac@herdagdelen.com

Katrin Erk
Linguistics Department
University of Texas at Austin
katrin.erk@mail.utexas.edu

Marco Baroni
Center for Mind/Brain Sciences
University of Trento
marco.baroni@unitn.it

Abstract

Both vector space models and graph random walk models can be used to determine similarity between concepts. Noting that vectors can be regarded as local views of a graph, we directly compare vector space models and graph random walk models on standard tasks of predicting human similarity ratings, concept categorization, and semantic priming, varying the size of the dataset from which vector space and graph are extracted.

1 Introduction

Vector space models, representing word meanings as points in high-dimensional space, have been used in a variety of semantic relatedness tasks (Sahlgren, 2006; Padó and Lapata, 2007). Graphs are another way of representing relations between linguistic entities, and they have been used to capture semantic relatedness by using both corpus-based evidence and the graph structure of WordNet and Wikipedia (Pedersen et al., 2004; Widdows and Dorow, 2002; Minkov and Cohen, 2008). We study the relationship between vector space models and graph random walk models by embedding vector space models in graphs. The flexibility offered by graph random walk models allows us to compare the vector space-based similarity measures to extended notions of relatedness and similarity. In particular, a random walk model can be viewed as smoothing direct similarity between two vectors using second-order and even higher-order vectors. This view leads to the second focal point of this paper: We investigate whether random walk models can simulate the smoothing effects obtained by methods like Singular Value Decomposition (SVD). To answer this question, we compute models on reduced (downsampled) versions of our dataset and evaluate the robustness of random walk models, a classic vector-based model, and SVD-based models against data sparseness.

2 Model definition and implementation

We use directed graphs with weighted edges, $G = (V, E, w)$ where V is a set of nodes, $E = V \times V$ is a set of edges and $w : E \rightarrow \mathbb{R}$ is the weighting function on edges. For simplicity, we assume that G is fully connected, edges with zero weights can be considered as non-existing in the graph. On these graphs, we perform random walks with an initial probability distribution $\mathbf{q}$ over the nodes (a $1 \times |V|$ vector). We then follow edges with probability proportional to their weights, so that the probability of walking from node v_1 to node v_2 is $w(v_1, v_2)/\sum_v w(v_1, v)$. A *fixed length* random walk ends after a predetermined number of steps. In *flexible* walks, there is a constant probability γ of stopping at each step. Thus, walk length follows a geometric distribution with parameter γ, the probability of a walk of length k is $\gamma(1-\gamma)^{k-1}$ and the expected walk length is $1/\gamma$. For example, a flexible walk with $\gamma = 1/2$ will produce 1-step, 2-step, and higher-step walks while the expected average length is 2.

Relating vectors and graphs. Corpus co-occurrence (e_1, e_2, a_{12}) of two entities e_1 and e_2 that co-occur with (potentially transformed) count a_{12} can be represented in either a vector or a graph. In a vector, it corresponds to a dimension value of a_{12} for the dimension e_2 of entity e_1. In a graph, it corresponds to two nodes labeled e_1 and e_2 connected by an edge with weight a_{12}.

Similarity measures. Let $R(\mathbf{q}) = \mathbf{p}$ denote a specific random walk process which transforms an

Proceedings of the 2009 Workshop on Graph-based Methods for Natural Language Processing, ACL-IJCNLP 2009, pages 50–53,
Suntec, Singapore, 7 August 2009.

initial probability distribution $\mathbf{q}$ to a final probability distribution $\mathbf{p}$ over the nodes. We write $q(m)$ for the probability assigned to the node m under $\mathbf{q}$. If the initial distribution $\mathbf{q}$ concentrates all probability on a single node n, i.e., $q(n) = 1$ and $q(x) = 0$ for all nodes $x \neq n$, we write $pr(n \rightarrow m)$ for the probability $p(m)$ of ending up at node m.

The simplest way of measuring relatedness through random walks is to consider the probability $p(m)$ of a single node m as an endpoint for a walk starting with start probability distribution $\mathbf{q}$, that is, $\mathbf{p} = R(\mathbf{q})$. We call this a **direct, one-direction** measure of relatedness between $\mathbf{q}$ and m. Direct, one-direction measures are typically asymmetric. In case all start probability is concentrated on a single node n, we can also consider **direct, two-direction** measures, which will be a combination of $pr(m \rightarrow n)$ and $pr(n \rightarrow m)$. The point of using two-direction measures is that these can be made symmetric, which is an advantage when we are modeling undirected semantic similarity. In the experiments below we focus on the average of the two probabilities.

In addition to direct measures, we will use **indirect measures**, in which we compute the relatedness of endpoint probability distributions $\mathbf{p_1} = R(\mathbf{q_1})$ and $\mathbf{p_2} = R(\mathbf{q_2})$. As endpoint distributions can be viewed both as probability distributions and as vectors, we used three indirect measures: 1) Jensen/Shannon divergence, a symmetric variant of the Kullback/Leibler divergence between probability distributions. 2) cosine similarity, and 3) dot product. Dot product is a natural choice in a graph setting because we can view it as the probability of a pair of walks, one starting at a node determined by $\mathbf{q_1}$ and the other starting at a node governed by $\mathbf{q_2}$, ending at the same node.

Discussion. Direct and indirect relatedness measures together with variation in walk length give us a simple, powerful and flexible way to capture different kinds of similarity (with traditional vector-based approach as a special case). Longer walks or flexible walks will capture higher order effects that may help coping with data sparseness, similar to the use of second-order vectors. Dimensionality reduction techniques like Singular Value Decomposition (SVD) also capture these higher-order effects, and it has been argued that that makes them more resistant against sparseness (Schütze, 1997). To our knowledge, no systematic comparison of SVD and classical vector-based methods has been done on different corpus sizes. In our experiments, we will compare the performance of SVD and flexible-walk smoothing at different corpus sizes and for a variety of tasks.

Implementation: We extract tuples from the 2-billion word ukWaC corpus,[1] dependency-parsed with MINIPAR.[2] Following Padó and Lapata (2007), we only consider co-occurrences where two target words are connected by certain dependency paths, namely: the top 30 most frequent preposition-mediated noun-to-noun paths (*soldier+with+gun*), the top 50 transitive-verb-mediated noun-to-noun paths (*soldier+use+gun*), the top 30 direct or preposition-mediated verb-noun paths (*kill+obj+victim*, *kill+in+school*), and the modifying and predicative adjective-to-noun paths. Pairs (w_1, w_2) that account for 0.01% or less of the marginal frequency of w_1 were trimmed. The resulting tuple list, with raw counts converted to mutual information scores, contains about 25 million tuples.

To test how well graph-based and alternative methods "scale down" to smaller corpora, we sampled random subsets of tuples corresponding to 0.1%, 1%, 10%, and 100% of the full list. To put things into perspective, the full list was extracted from a corpus of about 2 billion words; so, the 10% list is on the order of magnitude of the BNC, and the 0.1% list is on the order of magnitude of the Brown corpus. From each of the 4 resulting datasets, we built one graph and two vector space models: one space with full dimensionality, and one space reduced to 300 dimensions using singular value decomposition.

3 Experiments

First, we report the results for all tasks obtained on the full data-set and then proceed with the comparison of different models on differing graph sizes to see the robustness of the models against data sparseness.

Human similarity ratings: We use the dataset of Rubenstein and Goodenough (1965), consisting of averages of subject similarity ratings for 65 noun pairs. We use the Pearson's coefficient between estimates and human judgments as our performance measure. The results obtained for

[1] `http://wacky.sslmit.unibo.it`

[2] `http://www.cs.ualberta.ca/~lindek/minipar.htm`

	Direct (average)			Vector (cosine)		Indirect (dot product)			Previous
	0.5	1	2	svd	vector	0.5	1	2	
RG	0.409	0.326	0.571	0.798	0.689	0.634	0.673	0.400	BL: 0.70 CLW: 0.849
AAMP Purity	0.480	0.418	0.669	0.701	0.704	0.664	0.667	0.612	AP: 0.709 RS: 0.791
				Hodgson					
synonym	$2,563$	1.289	$5,408^{**}$	10.015^{**}	$6,623^{**}$	$5,462^{**}$	$5,954^{**}$	$5,537^{**}$	
coord	$4,275^{**}$	$3,969^{**}$	$6,319^{**}$	11.157^{**}	$7,593^{**}$	$8,466^{**}$	$8,477^{**}$	$4,854^{**}$	
antonym	$2,853*$	$2,237$	$5,319^{**}$	$7,724^{**}$	$5,455^{**}$	$4,589^{**}$	$4,859^{**}$	$6,810^{**}$	
conass	$9,209^{**}$	10.016^{**}	$5,889^{**}$	$9,299^{**}$	$6,950^{**}$	$5,993^{**}$	$5,455^{**}$	$4,994^{**}$	
supersub	$4,038^{**}$	$4,113^{**}$	$6,773^{**}$	10.422^{**}	$7,901^{**}$	$6,792^{**}$	$7,165^{**}$	$4,828^{**}$	
phrasacc	$4,577^{**}$	$4,718^{**}$	$2,911^{*}$	$3,532^{*}$	$3,023^{*}$	$3,506^{*}$	$3,612^{*}$	1.038	

Table 1: All datasets. * (**) indicates significance level $p < 0.01$ ($p < 0.001$). BL: (Baroni and Lenci, 2009), CLW: (Chen et al., 2006), AP: (Almuhareb, 2006), RS: (Rothenhäusler and Schütze, 2009)

	0.1%			1%			10%		
	cos svd	cos vector	dot 2	cos svd	cos vector	dot 2	cos svd	cos vector	dot 2
RG	0.219	0.244	**0.669**	0.676	0.700	**1.159**	0.911	0.829	**1.068**
AAMP	**0.379**	0.339	0.366	**0.723**	0.622	0.634	0.923	0.886	**0.948**
Synonym	0.369	0.464	**0.610**	0.493	0.590	**0.833**	0.857	0.770	**1.081**
Antonym	0.449	**0.493**	0.231	**0.768**	0.585	0.730	**1.044**	0.849	0.977
Conass	0.187	0.260	**0.261**	0.451	0.498	**0.942**	0.857	0.704	**1.062**
Coord	0.282	0.362	**0.456**	0.527	0.570	**1.050**	0.927	0.810	**1.187**
Phrasacc	0.268	0.132	**0.761**	0.849	0.610	**1.215**	0.920	0.868	**1.049**
Supersub	0.313	**0.353**	0.285	0.645	0.601	**1.029**	0.936	0.752	**1.060**

Table 2: Each cell contains the ratio of the performance of the corresponding model for the corresponding downsampling ratio to the performance of the same model on the full graph. The higher ratio means the less deterioration due to data sparseness.

the full graph are in Table 1, line 1. The SVD model clearly outperforms the pure-vector based approach and the graph-based approaches. Its performance is above that of previous models trained on the same corpus (Baroni and Lenci, 2009). The best model that we report is based on web search engine results (Chen et al., 2006). Among the graph-based random walk models, flexible walk with parameter 0.5 and fixed 1-step walk with indirect relatedness measures using dot product similarity achieve the highest performance.

Concept categorization: Almuhareb (2006) proposed a set of 402 nouns to be categorized into 21 classes of both concrete (animals, fruit...) and abstract (feelings, times...) concepts. Our results on this clustering task are given in Table 1 (line 2). The difference between SVD and pure-vector models is negligible and they both obtain the best performance in terms of both cluster entropy (not shown in the table) and purity. Both models' performances are comparable with the previously reported studies, and above that of random walks.

Semantic priming: The next dataset comes from Hodgson (1991) and it is of interest since it requires capturing different forms of semantic relatedness between prime-target pairs: synonyms (*synonym*), coordinates (*coord*), antonyms (*antonym*), free association pairs (*conass*), super- and subordinate pairs (*supersub*) and phrasal associates (*phrasacc*). Following previous simulations of this data-set (Padó and Lapata, 2007), we measure the similarity of each related target-prime pair, and we compare it to the average similarity of the target to all the other primes instantiating the same relation, treating the latter quantity as our surrogate of an unrelated target-prime pair. We report results in terms of differences between unrelated and related pairs, normalized to t-scores, marking significance according to two-tailed paired t-tests for the relevant degrees of freedom. Even though the SVD-based and pure-vector models are among the top achievers in general, we see that in different tasks different random walk models achieve comparable or even better performances. In particular, for phrasal associates and conceptual associates, the best results are obtained by random walks based on direct measures.

3.1 Robustness against data sparseness

So far, we reported only the results obtained on the full graph. However, in order to see the response of the models to using smaller corpora we ran another set of experiments on artificially down-sampled graphs as explained above. In this case, we are not interested in the absolute performance of the models per se but the relative performance. Thus, for ease of comparison we fixed each model's performance on the full graph to 1 for each task and linearly scaled its performance on smaller graphs. For example saying that the SVD-based model achieves a score of 0.911 on 10% graph for the Rubenstein and Goodenough dataset means that the ratio of the performance of SVD-based model on 10% graph to the performance of the same model on the full graph is 0.911. The results are given in Table 2, where the only random walk model we report is *dot 2*, i.e., a 2-step random walk coupled with the dot product-based indirect measure. This is by far the random walk model most robust to downsampling. In the 10% graph, we see that on all tasks but one, dot 2 is the model least affected by the data reduction. On the contrary, down-sampling has a positive effect on this model because on 6 tasks, it actually performs better than it does on the full graph! The same behavior is also observed on the 1% graph - as an example, for phrasal associates relations, dot 2 performance increases by a factor of around 1.2 when we use one hundredth of the graph instead of the full one. For the smallest graph we used, 0.1%, still dot 2 provides the highest relative performance in 5 out of the 8 tasks.

4 Conclusion

We compared graph-based random walk models and vector models. For this purpose, we showed how corpus co-occurrences could be represented both as a graph and a vector, and we identified two different ways to calculate relatedness based on the outcomes of random walks, by direct and indirect measures. The experiments carried out on 8 different tasks by using the full graph revealed that SVD-based model performs very well across all types of semantic relatedness. However, there is also evidence that -depending on the particular relation- some random walk models can achieve results as good as or even better than those of SVD-based models. Our second question was whether the random walk models would be able to simulate the smoothing effects obtained by SVD. While answering this question, we also carried out a systematic comparison of plain and SVD-based models on different tasks with different sizes of data. One interesting result is that an SVD-based model is not necessarily more robust to data sparseness than the plain vector model. The more interesting result is that a 2-step random walk model, based on indirect measures with dot product, consistently outperforms both SVD-based and plain vector models in terms of relative performance, thus it is able to achieve comparable results on very small datasets. Actually, the improvement on absolute performance measures of this random walk by making the dataset even smaller calls for future research.

References

A. Almuhareb. 2006. *Attributes in lexical acquisition*. Dissertation, University of Essex.

M. Baroni and A. Lenci. 2009. One distributional memory, many semantic spaces. In *Proceedings of GEMS*, Athens, Greece.

Hsin-Hsi Chen, Ming-Shun Lin, and Yu-Chuan Wei. 2006. Novel association measures using web search with double checking. In *Proceedings of ACL*, pages 1009–16.

J. Hodgson. 1991. Informational constraints on pre-lexical priming. *Language and Cognitive Processes*, 6:169–205.

Einat Minkov and William W. Cohen. 2008. Learning graph walk based similarity measures for parsed text. In *Proceedings of EMNLP'08*.

S. Padó and M. Lapata. 2007. Dependency-based construction of semantic space models. *Computational Linguistics*, 33(2):161–199.

T. Pedersen, S. Patwardhan, and J. Michelizzi. 2004. Wordnet::similarity: Measuring the relatedness of concepts. In *Proceedings of NAACL*, pages 38–41.

Klaus Rothenhäusler and Hinrich Schütze. 2009. Unsupervised classification with dependency based word spaces. In *Proceedings of GEMS*, pages 17–24.

H. Rubenstein and J.B. Goodenough. 1965. Contextual correlates of synonymy. *Communications of the ACM*, 8(10):627–633.

M. Sahlgren. 2006. *The Word-Space Model*. Dissertation, Stockholm University.

H. Schütze. 1997. *Ambiguity Resolution in Natural Language Learning*. CSLI, Stanford.

Dominic Widdows and Beate Dorow. 2002. A graph model for unsupervised lexical acquisition. In *19th International Conference on Computational Linguistics*, pages 1093–1099.

Graph-based Event Coreference Resolution

Zheng Chen
The Graduate Center
The City University of New York
zchen1@gc.cuny.edu

Heng Ji
Queens College and The Graduate Center
The City University of New York
hengji@cs.qc.cuny.edu

Abstract

In this paper, we address the problem of event coreference resolution as specified in the Automatic Content Extraction (ACE[1]) program. In contrast to entity coreference resolution, event coreference resolution has not received great attention from researchers. In this paper, we first demonstrate the diverse scenarios of event coreference by an example. We then model event coreference resolution as a spectral graph clustering problem and evaluate the clustering algorithm on ground truth event mentions using ECM F-Measure. We obtain the ECM-F scores of 0.8363 and 0.8312 respectively by using two methods for computing coreference matrices.

1 Introduction

Typically, an ACE Event Detection and Recognition (VDR) system consists of two steps: first, it detects all mentions of events with certain specified types occurring in the raw text (event mention detection) and second, it unifies the event mentions into equivalence classes so that all the mentions in a given class refer to an event (event coreference resolution). ACE defines the following terminologies related with VDR:

- Event: a specific occurrence involving participants. An ACE event has six attributes (type, subtype, modality, polarity, genericity and tense), zero or more event arguments, and a cluster of event mentions.
- Event trigger: the word that most clearly expresses an event's occurrence.
- Event argument: an *entity*, or a *temporal expression* or a *value* that has a certain role (e.g., Time-Within, Place) in an event.
- Event mention: a sentence (or a text span *extent*) that mentions an event, including a distinguished trigger and involving arguments.

In contrast to entity coreference, the scenarios in event coreference are more complicated, mainly because entity coreference is word (or phrase)-level coreference whereas event coreference is sentence-level coreference and therefore the coreferring event mentions may have more flexible linguistic structures than entity mentions. We provide an example to demonstrate this diversity.

[EM1]An {explosion} in a cafe at one of the capital's busiest intersections killed one woman and injured another Tuesday, police said. [EM2]Police were investigating the cause of the {explosion} in the restroom of the multistory Crocodile Cafe in the commercial district of Kizilay during the morning rush hour. [EM3]The {blast} shattered walls and windows in the building. [EM4]Ankara police chief Ercument Yilmaz visited the site of the morning blast but refused to say if a bomb had caused the {explosion}. [EM5]The {explosion} comes a month after [EM6]a bomb {exploded} at a McDonald's restaurant in Istanbul, causing damage but no injuries. [EM7]Radical leftist, Kurdish and Islamic groups are active in the country and have carried out {bombings} in the past.

Table 1. Source text and event mentions

Table 1 shows the source text of a news story. As an example, we only tag the event mentions which have the event type and subtype of (Conflict:Attack). In each event mention, the trigger is surrounded by curly brackets, and arguments are underlined.

Table 2 shows the tabular representation of those event mentions.

Table 3 shows that the five event mentions in event EV1 corefer with each other. We summarize EV1 as follows: a bomb (E4-1) exploded in the restroom (E2-1) of a café (E1-1 or E1-2) during Tuesday morning's rush hour (combination of T1-1, T2-1 and T3-1). EV2 is a different attack event because the target (E6-1) in EV2 differs from the one (E1-3) in EV1. EV3 tells that the bombing attacks have occurred generically

[1] http://www.nist.gov/speech/tests/ace/

Proceedings of the 2009 Workshop on Graph-based Methods for Natural Language Processing, ACL-IJCNLP 2009, pages 54–57,
Suntec, Singapore, 7 August 2009.

(thus the event attribute "genericity" is "General" whereas it is "Specific" in EV1 and EV2).

EM1	Trigger: explosion
	Arguments (ID: ROLE): (E1-1: Place) a cafe at one of the capital's busiest intersections (T1-1: Time-Within) Tuesday
EM2	Trigger: explosion
	Arguments: (E2-1: Place) the restroom of the multistory Crocodile Cafe (E3-1: Place) the commercial district of Kizilay (T2-1: Time-Within) the morning rush hour
EM3	Trigger: blast
	Arguments: (E1-2: Place) the building
EM4	Trigger: explosion
	Arguments: (E4-1: Instrument) a bomb (E1-3: Target) the site of the morning blast (T3-1: Time-Within) morning
EM5	Trigger: explosion
	Arguments: None
EM6	Trigger: exploded
	Arguments: (E5-1: Instrument) a bomb (E6-1: Target) a McDonald's restaurant (E7-1: Place) Istanbul
EM7	Trigger: bombings
	(E8-1: Attacker) Radical leftist, Kurdish and Islamic groups (E9-1: Place) the country (T4-1: Time-Within) the past

Table 2. Tabular representation of event mentions

Event	Included event mentions
EV1	{EM1,EM2,EM3,EM4,EM5}
EV2	{EM6}
EV3	{EM7}

Table 3. Event coreference results

2 Event Coreference Resolution as Spectral Graph Clustering

We view the event coreference space as an undirected weighted graph in which the nodes represent all the event mentions in a document and the edge weights indicate the coreference confidence between two event mentions. In real implementation, we initially construct different graphs for separate event types[2], such that, in each graph, all the event mentions have the same event type. Similar to (Nicolae and Nicolae, 2006), we formally define a framework for event coreference resolution.

[2] We view the 33 ACE event subtypes as event types

Let $EM = \{em_m: 1 \leq m \leq M\}$ be M event mentions in the document and $EV = \{ev_n: 1 \leq n \leq N\}$ be N events. Let $f: EM \rightarrow EV$ be the function mapping from an event mention $em_m \in EM$ to an event $ev_n \in EV$. Let $coref: EM \times EM \rightarrow [0,1]$ be the function that computes the coreference confidence between two event mentions $em_i, em_j \in EM$. Let $T = \{t_k: 1 \leq k \leq K\}$ be K event types. Thus for each event type k, we have a graph $G_k(V_k, E_k)$, where $V_k = \{em_m | f(em_m).type = t_k, em_m \in EM\}$ and $E_k = \{(em_i, em_j, coref(em_i, em_j)) | em_i, em_j \in EM\}$.

We then model event coreference resolution as a spectral graph clustering problem that optimizes the normalized-cut criterion (Shi and Malik, 2000). Such optimization can be achieved by computing the second generalized eigenvector, thus the name "spectral". In this paper, we do not try to propose a new spectral clustering algorithm or improve the existing algorithm. Instead, we focus on how to compute the coreference matrix (equivalently, the affinity matrix in Shi and Malik's algorithm) because a better estimation of coreference matrix can reduce the burden on clustering algorithm.

3 Coreference Matrix *W*

3.1 Method 1: Computing a Coreference Formula

Obviously, the trigger pair and the argument sets owned by two event mentions carry much information about whether one event mention corefers with the other. Based on a corpus, we compute the statistics about event mention pairs (with the same event type) listed in Table 4.

Let $em_i.trigger$ be the trigger in em_i, $stem(em_i.trigger)$ be the stem of the trigger in em_i, $wordnet(em_i.trigger, em_j.trigger)$ be the semantic similarity between the two triggers in em_i and em_j as computed in (Seco et al., 2004), $em_i.arg$ be the argument (ID and ROLE) set in em_i. Let $\cap_1$ be the conjunction operator on argument pairs whose ID[3] and ROLE match, $\cap_2$ be the conjunction operator on argument pairs whose ID matches but ROLE does not match, $\cap_3$ be the conjunction operator on argument pairs whose ROLE matches but ID does not match, $\cap_4$ be the conjunction operator on argument pairs whose ID and ROLE do not match. We then propose the following formula to measure the coreference value between em_i and em_j.

$$w_{ij} = e^{-\frac{1}{w_{ij}^T + w_{ij}^A}} \text{ where}$$

[3] We view two argument IDs "E1-1" and "E1-2" as a match if they mention the same entity which is "E1"

$$w_{ij}^{T} = \begin{cases} \frac{T11}{T11+T12} & \text{if } em_i.\,trigger = em_j.\,trigger \\ \frac{T21}{T21+T22} & \text{elseif } stem(em_i.\,trigger) = stem(em_j.\,trigger) \\ \frac{T31}{T31+T32} & \text{elseif } wordnet(em_i.\,trigger, em_j.\,trigger) > 0 \\ \frac{T41}{T41+T42} & \text{otherwise} \end{cases}$$

and

$$w_{ij}^{A} = \frac{1}{\min\{|em_i.\arg|, |em_j.\arg|\}} \times$$
$$[\frac{A11}{A11+A12}|em_i.\arg \cap_1 em_j.\arg| + \frac{A21}{A21+A22}|em_i.\arg \cap_2 em_j.\arg| +$$
$$\frac{A31}{A31+A32}|em_i.\arg \cap_3 em_j.\arg| + \frac{A41}{A41+A42}|em_i.\arg \cap_4 em_j.\arg|]$$

The strength of this formula is that it allows to give credit to different cases of trigger matching and argument pair matching between two event mentions.

T11	in those coreferring event mention pairs, how many pairs use exactly the same triggers
T12	in those non-coreferring event mention pairs, how many pairs use exactly the same triggers
T21	in those coreferring event mention pairs, how many pairs do not have the same triggers, but have the same stems of triggers
T22	non-coreferring version of T21
T31	in those coreferring event mention pairs, how many pairs do not have the same triggers nor the same stems, but the semantic similarity between two triggers is higher than 0 in WordNet.
T32	non-coreferring version of T31
T41	in those non-coreferring event mention pairs, how many pairs are not in T11 or T21 or T31
T42	non- coreferring version that is not T12 or T22 or T32
A11	in those coreferring event mention pairs, how many argument pairs whose ID and ROLE match
A12	non-coreferring version of A11
A21	in those coreferring event mention pairs, how many argument pairs whose ID matches but ROLE does not match
A22	non-coreferring version of A21
A31	in those coreferring event mention pairs, how many argument pairs whose ROLE matches but ID does not match
A32	non-coreferring version of A31
A41	in those non-coreferring event mention pairs, how many argument pairs whose ID and ROLE do not match
A42	non-coreferring version of A41

Table 4. Statistics of event mention pairs

3.2 Method 2: Applying a Maximum Entropy Model

We train a maximum entropy model to produce the confidence values for W. Each confidence value tells the probability that there exists coreference C between event mention em_i and em_j.

$$P(C|em_i, em_j) = \frac{e^{(\sum_k \lambda_k g_k(em_i, em_j, C))}}{Z(em_i, em_j)}$$

where $g_k(em_i, em_j, C)$ is a feature and λ_k is its weight; $Z(em_i, em_j)$ is the normalizing factor.

The feature sets applied in the model are listed in Table 5 by categories.

4 Experiments and Results

4.1 Data and Evaluation Metrics

We developed and tested the spectral clustering algorithm for event coreference resolution using the ACE 2005 English corpus which contains 560 documents. We used the ground truth event mentions and evaluated our algorithm based on ECM F-Measure (Luo, 2005). We reserved 60 documents for testing purpose and used the left 500 documents for training/developing purpose and for computing the statistics discussed above. We applied 10-fold cross-validation in the experiment of comparing two methods for computing coreference matrix.

4.2 Statistics of Event Mention Pairs

The results of the statistics discussed in Section 3.1 are presented in Table 6.

T11=1042,T12=1297, T21=240,T22=840, T31=257, T32=2637, T41=784,T42=5628
A11=888, A12= 1485, A21=31, A22=146, A31=542, A32=6849, A41=323, A42=3000

Table 6. Results of statistics in 500 documents

From Table 6, we observe that if two event mentions use the same trigger or if they have arguments whose ID and ROLE match, it is more probable for them to corefer with each other than other cases.

4.3 Comparison of the Two Methods for Computing Coreference Matrix

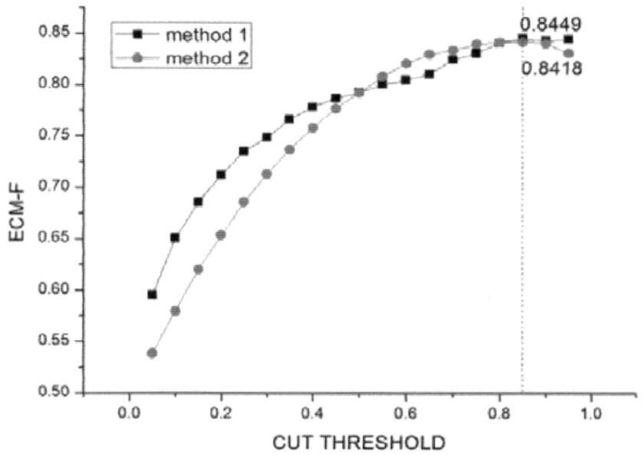

Figure 1. ECM-F scores for both methods

Category	Features	Remarks (EM1: the first event mention, EM2: the second event mention)
Lexicon	type_subtype	pair of event type and subtype in EM1
	trigger_pair	trigger pair of EM1 and EM2
	pos_pair	part-of-speech pair of triggers of EM1 and EM2
	nominal	1 if the trigger of EM2 is nominal
	exact_match	1 if the spellings of triggers in EM1 and EM2 exactly match
	stem_match	1 if the stems of triggers in EM1 and EM2 match
	trigger_sim	quantized semantic similarity score (0-5) using WordNet resource
Distance	token_dist	how many tokens between triggers of EM1 and EM2 (quantized)
	sentence_dist	how many sentences EM1 and EM2 are apart (quantized)
	event_dist	how many event mentions in between EM1 and EM2 (quantized)
Arguments	overlap_num,overlap_roles	overlap number of arguments and their roles (role and id exactly match) between EM1 and EM2
	prior_num, prior_roles	the number and the roles of arguments that only appear in EM1
	act_num, act_roles	the number and the roles of arguments that only appear in EM2
	coref_num	the number of arguments that corefer each other but have different roles between EM1 and EM2

Table 5. EM(Event Mention)-pair features for the maximum entropy model

Figure 1 shows the ECM-F scores for both methods by varying the cut threshold in the clustering algorithm. Both methods obtain the highest ECM-F score at threshold 0.85 and method 1 performs slightly better than method 2 (0.8449 vs. 0.8418, significant at 85% confidence level, $p<=0.1447$). We obtained the ECM-F scores of 0.8363 and 0.8312 on the test set for method 1 and method 2 respectively. We also obtained two baseline ECM-F scores, one is 0.535 if we consider all the event mentions with the same event type as a cluster, the other is 0.7635 if we consider each event mention as a cluster.

5 Related Work

Earlier work on event coreference (e.g. Humphreys et al., 1997; Bagga and Baldwin, 1999) in MUC was limited to several scenarios, e.g., terrorist attacks, management succession, resignation. The ACE program takes a further step towards processing more fine-grained events. To the best of our knowledge, this paper is the first effort to apply graph-based algorithm to the problem of event coreference resolution.

Nicolae and Nicolae (2006) proposed a similar graph-based framework for entity coreference resolution. However, in our task, the event mention has much richer structure than the entity mention, thus, it is possible for us to harness the useful information from both the triggers and the attached arguments in the event mentions.

6 Conclusions and Future Work

In this paper, we addressed the problem of event coreference resolution in a graph-based framework, and presented two methods for computing the coreference matrix. A practical event coreference resolver also depends on high-performance event extractor. We will further study the impact of system generated event mentions on the performance of our coreference resolver.

Acknowledgments
This material is based upon work supported by the Defense Advanced Research Projects Agency under Contract No. HR0011-06-C-0023 via 27-001022, and the CUNY Research Enhancement Program and GRTI Program.

References

A. Bagga and B. Baldwin. 1999. Cross-document event coreference: Annotations, experiments, and observations. In *Proc. ACL-99 Workshop on Coreference and Its Applications*.

C. Nicolae and G. Nicolae. 2006. Bestcut: A graph algorithm for coreference resolution. In *EMNLP*, pages 275–283, Sydney, Australia, July.

J. Shi and J. Malik.1997. Normalized Cuts and Image Segmentation. In *Proc. of IEEE Conf. on Comp. Vision and Pattern Recognition*, Puerto Rico

K. Humphreys, R. Gaizauskas, S. Azzam. 1997. Event coreference for information extraction. In *Proceedings of the ACL Workshop on Operational Factors in Practical Robust Anaphora Resolution for Unrestricted Texts*.

N. Seco, T. Veale, J. Hayes. 2004. An intrinsic information content metric for semantic similarity in WordNet. In *Proc. of ECAI-04*, pp. 1089–1090.

X. Luo. 2005. On coreference resolution performance metrics. *Proc. of HLT-EMNLP*.

Ranking and Semi-supervised Classification on Large Scale Graphs Using Map-Reduce

Delip Rao
Dept. of Computer Science
Johns Hopkins University
delip@cs.jhu.edu

David Yarowsky
Dept. of Computer Science
Johns Hopkins University
yarowsky@cs.jhu.edu

Abstract

Label Propagation, a standard algorithm for semi-supervised classification, suffers from scalability issues involving memory and computation when used with large-scale graphs from real-world datasets. In this paper we approach Label Propagation as solution to a system of linear equations which can be implemented as a scalable parallel algorithm using the map-reduce framework. In addition to semi-supervised classification, this approach to Label Propagation allows us to adapt the algorithm to make it usable for ranking on graphs and derive the theoretical connection between Label Propagation and PageRank. We provide empirical evidence to that effect using two natural language tasks – lexical relatedness and polarity induction. The version of the Label Propagation algorithm presented here scales linearly in the size of the data with a constant main memory requirement, in contrast to the quadratic cost of both in traditional approaches.

1 Introduction

Natural language data often lend themselves to a graph-based representation. Words can be linked by explicit relations as in WordNet (Fellbaum, 1989), and documents can be linked to one another via hyperlinks. Even in the absence of such a straightforward representation it is possible to derive meaningful graphs such as the nearest neighbor graphs, as done in certain manifold learning methods, e.g. Roweis and Saul (2000); Belkin and Niyogi (2001). Typically, these graphs share the following properties:

- They are edge-weighted.
- The edge weight encodes some notion of relatedness between the vertices.
- The relation represented by edges is at least weakly transitive. Examples of such relations include, "is similar to", "is more general than", and so on. It is important that the relations selected are transitive for the graph-based learning methods using random walks.

Such graphs present several possibilities for solving natural language problems involving ranking, classification, and clustering. Graphs have been successfully employed in machine learning in a variety of supervised, unsupervised, and semi-supervised tasks. Graph based algorithms perform better than their counterparts as they capture the latent structure of the problem. Further, their elegant mathematical framework allows simpler analysis to gain a deeper understanding of the problem. Despite these advantages, implementations of most graph-based learning algorithms do not scale well on large datasets from real world problems in natural language processing. With large amounts of unlabeled data available, the graphs can easily grow to millions of nodes and most existing non-parallel methods either fail to work due to resource constraints or find the computation intractable.

In this paper we describe a scalable implementation of Label Propagation, a popular random walk based semi-supervised classification method. We show that our framework can also be used for ranking on graphs. Our parallel formulation shows a theoretical connection between Label Propagation and PageRank. We also confirm this empirically using the lexical relatedness task. The

Proceedings of the 2009 Workshop on Graph-based Methods for Natural Language Processing, ACL-IJCNLP 2009, pages 58–65,
Suntec, Singapore, 7 August 2009.

proposed Parallel Label Propagation scales up linearly in the data and the number of processing elements available. Also, the main memory required by the method does not grow with the size of the graph.

The outline of this paper is as follows: Section 2 introduces the manifold assumption and explains why graph-based learning algorithms perform better than their counterparts. Section 3 motivates the random walk based approach for learning on graphs. Section 4 introduces the Label Propagation method by Zhu et al. (2003). In Section 5 we describe a method to scale up Label Propagation using Map-Reduce. Section 6 shows how Label Propagation could be used for ranking on graphs and derives the relation between Label Propagation and PageRank. Parallel Label Propagation is evaluated on ranking and semi-supervised classification problems in natural language processing in Section 8. We study scalability of this algorithm in Section 9 and describe related work in the area of parallel algorithms and machine learning in Section 10.

2 Manifold Assumption

The training data $\mathcal{D}$ can be considered as a collection of tuples $\mathcal{D} = (\mathcal{X}, \mathcal{Y})$ where $\mathcal{Y}$ are the labels and $\mathcal{X}$ are the features, and the learned model $\mathcal{M}$ is a surrogate for an underlying physical process which generates the data $\mathcal{D}$. The data $\mathcal{D}$ can be considered as a sampling from a smooth surface or a manifold which represents the physical process. This is known as the manifold assumption (Belkin et al., 2005). Observe that even in the simple case of Euclidean data ($\mathcal{X} = \{x : x \in \mathbb{R}^d\}$) as shown in Figure 1, points that lie close in the Euclidean space might actually be far off on the manifold. A graph, as shown in Figure 1c, approximates the structure of the manifold which was lost in vectorized algorithms operating in the Euclidean space. This explains the better performance of graph algorithms for learning as seen in the literature.

3 Distance measures on graphs

Most learning tasks on graphs require some notion of distance or similarity to be defined between the vertices of a graph. The most obvious measure of distance in a graph is the shortest path between the vertices, which is defined as the minimum number of intervening edges between two vertices. This is also known as the geodesic distance. To convert this distance measure to a similarity measure, we take the reciprocal of the shortest-path length. We refer to this as the geodesic similarity.

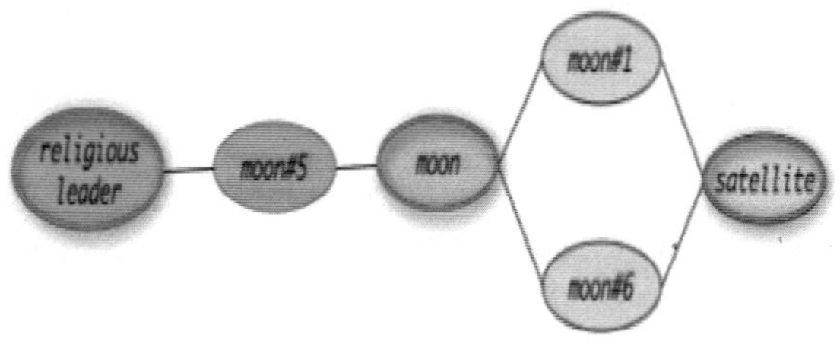

Figure 2: Shortest path distances on graphs ignore the connectivity structure of the graph.

While shortest-path distances are useful in many applications, it fails to capture the following observation. Consider the subgraph of WordNet shown in Figure 2. The term `moon` is connected to the terms `religious_leader` and `satellite`.[1] Observe that both `religious_leader` and `satellite` are at the same shortest path distance from `moon`. However, the connectivity structure of the graph would suggest `satellite` to be more similar than `religious_leader` as there are multiple senses, and hence multiple paths, connecting `satellite` and `moon`.

Thus it is desirable to have a measure that captures not only path lengths but also the connectivity structure of the graph. This notion is elegantly captured using random walks on graphs.

4 Label Propagation: Random Walk on Manifold Graphs

An efficient way to combine labeled and unlabeled data involves construction of a graph from the data and performing a Markov random walk on the graph. This has been utilized in Szummer and Jaakkola (2001), Zhu et. al. (2003), and Azran (2007). The general idea of Label Propagation involves defining a probability distribution F over the labels for each node in the graph. For labeled nodes, this distribution reflects the true labels and the aim is to recover this distribution for the unlabeled nodes in the graph.

Consider a graph $G(V, E, W)$ with vertices V, edges E, and an $n \times n$ edge weight matrix $W =$

[1] The `religious_leader` sense of `moon` is due to Sun Myung Moon, a US religious leader.

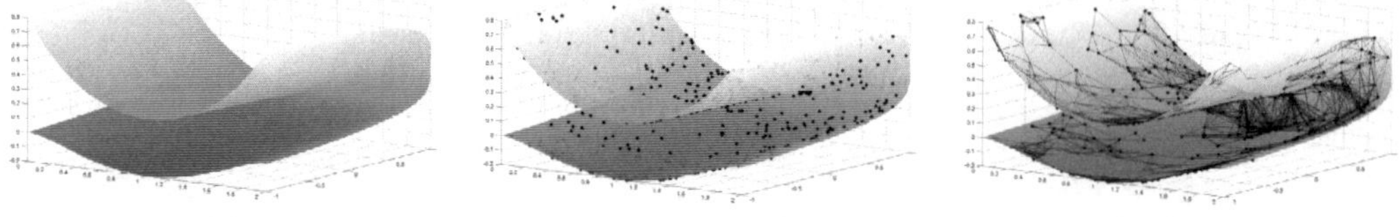

(a) (b) (c)

Figure 1: Manifold Assumption [Belkin *et al.*, 2005]: Data lies on a manifold (a) and points along the manifold are locally similar (b).

$[w_{ij}]$, where $n = |V|$. The Label Propagation algorithm minimizes a quadratic energy function

$$\mathcal{E} = \frac{1}{2} \sum_{(i,j) \in E} w_{ij}(F_i - F_j)^2 \quad (1)$$

The general recipe for using random walks for classification involves constructing the graph Laplacian and using the pseudo-inverse of the Laplacian as a kernel (Xiao and Gutman, 2003). Given a weighted undirected graph, $G(V, E, W)$, the Laplacian is defined as follows:

$$L_{ij} = \begin{cases} d_i & \text{if } i = j \\ -w_{ij} & \text{if } i \text{ is adjacent to } j \\ 0 & \text{otherwise} \end{cases} \quad (2)$$

where $d_i = \sum_j w_{ij}$.

It has been shown that the pseudo-inverse of the Laplacian L is a kernel (Xiao and Gutman, 2003), i.e., it satisfies the Mercer conditions. However, there is a practical limitation to this approach. For very large graphs, even if the graph Laplacians are sparse, their pseudo-inverses are dense matrices requiring $O(n^2)$ space. This can be prohibitive in most computing environments.

5 Parallel Label Propagation

In developing a parallel algorithm for Label Propagation we instead take an alternate approach and completely avoid the use of inverse Laplacians for the reasons stated above. Our approach follows from the observation made from Zhu et al.'s (2003) Label Propagation algorithm:

Observation: In a weighted graph $G(V, E, W)$ with $n = |V|$ vertices, minimization of Equation (1) is equivalent to solving the following system of linear equations.

$$\sum_{(i,j) \in E} w_{ij} F_i = \sum_{(i,j) \in E} w_{ij} F_j \quad (3)$$
$$\sum_{c \in \text{classes}(i)} F_i(c) = 1 \qquad \forall i, j \in V.$$

We use this observation to derive an iterative Label Propagation algorithm that we will later parallelize. Consider a weighted undirected graph $G(V, E, W)$ with the vertex set partitioned into V_L and V_U (i.e., $V = V_L \cup V_U$) such that all vertices in V_L are labeled and all vertices in V_U are unlabeled. Typically only a small set of vertices are labeled, i.e., $|V_U| \gg |V_L|$. Let F_u denote the probability distribution over the labels associated with vertex $u \in V$. For $v \in V_L$, F_v is known, and we also add a "dummy vertex" v' to the graph G such that $w_{vv'} = 1$ and $F_{v'} = F_v$. This is equivalent to the "clamping" done in (Zhu et al., 2003). Let V_D be the set of dummy vertices.

Algorithm 1: Iterative Label Propogation

repeat
  forall $v \in (V \cup V_D)$ **do**
    $F_v = \sum_{(v,u) \in E} w_{uv} F_v$
    Row normalize F_v.
  end
until *convergence or maxIterations*

Observe that every iteration of Algorithm 1 performs certain operations on each vertex of the graph. Further, these operations only rely on local information (from neighboring vertices of the graph). This leads to the parallel algorithm (Algorithm 2) implemented using the map-reduce model. Map-Reduce (Dean and Ghemawat, 2004) is a paradigm for implementing distributed algorithms with two user supplied functions "map" and "reduce". The map function processes the input key/value pairs with the key being a unique identifier for a node in the graph and the value corresponds to the data associated with the node. The mappers run on different machines operating on different parts of the data and the reduce function aggregates results from various mappers.

Algorithm 2: Parallel Label Propagation

```
map(key, value):
begin
    d = 0
    neighbors = getNeighbors(value);
    foreach n ∈ neighbors do
        w = n.weight();
        d += w * n.getDistribution();
    end
    normalize(d);
    value.setDistribution(d);
    Emit(key, value);
end
reduce(key, values): Identity Reducer
```

Algorithm 2 represents one iteration of Algorithm 1. This is run repeatedly until convergence or for a specified number of iterations. The algorithm is considered to have converged if the label distributions associated with each node do not change significantly, i.e., $\left|\left|\mathbf{F}_{(i+1)} - \mathbf{F}_{(i)}\right|\right|_2 < \epsilon$ for a fixed $\epsilon > 0$.

6 Label Propagation for Ranking

Graph ranking is applicable in a variety of problems in natural language processing and information retrieval. Given a graph, we would like to rank the vertices of a graph with respect to a node, called the pivot node or query node. Label Propagation and its variants (Szummer and Jaakkola, 2001; Zhu et al., 2003; Azran, 2007) have been traditionally used for semi-supervised classification. Our view of Label Propagation (via Algorithm 1) suggests a way to perform ranking on graphs.

Ranking on graphs can be performed in the Parallel Label Propagation framework by associating a single point distribution with all vertices. The pivot node has a mass fixed to the value 1 at all iterations. In addition, the normalization step in Algorithm 2 is omitted. At the end of the algorithm, the mass associated with each node determines its rank.

6.1 Connection to PageRank

It is interesting to note that Algorithm 1 brings out a connection between Label Propagation and PageRank (Page et al., 1998). PageRank is a random walk model that allows the random walk to "jump" to its initial state with a nonzero probability (α). Given the probability transition matrix $\mathbf{P} = [P_{rs}]$, where P_{rs} is the probability of jumping from node r to node s, the weight update for any vertex (say v) is derived as follows

$$v_{t+1} = \alpha v_t \mathbf{P} + (1 - \alpha) v_0 \tag{4}$$

Notice that when $\alpha = 0.5$, PageRank is reduced to Algorithm 1, by a constant factor, with the additional $(1 - \alpha)v_0$ term corresponding to the contribution from the "dummy vertices" V_D in Algorithm 1.

We can in fact show that Algorithm 1 reduces to PageRank as follows:

$$\begin{aligned} v_{t+1} &= \alpha v_t \mathbf{P} + (1 - \alpha) v_0 \\ &\propto v_t \mathbf{P} + \frac{(1 - \alpha)}{\alpha} v_0 \\ &= v_t \mathbf{P} + \beta v_0 \end{aligned} \tag{5}$$

where $\beta = \frac{(1-\alpha)}{\alpha}$. Thus by setting the edge weights to the dummy vertices to β, i.e., $\forall (z, z') \in E$ and $z' \in V_D, w_{zz'} = \beta$, Algorithm 1, and hence Algorithm 2, reduces to PageRank. Observe that when $\beta = 1$ we get the original Algorithm 1. We'll refer to this as the "β-correction".

7 Graph Representation

Since Parallel Label Propagation algorithm uses only local information, we use the adjacency list representation (which is same as the sparse adjacency matrix representation) for the graph. This representation is important for the algorithm to have a constant main memory requirement as no further lookups need to be done while computing the label distribution at a node. The interface definition for the graph is listed in Appendix A. Often graph data is available in an edge format, as <source, destination, weight> triples. We use another map-reduce step (Algorithm 3) to convert that data to the form shown in Appendix A.

8 Evaluation

We evaluate the Parallel Label Propagation algorithm for both ranking and semi-supervised classification. In ranking our goal is to rank the vertices of a graph with respect to a given node called the pivot/query node. In semi-supervised classification, we are given a graph with some vertices

Algorithm 3: Graph Construction

```
map(key, value):
begin
    edgeEntry = value;
    Node n(edgeEntry);
    Emit(n.id, n);
end

reduce(key, values):
begin
    Emit(key, serialize(values));
end
```

labeled and would like to predict labels for the remaining vertices.

8.1 Ranking

To evaluate ranking, we consider the problem of deriving lexical relatedness between terms. This has been a topic of interest with applications in word sense disambiguation (Patwardhan et al., 2005), paraphrasing (Kauchak and Barzilay, 2006), question answering (Prager et al., 2001), and machine translation (Blatz et al., 2004), to name a few. Following the tradition in previous literature we evaluate on the Miller and Charles (1991) dataset. We compare our rankings with the human judgements using the Spearman rank correlation coefficient. The graph for this task is derived from WordNet, an electronic lexical database. We compare Algorithm 2 with results from using geodesic similarity as a baseline.

As observed in Table 1, the parallel implementation in Algorithm 2 performs better than ranking using geodesic similarity derived from shortest path lengths. This reinforces the motivation of using random walks as described in Section 3.

Method	Spearman Correlation
Geodesic (baseline)	0.28
Parallel Label Propagation	**0.36**

Table 1: Lexical-relatedness results: Comparison with geodesic similarity.

We now empirically verify the equivalence of the β-corrected Parallel Label Propagation and PageRank established in Equation 4. To do this, we use $\alpha = 0.1$ in the PageRank algorithm and set $\beta = \frac{(1-\alpha)}{\alpha} = 9$ in the β-corrected Parallel Label Propagation algorithm. The results are seen in Table 2.

Method	Spearman Correlation
PageRank ($\alpha = 0.1$)	0.39
Parallel Label Propagation ($\beta = 9$)	**0.39**

Table 2: Lexical-relatedness results: Comparision of PageRank and β-corrected Parallel Label Propagation

8.2 Semi-supervised Classification

Label Propagation was originally developed as a semi-supervised classification method. Hence Algorithm 2 can be applied without modification. After execution of Algorithm 2, every node v in the graph will have a distribution over the labels F_v. The predicted label is set to $\arg\max_{c \in \text{classes}(v)} F_v(c)$.

To evaluate semi-supervised classification we consider the problem of learning sentiment polarity lexicons. We consider the polarity of a word to be either positive or negative. For example, words such as *good, beautiful*, and *wonderful* are considered as positive sentiment words; whereas words such as *bad, ugly*, and *sad* are considered negative sentiment words. Learning such lexicons has applications in sentiment detection and opinion mining. We treat sentiment polarity detection as a semi-supervised Label Propagation problem in a graph. In the graph, each node represents a word whose polarity is to be determined. Each weighted edge encodes a relation that exists between two words. Each node (word) can have two labels: positive or negative. It is important to note that Label Propagation, and hence Algorithms 1&2, support multi-class classification but for the purpose of this task we have two labels. The graph for the task is derived from WordNet. We use the General Inquirer (GI)[2] data for evaluation. General Inquirer is lexicon of English words hand-labeled with categorical information along several dimensions. One such dimension is called valence, with 1915 words labeled "Positiv" (sic) and 2291 words labeled "Negativ" for words with positive and negative sentiments respectively. We used a random 20% of the data as our seed labels and the rest as our unlabeled data. We compare our results

[2]http://www.wjh.harvard.edu/~inquirer/

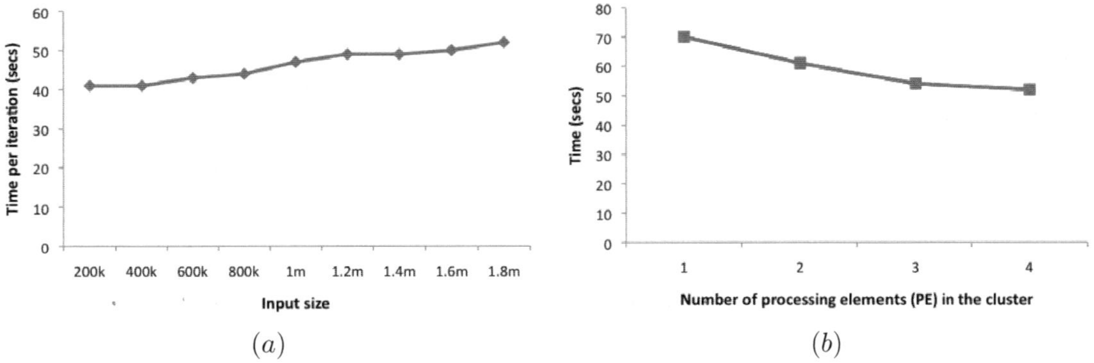

Figure 3: Scalability results: (a) Scaleup (b) Speedup

(F-scores) with another scalable previous work by Kim and Hovy (Kim and Hovy, 2006) in Table 2 for the same seed set. Their approach starts with a few seeds of positive and negative terms and bootstraps the list by considering all synonyms of positive word as positive and antonyms of positive words as negative. This procedure is repeated *mutatis mutandis* for negative words in the seed list until there are no more words to add.

Method	Nouns	Verbs	Adjectives
Kim & Hovy	34.80	53.36	47.28
Parallel Label Propagation	**58.53**	**83.40**	**72.95**

Table 3: Polarity induction results (F-scores)

The performance gains seen in Table 3 should be attributed to the Label Propagation in general as the previous work (Kim and Hovy, 2006) did not utilize a graph based method.

9 Scalability experiments

We present some experiments to study the scalability of the algorithm presented. All our experiments were performed on an experimental cluster of four machines to test the concept. The machines were Intel Xeon 2.4 GHz with 1Gb main memory. All performance measures were averaged over 20 runs.

Figure 3a shows scaleup of the algorithm which measures how well the algorithm handles increasing data sizes. For this experiment, we used all nodes in the cluster. As observed, the increase in time is at most linear in the size of the data. Figure 3b shows speedup of the algorithm. Speedup shows how well the algorithm performs with increase in resources for a fixed input size. In this case, we progressively increase the number of nodes in the cluster. Again, the speedup achieved is linear in the number of processing elements (CPUs). An appealing factor of Algorithm 2 is that the memory used by each mapper process is fixed regardless of the size of the graph. This makes the algorithm feasible for use with large-scale graphs.

10 Related Work

Historically, there is an abundance of work in parallel and distributed algorithms for graphs. See Grama et al. (2003) for survey chapters on the topic. In addition, the emergence of open-source implementations of Google's map-reduce (Dean and Ghemawat, 2004) such as Hadoop[3] has made parallel implementations more accessible.

Recent literature shows tremendous interest in application of distributed computing to scale up machine learning algorithms. Chu et al. (2006) describe a family of learning algorithms that fit the Statistical Query Model (Kearns, 1993). These algorithms can be written in a special summation form that is amenable to parallel speed-up. Examples of such algorithms include Naive Bayes, Logistic Regression, backpropagation in Neural Networks, Expectation Maximization (EM), Principal Component Analysis, and Support Vector Machines to name a few. The summation form can be easily decomposed so that the mapper can compute the partial sums that are then aggregated by a reducer. Wolfe et al. (2008) describe an approach to estimate parameters via the EM algorithm in a setup aimed to minimize communication latency.

The k-means clustering algorithm has been an archetype of the map-reduce framework with several implementations available on the web. In

[3]http://hadoop.apache.org/core

addition, the Netflix Million Dollar Challenge[4] generated sufficient interest in large scale clustering algorithms. (McCallum et al., 2000), describe algorithmic improvements to the k-means algorithm, called canopy clustering, to enable efficient parallel clustering of data.

While there is earlier work on scalable map-reduce implementations of PageRank (E.g., Gleich and Zhukov (2005)) there is no existing literature on parallel algorithms for graph-based semi-supervised learning or the relationship between PageRank and Label Propagation.

11 Conclusion

In this paper, we have described a parallel algorithm for graph ranking and semi-supervised classification. We derived this by first observing that the Label Propagation algorithm can be expressed as a solution to a set of linear equations. This is easily expressed as an iterative algorithm that can be cast into the map-reduce framework. This algorithm uses fixed main memory regardless of the size of the graph. Further, our scalability study reveals that the algorithm scales linearly in the size of the data and the number of processing elements in the cluster. We also showed how Label Propagation can be used for ranking on graphs and the conditions under which it reduces to PageRank. We evaluated our implementation on two learning tasks – ranking and semi-supervised classification – using examples from natural language processing including lexical-relatedness and sentiment polarity lexicon induction with a substantial gain in performance.

A Appendix A: Interface definition for Undirected Graphs

In order to guarantee the constant main memory requirement of Algorithm 2, the graph representation should encode for each node, the complete information about it's neighbors. We represent our undirected graphs in the Google's Protocol Buffer format.[5] Protocol Buffers allow a compact, portable on-disk representation that is easily extensible. This definition can be compiled into efficient Java/C++ classes.

The interface definition for undirected graphs is listed below:

[4] http://www.netflixprize.com

[5] Implementation available at http://code.google.com/p/protobuf/

```
package graph;

message NodeNeighbor {
   required string id = 1;
   required double edgeWeight = 2;
   repeated double labelDistribution = 3;
}

message UndirectedGraphNode {
   required string id = 1;
   repeated NodeNeighbor neighbors = 2;
   repeated double labelDistribution = 3;
}

message UndirectedGraph {
   repeated UndirectedGraphNode nodes = 1;
}
```

References

Arik Azran. 2007. The rendezvous algorithm: Multiclass semi-supervised learning with markov random walks. In *Proceedings of the International Conference on Machine Learning (ICML)*.

Micheal. Belkin, Partha Niyogi, and Vikas Sindhwani. 2005. On manifold regularization. In *Proceedings of AISTATS*.

John Blatz, Erin Fitzgerald, George Foster, Simona Gandrabur, Cyril Goutte, Alex Kulesza, Alberto Sanchis, and Nicola Ueffing. 2004. Confidence estimation for machine translation. In *Proceeding of COLING*.

Cheng T. Chu, Sang K. Kim, Yi A. Lin, Yuanyuan Yu, Gary R. Bradski, Andrew Y. Ng, and Kunle Olukotun. 2006. Map-reduce for machine learning on multicore. In *Proceedings of Neural Information Processing Systems*.

Jeffrey Dean and Sanjay Ghemawat. 2004. Map-reduce: Simplified data processing on large clusters. In *Proceedings of the symposium on Operating systems design and implementation (OSDI)*.

Christaine Fellbaum, editor. 1989. *WordNet: An Electronic Lexical Database*. The MIT Press.

D. Gleich and L. Zhukov. 2005. Scalable computing for power law graphs: Experience with parallel pagerank. In *Proceedings of SuperComputing*.

Ananth Grama, George Karypis, Vipin Kumar, and Anshul Gupta. 2003. *Introduction to Parallel Computing (2nd Edition)*. Addison-Wesley, January.

David Kauchak and Regina Barzilay. 2006. Paraphrasing for automatic evaluation. In *Proceedings of HLT-NAACL*.

Michael Kearns. 1993. Efficient noise-tolerant learning from statistical queries. In *Proceedings of the Twenty-Fifth Annual ACM Symposium on Theory of Computing (STOC)*.

Soo-Min Kim and Eduard H. Hovy. 2006. Identifying and analyzing judgment opinions. In *Proceedings of HLT-NAACL*.

Andrew McCallum, Kamal Nigam, and Lyle H. Ungar. 2000. Efficient clustering of high-dimensional data sets with application to reference matching. In *Knowledge Discovery and Data Mining (KDD)*, pages 169–178.

G. Miller and W. Charles. 1991. Contextual correlates of semantic similarity. In *Language and Cognitive Process*.

Larry Page, Sergey Brin, Rajeev Motwani, and Terry Winograd. 1998. The pagerank citation ranking: Bringing order to the web. *Technical report, Stanford University, Stanford, CA*.

Siddharth Patwardhan, Satanjeev Banerjee, and Ted Pedersen. 2005. Senserelate::targetword - A generalized framework for word sense disambiguation. In *Proceedings of ACL*.

John M. Prager, Jennifer Chu-Carroll, and Krzysztof Czuba. 2001. Use of wordnet hypernyms for answering what-is questions. In *Proceedings of the Text REtrieval Conference*.

M. Szummer and T. Jaakkola. 2001. Clustering and efficient use of unlabeled examples. In *Proceedings of Neural Information Processing Systems (NIPS)*.

Jason Wolfe, Aria Haghighi, and Dan Klein. 2008. Fully distributed EM for very large datasets. In *Proceedings of the International Conference in Machine Learning*.

W. Xiao and I. Gutman. 2003. Resistance distance and laplacian spectrum. *Theoretical Chemistry Association*, 110:284–289.

Xiaojin Zhu, Zoubin Ghahramani, and John Lafferty. 2003. Semi-supervised learning using Gaussian fields and harmonic functions. In *Proceedings of the International Conference on Machine Learning (ICML)*.

Opinion Graphs for Polarity and Discourse Classification *

Swapna Somasundaran
Univ. of Pittsburgh
Pittsburgh, PA 15260
swapna@cs.pitt.edu

Galileo Namata
Univ. of Maryland
College Park, MD 20742
namatag@cs.umd.edu

Lise Getoor
Univ. of Maryland
College Park, MD 20742
getoor@cs.umd.edu

Janyce Wiebe
Univ. of Pittsburgh
Pittsburgh, PA 15260
wiebe@cs.pitt.edu

Abstract

This work shows how to construct discourse-level opinion graphs to perform a joint interpretation of opinions and discourse relations. Specifically, our opinion graphs enable us to factor in discourse information for polarity classification, and polarity information for discourse-link classification. This inter-dependent framework can be used to augment and improve the performance of local polarity and discourse-link classifiers.

1 Introduction

Much research in opinion analysis has focused on information from words, phrases and semantic orientation lexicons to perform sentiment classification. While these are vital for opinion analysis, they do not capture discourse-level associations that arise from relations between opinions. To capture this information, we propose discourse-level opinion graphs for classifying opinion polarity.

In order to build our computational model, we combine a linguistic scheme *opinion frames* (Somasundaran et al., 2008) with a collective classification framework (Bilgic et al., 2007). According to this scheme, two opinions are related in the discourse when their targets (what they are about) are related. Further, these pair-wise discourse-level relations between opinions are either *reinforcing* or *non-reinforcing* frames. Reinforcing frames capture reinforcing discourse scenarios where the individual opinions reinforce one another, contributing to the same opinion polarity or stance. Non-reinforcing frames, on the other hand, capture discourse scenarios where the individual opinions do not support the same stance. The individual opinion polarities and the type of relation between their targets determine whether the discourse frame is reinforcing or non-reinforcing.

Our polarity classifier begins with information from opinion lexicons to perform polarity classification locally at each node. It then uses discourse-level links, provided by the opinion frames, to transmit the polarity information between nodes. Thus the opinion classification of a node is not just dependent on its local features, but also on the class labels of related opinions and the nature of these links. We design two discourse-level link classifiers: the target-link classifier, which determines if a given node pair has unrelated targets (*no link*), or if their targets have a *same* or *alternative* relation, and the frame-link classifier, which determines if a given node pair has *no link*, *reinforcing* or *non-reinforcing* link relation. Both these classifiers too first start with local classifiers that use local information. The opinion graph then provides a means to factor in the related opinion information into the link classifiers. Our approach enables using the information in the nodes (and links) to establish or remove links in the graph. Thus information flows to and fro between all the opinion nodes and discourse-level links to achieve a joint inference.

The paper is organized as follows: We first describe opinion graphs, a structure that can capture discourse-level opinion relationships in Section 2, and then describe our joint interpretation approach to opinion analysis in Section 3. Next, we describe our algorithm for joint interpretation in Section 4. Our experimental results are reported in Section 5. We discuss related work in Section 6 and conclude in Section 7.

2 Discourse-Level Opinion Graphs

The pairwise relationships that compose opinion frames can be used to construct a graph over opinion expressions in a discourse, which we refer to as the *discourse-level opinion graph (DLOG)*.

* This research was supported in part by the Department of Homeland Security under grant N000140710152.

Proceedings of the 2009 Workshop on Graph-based Methods for Natural Language Processing, ACL-IJCNLP 2009, pages 66–74,
Suntec, Singapore, 7 August 2009.

Figure 1 Opinion Frame Annotations.

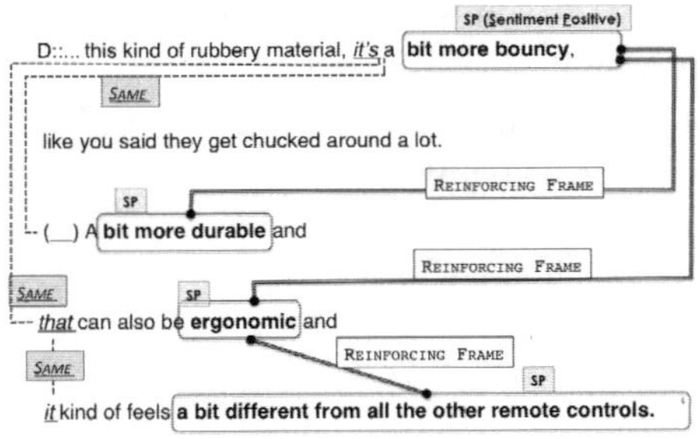

In this section, we describe these graphs and illustrate their applicability to goal-oriented multi-party conversations.

The nodes in the DLOG represent opinions, and there are two kinds of links: target links and frame links. Each opinion node has a polarity (*positive*, *negative* or *neutral*) and type (*sentiment* or *arguing*). *Sentiment* opinions are evaluations, feelings or judgments about the target. *Arguing* opinions argue for or against something. Target links are labeled as either *same* or *alternatives*. *Same* links hold between targets that refer to the same entity or proposition, while *alternative* links hold between targets that are related by virtue of being opposing (mutually exclusive) options in the context of the discourse. The frame links correspond to the *opinion frame* relation between opinions.

We illustrate the construction of the opinion graph with an example (Example 1, from Somasundaran et al. (2008)) from a multi-party meeting corpus where participants discuss and design a new TV remote control. The opinion expressions are in bold and their targets are in italics. Notice here that speaker D has a positive sentiment towards the rubbery material for the TV remote.

(1) D:: ... this kind of rubbery material, *it's* a **bit more bouncy**, like you said they get chucked around a lot. A **bit more durable** and *that* can also be **ergonomic** and *it* kind of feels **a bit different from all the other remote controls**.

All the individual opinions in this example are essentially regarding the same thing – the rubbery material. The speaker's positive sentiment is apparent from the text spans **bit more bouncy**, **bit more durable**, **ergonomic** and **a bit different from all the other remote controls**. The explicit targets of these opinions (*it's*, *that*, and *it*) and the implicit target of "a bit more durable" are thus all linked with *same* relations.

Figure 1 illustrates the individual opinion annotations, target annotations (shown in italics) and the relations between the targets (shown in dotted lines). Note that the target of **a bit more durable** is a zero span ellipsis that refers back to the rubbery material. The opinion frames resulting from the individual annotations make pairwise connections between opinion instances, as shown in bold lines in the figure. For example, the two opinions **bit more bouncy** and **ergonomic**, and the *same* link between their targets (*it's* and *that*), make up an opinion frame. An opinion frame type is derived from the details (type and polarity) of the opinions it relates and the target relation involved. Even though the different combinations of opinion type (sentiment and arguing), polarity (positive and negative) and target links (same and alternative) result in many distinct frames types (32 in total), they can be grouped, according to their discourse-level characteristics, into the two categories reinforcing and non-reinforcing. In this work, we only make this category distinction for opinion frames and the corresponding frame links.

The next example (Example 2, also from Somasundaran et al. (2008)) illustrates an *alternative* target relation. In the domain of TV remote controls, the set of all shapes are alternatives to one another, since a remote control may have only one shape at a time. In such scenarios, a positive opinion regarding one choice may imply a negative opinion toward competing choices, and vice versa. In this passage, speaker C's positive stance towards the curved shape is brought out even more strongly with his negative opinions toward the alternative, square-like, shapes.

(2) C:: ... shapes **should be** *curved*, so round shapes. **Nothing** *square-like*.

:

C:: ... So we **shouldn't have too** *square corners* and that kind of thing.

The reinforcing frames characteristically show a reinforcement of an opinion or stance in the discourse. Both the examples presented above depict a reinforcing scenario. In the first example, the opinion towards the rubbery material is reinforced by repeated positive sentiments towards it, while in the second example the positive stance towards the curved shapes is further reinforced by negative opinions toward the alternative option. Examples of non-reinforcing scenarios are ambivalence between alternative options (for e.g., "I **like** *the rubbery material* but *the plastic* will be **much**

cheaper") or mixed opinions about the same target (for e.g., weighing pros and cons "*The rubbery material* is **good** but *it* will be **just so expensive**").

3 Interdependent Interpretation

Our interdependent interpretation in DLOGs is motivated by the observation that, when two opinions are related, a clear knowledge of the polarity of one of them makes interpreting the other much easier. For instance, suppose an opinion classifier wants to find the polarity of all the opinion expressions in Example 1. As a first step, it can look up opinion lexicons to infer that words like **"bouncy"**, **"durable"** and **" ergonomic"** are positive. However, **"a bit different "** cannot be resolved via this method, as its polarity can be different in different scenarios.

Suppose now we relate the targets of opinions. There are clues in the passage that the targets are related via the *same* relation; for instance they are all third person pronouns occurring in adjacent clauses and sentences. Once we relate the targets, the opinions of the passage are related via target links in the discourse opinion graph. We are also able to establish frames using the opinion information and target link information wherever they are available, i.e., a reinforcing link between **bit more bouncy** and **ergonomic**. For the places where all the information is not available (between **ergonomic** and **a bit different**) there are multiple possibilities. Depending on the polarity, either a reinforcing frame (if **a bit different** has positive polarity) or a non-reinforcing frame (if **a bit different** has negative polarity) can exist. There are clues in the discourse that this passage represents a reinforcing scenario. For instance there are reinforcing frames between the first few opinions, the repeated use of "and" indicates a *list*, *conjunction* or *expansion* relation between clauses (according to the Penn Discourse TreeBank (PDTB) (Prasad et al., 2008)), and there is a lack of contrastive clues that would indicate a change in the opinion. Thus the reinforcing frame link emerges as being the most likely candidate. This in turn disambiguates the polarity of **a bit different**. Thus, by establishing target links and frame links between the opinion instances, we are able to perform a joint interpretation of the opinions.

The interdependent framework of this example is iterative and dynamic — the information in the nodes can be used to change the structure (i.e., establish new links), and the structure provides a framework to change node polarity. We build our classification framework and feature sets with respect to this general framework, where the node labels as well as the structure of the graph are predicted in a joint manner.

Thus our interdependent interpretation framework has three main units: an instance polarity classifier (IPC), a target-link classifier (TLC), and a frame-link classifier (FLC). IPC classifies each node (instance), which may be a sentence, utterance or an other text span, as *positive*, *negative* or *neutral*. The TLC determines if a given node pair has related targets and whether they are linked by a *same* or *alternative* relation. The FLC determines if a given node pair is related via frames, and whether it is a reinforcing or non-reinforcing link. As we saw in the example, there are local clues available for each unit to arrive at its classification. The discourse augments this information to aid in further disambiguation.

4 Collective Classification Framework

For our collective classification framework, we use a variant of the iterative classification algorithm (ICA) proposed by Bilgic et al (2007). It combines several common prediction tasks in graphs: object classification (predicting the label of an object) and link prediction (predicting the existence and class of a link between objects). For our tasks, object classification directly corresponds to predicting opinion polarity and the link prediction corresponds to predicting the existence of a *same* or *alternative* target link or a *reinforcing* or *non-reinforcing* frame link between opinions. We note that given the nature of our problem formulation and approach, we use the terms link prediction and link classification interchangeably.

In the collective classification framework, there are two sets of features to use. The first are local features which can be generated for each object or link, independent of the links in which they participate, or the objects they connect. For example, the opinion instance may contain words that occur in sentiment lexicons. The local features are described in Section 4.2. The second set of features, the relational features, reflect neighborhood information in the graph. For frame link classification, for example, there is a feature indicating whether the connected nodes are predicted to have the same polarity. The relational features are described in Section 4.3.

4.1 DLOG-ICA Algorithm

Our variant of the ICA algorithm begins by predicting the opinion polarity, and link type using only the local features. We then randomly order the set of all opinions and links and, in turn, predict the polarity or class using the local features and the values of the currently predicted relational features based on previous predictions. We repeat this until some stopping criterion is met. For our experiments, we use a fixed number of 30 iterations which was sufficient, in most of our datasets, for ICA to converge to a solution. The pseudocode for the algorithm is shown in Algorithm 4.1.

Algorithm 1 DLOG-ICA Algorithm

```
for each opinion o do {bootstrapping}
  Compute polarity for o using local attributes
end for
for each target link t do {bootstrapping}
  Compute label for t using local attributes
end for
for each frame link f do {bootstrapping}
  Compute label for f using local attributes
end for
repeat {iterative classification}
  Generate ordering I over all nodes and links
  for each i in I do
    if i is an opinion instance then
      Compute polarity for i using local and
      relational attributes
    else if i is a target link then
      Compute class for i using local and re-
      lational attributes
    else if i is a frame link then
      Compute class for i using local and re-
      lational attributes
    end if
  end for
until Stopping criterion is met
```

The algorithm is one very simple way of making classifications that are interdependent. Once the local and relational features are defined, a variety of classifiers can be used. For our experiments, we use SVMs. Additional details are provided in the experiments section.

4.2 Local Features

For the local polarity classifier, we employ opinion lexicons, dialog information, and unigram features. We use lexicons that have been successfully used in previous work (the polarity lexicon from (Wilson et al., 2005) and the arguing lexicon (Somasundaran et al., 2007)). Previous work used features based on parse trees, e.g., (Wilson et al., 2005; Kanayama and Nasukawa, 2006), but our data has very different characteristics from monologic texts – the utterances and sentences are much shorter, and there are frequent disfluencies, restarts, hedging and repetitions. Because of this, we cannot rely on parsing features. On the other hand, in this data, we have dialog act information[1] (Dialog Acts), which we can exploit. Note that the IPC uses only the Dialog Act tags (instance level tags like *Inform*, *Suggest*) and not the dialog structure information.

Feature	Task
Time difference between the node pair	TLC, FLC
Number of intervening instances	TLC, FLC
Content word overlap between the node pair	TLC,FLC
Focus space overlap between the node pair	TLC, FLC
Bigram overlap between the node pair *	TLC, FLC
Are both nodes from same speaker *	TLC, FLC
Bag of words for each node	TLC, FLC
Anaphoric indicator in the second node	TLC
Adjacency pair between the node pair	FLC
Discourse relation between node pair *	FLC

Table 1: Features and the classification task it is used for; TLC = target-link classification, FLC = Frame-link classification

Opinion frame detection between sentences has been previously attempted (Somasundaran et al., 2008) by using features that capture discourse and dialog continuity. Even though our link classification tasks are not directly comparable (the previous work performs binary classification of frame-present/frame-absent between opinion bearing sentences, while this work performs three-way classification: no-link/reinforcing/non-reinforcing between DA pairs), we adapt the features for the link classification tasks addressed here. These features depend on properties of the nodes that the link connects. We also create some new features that capture discourse relations and lexical overlap.

Table 1 lists the link classification features. New features are indicated with a '*'. Continuous discourse indicators, like *time difference between the node pair* and *number of intervening instances* are useful for determining if the two nodes can be related. The *content word over-*

[1]Manual annotations for Dialog act tags and *adjacency pairs* are available for the AMI corpus.

lap, and *focus space overlap* features (the focus space for an instance is a list of the most recently used NP chunks; i.e., NP chunks in that instance and a few previous instances) capture the overlap in topicality within the node pair; while the *bigram overlap* feature captures the alignment between instances in terms of function words as well as content words. The entity-level relations are captured by the *anaphoric indicator feature* that checks for the presence of pronouns such as *it* and *that* in the second node in the node pair. The *adjacency pair* and *discourse relation* are actually feature sets that indicate specific dialog-structure and discourse-level relations. We group the list of discourse relations from the PDTB into the following sets: *expansion*, *contingency*, *alternative*, *temporal*, *comparison*. Each discourse relation in PDTB is associated with a list of discourse connective words.[2] Given a node pair, if the first word of the later instance (or the last word first instance) is a discourse connective word, then we assume that this node is connecting back (or forward) in the discourse and the feature set to which the connective belongs is set to true (e.g., if a latter instance is "because we should ...", it starts with the connective "because", and connects backwards via a *contingency* relation). The *adjacency pair* feature indicates the presence of a particular dialog structure (e.g., *support*, *positive-assessment*) between the nodes.

4.3 Relational Features

In addition to the local features, we introduce relational features (Table 2) that incorporate related class information as well as transfer label information between classifiers. As we saw in our example in Figure 1, we need to know not only the polarity of the related opinions, but also the type of the relation between them. For example, if the frame relation between **ergonomic** and **a bit different** is non-reinforcing, then the polarity of **a bit different** is likely to be negative. Thus link labels play an important role in disambiguating the polarity. Accordingly, our relational features transfer information of class labels from other instances of the same classifier as well as between different classifiers. Table 2 lists our relational features. Each row represents a set of features. Features are generated for all combinations of x, y and z for each row. For example, one of the features in the first row is *Number of neighbors with polarity type positive, that are related via a reinforcing frame link.* Thus each feature for the polarity classifier identifies neighbors for a given node via a specific relation (z or y) and factors in their polarity values. Similarly, both link classifiers use polarity information of the node pair, and other link relations involving the nodes of the pair.

5 Evaluation

We experimentally test our hypothesis that discourse-level information is useful and non-redundant with local information. We also wanted to test how the DLOG performs for varying amounts of available annotations: from full neighborhood information to absolutely no neighborhood information.

Accordingly, for polarity classification, we implemented three scenarios: ICA-LinkNeigh, ICA-LinkOnly and ICA-noInfo. The ICA-LinkNeigh scenario measures the performance of the DLOG under ideal conditions (full neighborhood information) — the structure of the graph (link information) as well as the neighbors' class are provided (by an oracle). Here we do not need the TLC, or the FLC to predict links and the Instance Polarity Classifier (IPC) is not dependent on its predictions from the previous iteration. On the other hand, the ICA-noInfo scenario is the other extreme, and has absolutely no neighborhood information. Each node does not know which nodes in the network it is connected to apriori, and also has no information about the polarity of any other node in the network. Here, the structure of the graph, as well as the node classes, have to be inferred via the collective classification framework described in Sections 3 and 4. The ICA-LinkOnly is an intermediate condition, and is representative of scenarios where the discourse relationships between nodes is known. Here we start with the link information (from an oracle) and the IPC uses the collective classification framework to infer neighbor polarity information.

Similarly, we vary the amounts of neighborhood information for the TLC and FLC classifiers. In the ICA-LinkNeigh condition, TLC and FLC have full neighborhood information. In the ICA-noInfo condition, TLC and FLC are fully dependent on the classifications of the previous rounds. In the ICA-Partial condition, the TLC classifier

[2]The PDTB provides a list of discourse connectives and the list of discourse relations each connective signifies.

Feature
Opinion Polarity Classification
Number of neighbors with polarity type x linked via frame link z
Number of neighbors with polarity type x linked via target link y
Number of neighbors with polarity type x and same speaker linked via frame link z
Number of neighbors with polarity type x and same speaker linked via target link y
Target Link Classification
Polarity of the DA nodes
Number of other target links y involving the given DA nodes
Number of other target links y involving the given DA nodes and other same-speaker nodes
Presence of a frame link z between the nodes
Frame Link Classification
Polarity of the DA nodes
Number of other frame links z involving the given DA nodes
Number of other frame links z involving the given DA nodes and other same-speaker nodes
Presence of a target link y between the nodes

Table 2: Relational features: $x \in$ {non-neutral (i.e., positive or negative), positive, negative}, $y \in$ {same, alt}, $z \in$ {reinforcing, non-reinforcing}

uses true frame-links and polarity information, and previous-stage classifications for information about neighborhood target links; the FLC classifier uses true target-links and polarity information, and previous-stage classifications for information about neighborhood frame-links.

5.1 Data

For our experiments, we use the opinion frame annotations from previous work (Somasundaran et al., 2008). These annotations consist of the opinion spans that reveal opinions, their targets, the polarity information for opinions, the labeled links between the targets and the frame links between the opinions. The annotated data consists of 7 scenario-based, multi-party meetings from the AMI meeting corpus (Carletta et al., 2005). The manual Dialog Act (DA) annotations, provided by AMI, segment the meeting transcription into separate dialog acts. We use these DAs as nodes or instances in our opinion graph.

A DA is assigned the opinion orientation of the words it contains (for example, if a DA contains a positive opinion expression, then the DA assigned the positive opinion category). We filter out very small DAs (DAs with fewer than 3 tokens, punctuation included) in order to alleviate data skewness problem in the link classifiers. This gives us a total of 4606 DA instances, of which 1935 (42%) have opinions. Out of these 1935, 61.7% are positive, 30% are negative and the rest are neutral. The DAs that do not have opinions are considered neutral, and have no links in the DLOG. We create DA pairs by first ordering the DAs by their start time, and then pairing a DA with five DAs before it, and five DAs after it. The classes for target-link classification are *no-link, same, alt*. The gold standard target-link class is decided for a DA pair based on the target link between the targets of the opinions contained in that pair. Similarly, the labels for the frame-link labeling task are *no-link, reinforcing, non-reinforcing*. The gold standard frame link class is decided for a DA pair based on the frame between opinions contained by that pair. In our data, of the 4606 DAs, 1118 (24.27%) participate in target links with other DAs, and 1056 (22.9%) form frame links. The gold standard data for links, which has pair-wise information, has a total of 22,925 DA pairs, of which 1371 (6%) pairs have target links and 1264 (5.5%) pairs have frame links.

We perform 7-fold cross-validation experiments, using the 7 meetings. In each fold, 6 meetings are used for training and one meeting is used for testing.

5.2 Classifiers

Our baseline (Base) classifies the test data based on the distribution of the classes in the training data. Note that due to the heavily skewed nature of our link data, this classifier performs very poorly for minority class prediction, even though it may achieve good overall accuracy.

For our local classifiers, we used the classifiers from the Weka toolkit (Witten and Frank, 2002). For opinion polarity, we used the Weka's SVM implementation. For the target link and frame link classes, the huge class skew caused SVM to learn a trivial model and always predict the majority class. To address this, we used a cost sensitive classifier in Weka where we set the cost of misclassifying a less frequent class, A, to a more frequent class, B,

	Base	Local	ICA		
			LinkNeigh	LinkOnly	noInfo
Acc	45.9	68.7	78.8	72.9	68.4
Class: neutral (majority class)					
Prec	61.2	76.3	83.9	78.2	73.5
Rec	61.5	83.9	89.6	89.1	86.6
F1	61.1	79.6	86.6	83.2	79.3
Class: positive polarity					
Prec	26.3	56.2	70.9	63.3	57.6
Rec	26.1	46.6	62.0	47.0	42.8
F1	25.8	50.4	65.9	53.5	48.5
Class: negative polarity					
Prec	12.4	52.3	64.6	56.3	55.2
Rec	12.2	44.3	60.2	48.2	38.2
F1	12.2	46.0	61.9	51.2	43.9

Table 3: Performance of Polarity Classifiers

	Base	Local	ICA		
			LinkNeigh	Partial	noInfo
TLC					
Acc	88.5	85.8	98.1	98.2	86.3
P-M	33.3	35.9	76.1	76.1	36.3
R-M	33.3	38.1	78.1	78.1	38.1
F1-M	33.1	36.0	74.6	74.6	36.5
FLC					
Acc	89.3	86.2	98.9	98.9	87.6
P-M	33.3	36.9	81.3	82.8	38.0
R-M	33.4	41.2	82.2	84.4	41.7
F1-M	33.1	37.2	80.7	82.3	38.1

Table 4: Performance of Link Classifiers

as $|B|/|A|$ where $|class|$ is the size of the class in the training set. All other misclassification costs are set to 1.

For our collective classification, we use the above classifiers for local features (l) and use similar, separate classifiers for relational features (r). For example, we learned an SVM for predicting opinion polarity using only the local features and learned another SVM using only relational features. For the ICA-noInfo condition, where we use TLC and FLC classifiers, we combine the predictions using a weighted combination where $P(class|l, r) = \alpha * P(class|l) + (1 - \alpha) * P(class|r)$. This allows us to vary the influence each feature set has to the overall prediction. The results for ICA-noInfo are reported on the best performing α (0.7).

5.3 Results

Our polarity classification results are presented in Table 3, specifically accuracy (Acc), precision (Prec), recall (Rec) and F-measure (F1). As we can see, the results are mixed. First, we notice that the Local classifier shows substantial improvement over the baseline classifier. This shows that the lexical and dialog features we use are informative of opinion polarity in multi-party meetings.

Next, notice that the ICA-LinkNeigh classifier performs substantially better than the Local classifier for all metrics and all classes. The accuracy improves by 10 percentage points, while the F-measure improves by about 15 percentage points for the minority (positive and negative) classes. This result confirms that our discourse-level opinion graphs are useful and discourse-level information is non-redundant with lexical and dialog-act information.

The results for ICA-LinkOnly follow the same trend as for ICA-LinkNeigh, with a 3 to 5 percentage point improvement. These results show that even when the neighbors' classes are not known a priori, joint inference using discourse-level relations helps reduce errors from local classification.

However, the performance of the ICA-noInfo system, which is given absolutely no starting information, is comparable to the Local classifier for the overall accuracy and F-measure metrics for the neutral class. There is slight improvement in precision for both the positive and negative classes, but there is a drop in their recall. The reason this classifier does no better than the Local classifier is because the link classifiers TLC and FLC predict "none" predominantly due to the heavy class skew.

The performance of the link classifiers are reported in Table 4, specifically the accuracy (Acc) and macro averages over all classes for precision (P-M), recall (R-M) and F-measure (F1-M). Due to the heavy skew in the data, accuracy of all classifiers is high; however, the macro F-measure, which depends on the F1 of the minority classes, is poor for the ICA-noInfo. Note, however, that when we provide some (Partial) or full (LinkNeigh) neighborhood information for the Link classifiers, the performance of these classifiers improve considerably. This overall observed trend is similar to that observed with the polarity classifiers.

6 Related Work

Previous work on polarity disambiguation has used contextual clues and reversal words (Wilson et al., 2005; Kennedy and Inkpen, 2006; Kanayama and Nasukawa, 2006; Devitt and Ahmad, 2007; Sadamitsu et al., 2008). However, these do not capture discourse-level relations.

Polanyi and Zaenen (2006) observe that a central topic may be divided into subtopics in order to perform evaluations. Similar to Somasundaran et al. (2008), Asher et al. (2008) advocate a discourse-level analysis in order to get a deeper understanding of contextual polarity and the strength of opinions. However, these works do not provide an implementation for their insights. In this work we demonstrate a concrete way that discourse-level interpretation can improve recognition of individual opinions and their polarities.

Graph-based approaches for joint inference in sentiment analysis have been explored previously by many researchers. The biggest difference between this work and theirs is in what the links represent linguistically. Some of these are not related to discourse at all (e.g., lexical similarities (Takamura et al., 2007), morphosyntactic similarities (Popescu and Etzioni, 2005) and word based measures like TF-IDF (Goldberg and Zhu, 2006)). Some of these work on sentence cohesion (Pang and Lee, 2004) or agreement/disagreement between speakers (Thomas et al., 2006; Bansal et al., 2008). Our model is not based on sentence cohesion or structural adjacency. The relations due to the opinion frames are based on relationships between targets and discourse-level functions of opinions being mutually reinforcing or non-reinforcing. Adjacent instances need not be related via opinion frames, while long distant relations can be present if opinion targets are same or alternatives. Also, previous efforts in graph-based joint inference in opinion analysis has been text-based, while our work is over multi-party conversations.

McDonald et al. (2007) propose a joint model for sentiment classification based on relations defined by granularity (sentence and document). Snyder and Barzilay (2007) combine an agreement model based on contrastive RST relations with a local aspect (topic) model. Their aspects would be related as same and their high contrast relations would correspond to (a subset of) the non-reinforcing frames.

In the field of product review mining, sentiments and features (aspects or targets) have been mined (for example, Yi et al. (2003), Popescu and Etzioni (2005), and Hu and Liu (2006)). More recently there has been work on creating joint models of topic and sentiments (Mei et al., 2007; Titov and McDonald, 2008) to improve topic-sentiment summaries. We do not model topics; instead we directly model the relations between targets. The focus of our work is to jointly model opinion polarities via target relations. The task of finding coreferent opinion topics by (Stoyanov and Cardie, 2008) is similar to our target link classification task, and we use somewhat similar features. Even though their genre is different, we plan to experiment with their full feature set for improving our TLC system.

Turning to collective classification, there have been various collective classification frameworks proposed (for example, Neville and Jensen (2000), Lu and Getoor (2003), Taskar et al. (2004), Richardson and Domingos (2006)). In this paper, we use an approach proposed by (Bilgic et al., 2007) which iteratively predicts class and link existence using local classifiers. Other joint models used in sentiment classification include the spin model (Takamura et al., 2007), relaxation labeling (Popescu and Etzioni, 2005), and label propagation (Goldberg and Zhu, 2006).

7 Conclusion

This work uses an opinion graph framework, DLOG, to create an interdependent classification of polarity and discourse relations. We employed this graph to augment lexicon-based methods to improve polarity classification. We found that polarity classification in multi-party conversations benefits from opinion lexicons, unigram and dialog-act information. We found that the DLOGs are valuable for further improving polarity classification, even with partial neighborhood information. Our experiments showed three to five percentage points improvement in F-measure with link information, and 15 percentage point improvement with full neighborhood information. These results show that lexical and discourse information are non-redundant for polarity classification, and our DLOG, that employs both, improves performance.

We discovered that link classification is a difficult problem. Here again, we found that by using the DLOG framework, and using even partial neighborhood information, improvements can be achieved.

References

N. Asher, F. Benamara, and Y. Mathieu. 2008. Distilling opinion in discourse: A preliminary study.

COLING-2008.

M. Bansal, C. Cardie, and L. Lee. 2008. The power of negative thinking: Exploiting label disagreement in the min-cut classification framework. In *COLING-2008*.

M. Bilgic, G. M. Namata, and L. Getoor. 2007. Combining collective classification and link prediction. In *Workshop on Mining Graphs and Complex Structures at the IEEE International Conference on Data Mining*.

J. Carletta, S. Ashby, S. Bourban, M. Flynn, M. Guillemot, T. Hain, J. Kadlec, V. Karaiskos, W. Kraaij, M. Kronenthal, G. Lathoud, M. Lincoln, A. Lisowska, I. McCowan, W. Post, D. Reidsma, and P. Wellner. 2005. The AMI Meetings Corpus. In *Proceedings of the Measuring Behavior Symposium on "Annotating and measuring Meeting Behavior"*.

A. Devitt and K. Ahmad. 2007. Sentiment polarity identification in financial news: A cohesion-based approach. In *ACL 2007*.

A. B. Goldberg and X. Zhu. 2006. Seeing stars when there aren't many stars: Graph-based semi-supervised learning for sentiment categorization. In *HLT-NAACL 2006 Workshop on Textgraphs: Graph-based Algorithms for Natural Language Processing*.

M. Hu and B. Liu. 2006. Opinion extraction and summarization on the Web. In *21st National Conference on Artificial Intelligence (AAAI-2006)*.

H. Kanayama and T. Nasukawa. 2006. Fully automatic lexicon expansion for domain-oriented sentiment analysis. In *EMNLP-2006*, pages 355–363, Sydney, Australia.

A. Kennedy and D. Inkpen. 2006. Sentiment classification of movie reviews using contextual valence shifters. *Computational Intelligence*, 22(2):110–125.

Q. Lu and L. Getoor. 2003. Link-based classification. In *Proceedings of the International Conference on Machine Learning (ICML)*.

R. McDonald, K. Hannan, T. Neylon, M. Wells, and J. Reynar. 2007. Structured models for fine-to-coarse sentiment analysis. In *ACL 2007*.

Q. Mei, X. Ling, M. Wondra, H. Su, and C Zhai. 2007. Topic sentiment mixture: modeling facets and opinions in weblogs. In *WWW '07*. ACM.

J. Neville and D. Jensen. 2000. Iterative classification in relational data. In *In Proc. AAAI-2000 Workshop on Learning Statistical Models from Relational Data*, pages 13–20. AAAI Press.

B. Pang and L. Lee. 2004. A sentimental education: Sentiment analysis using subjectivity summarization based on minimum cuts. In *ACl 2004*.

L. Polanyi and A. Zaenen, 2006. *Contextual Valence Shifters*. Computing Attitude and Affect in Text: Theory and Applications.

A.-M. Popescu and O. Etzioni. 2005. Extracting product features and opinions from reviews. In *HLT-EMNLP 2005*.

R. Prasad, A. Lee, N. Dinesh, E. Miltsakaki, G. Campion, A. Joshi, and B. Webber. 2008. Penn discourse treebank version 2.0. Linguistic Data Consortium.

M. Richardson and P. Domingos. 2006. Markov logic networks. *Mach. Learn.*, 62(1-2):107–136.

K. Sadamitsu, S. Sekine, and M. Yamamoto. 2008. Sentiment analysis based on probabilistic models using inter-sentence information. In *LREC'08*.

B. Snyder and R. Barzilay. 2007. Multiple aspect ranking using the good grief algorithm. In *HLT 2007: NAACL*.

S. Somasundaran, J. Ruppenhofer, and J. Wiebe. 2007. Detecting arguing and sentiment in meetings. In *SIGdial Workshop on Discourse and Dialogue 2007*.

S. Somasundaran, J. Wiebe, and J. Ruppenhofer. 2008. Discourse level opinion interpretation. In *Coling 2008*.

V. Stoyanov and C. Cardie. 2008. Topic identification for fine-grained opinion analysis. In *Coling 2008*.

H. Takamura, T. Inui, and M. Okumura. 2007. Extracting semantic orientations of phrases from dictionary. In *HLT-NAACL 2007*.

B. Taskar, M. Wong, P. Abbeel, and D. Koller. 2004. Link prediction in relational data. In *Neural Information Processing Systems*.

M. Thomas, B. Pang, and L. Lee. 2006. Get out the vote: Determining support or opposition from congressional floor-debate transcripts. In *EMNLP 2006*.

I. Titov and R. McDonald. 2008. A joint model of text and aspect ratings for sentiment summarization. In *ACL 2008*.

T. Wilson, J. Wiebe, and P. Hoffmann. 2005. Recognizing contextual polarity in phrase-level sentiment analysis. In *HLT-EMNLP 2005*.

I. H. Witten and E. Frank. 2002. Data mining: practical machine learning tools and techniques with java implementations. *SIGMOD Rec.*, 31(1):76–77.

J. Yi, T. Nasukawa, R. Bunescu, and W. Niblack. 2003. Sentiment analyzer: Extracting sentiments about a given topic using natural language processing techniques. In *ICDM-2003*.

A Cohesion Graph Based Approach for Unsupervised Recognition of Literal and Non-literal Use of Multiword Expressions

Linlin Li and **Caroline Sporleder**
Saarland University
Postfach 15 11 50
66041 Saarbrücken
Germany
{linlin,csporled}@coli.uni-saarland.de

Abstract

We present a graph-based model for representing the lexical cohesion of a discourse. In the graph structure, vertices correspond to the content words of a text and edges connecting pairs of words encode how closely the words are related semantically. We show that such a structure can be used to distinguish literal and non-literal usages of multi-word expressions.

1 Introduction

Multiword expressions (MWEs) are defined as "idiosyncratic interpretations that cross word boundaries or spaces" (Sag et al., 2001). Such expressions are pervasive in natural language; they are estimated to be equivalent in number to simplex words in mental lexicon (Jackendoff, 1997). MWEs exhibit a number of lexical, syntactic, semantic, pragmatic and statistical idiosyncrasies: syntactic peculiarities (e.g., *by and large*, *ad hoc*), semantic non-compositionality (e.g., as in *kick the bucket* (die) and *red tape* (bureaucracy)), pragmatic idiosyncrasies (the expression is sometimes associated with a fixed pragmatic point, e.g., *good morning, good night*), variation in syntactic flexibility (e.g., *I handed in my thesis* = *I handed my thesis in* vs. *Kim kicked the bucket* ≠ **the bucket was kicked by Kim*), variation in productivity (there are various levels of productivity for different MWEs, e.g., *kick/*beat/*hit the bucket, call/ring/phone/*telephone up*).

These idiosyncrasies pose challenges for NLP systems, which have to recognize that an expression is an MWE to deal with it properly. Recognizing MWEs has been shown to be useful for a number of applications such as information retrieval (Lewis and Croft, 1990; Rila Mandala and Tanaka, 2000; Wacholder and Song, 2003) and POS tagging (Piao et al., 2003). It has also been shown that MWEs account for 8% of parsing errors with precision grammars (Baldwin et al., 2004). Furthermore, MWE detection is used in information extraction (Lin, 1998b) and an integral component of symbolic MT systems (Gerber and Yang, 1997; Bond and Shirai, 1997).

However, the special properties of MWEs can also be exploited to recognize MWEs automatically. There have been many studies on MWEs: identification (determining whether multiple simplex words form a MWE in a given token context, e.g. *put the sweater on* vs. *put the sweater on the table*), extraction (recognizing MWEs as word units at the type level), detecting or measuring compositionality of MWEs, semantic interpretation (interpreting the semantic association among components in MWEs).

To extract MWEs, various methods have been proposed that exploit the syntactic and lexical fixedness exhibited by MWEs, or apply various statistical measures across all co-occurrence vectors between the whole expression and its component parts (see Section 2). These methods can be used to automatically identify potentially idiomatic expressions at a type level, but they do not say anything about the idiomaticity of an expression in a particular context. While some idioms (e.g., *ad hoc*) are always used idiomatically, there are numerous others that can be used both idiomatically (see Example 1) and non-idiomatically (see Example 2).

(1) When the members of De la Guarda aren't hanging around, they're yelling and bouncing off the wall.

(2) Blinded by the sun, Erstad leaped at the wall, but the ball bounced off the wall well below his glove.

Our work aims to distinguish the literal and non-literal usages of idiomatic expressions in a

Proceedings of the 2009 Workshop on Graph-based Methods for Natural Language Processing, ACL-IJCNLP 2009, pages 75–83, Suntec, Singapore, 7 August 2009.

discourse context (so-called *token based classification*). It is therefore different from *type-based approaches* which aim to detect the general idiomaticity of an expression rather than its actual usage in a particular context.

We utilize the cohesive structure of a discourse (Halliday and Hasan, 1976) to distinguish literal or non-literal usage of MWEs. The basic idea is that the component words of an MWE contribute to the cohesion of the discourse in the literal case, while in the non-literal case they do not. For instance, in the literal use of *break the ice* in Example 3, the content word *ice* contributes to the overall semantic connectivity of the whole sentence by the fact that *ice* is semantically related to *water.* In contrast, in the non-literal example in 4, the word *ice* does not contribute to the overall cohesion as it is poorly connected to all the other (content) words in this specific context (*play, party, games*).

(3) The water would break the ice into floes with its accumulated energy.

(4) We played a couple of party games to break the ice.

Our approach bears similarities to Hirst and St-Onge's (1998) method for detecting malapropisms based on their non-participation in cohesive chains. However, computing such chains requires a pre-defined similarity threshold which governs whether a word is placed in a particular chain. Setting this threshold typically requires a manually labeled development set, which makes this method weakly supervised. We propose an alternative, parameter-free method in which we model the cohesive structure of a discourse as a graph structure (called *cohesion graph*), where the vertices of the graph correspond to the content words of the text and the edges encode the semantic relatedness between pairs of words. To distinguish between literal and non-literal use of MWEs, we look at how the average relatedness of the graph changes when the component words of the MWE are excluded or included in the graph (see Section 3).[1]

We first introduced the cohesion graph method in Sporleder and Li (2009). In the present paper, we provide a formalization of the graph and experiment with different vertex and edge weighting schemes. We also report on experiments with varying the size of the input context and also with pruning the graph structure automatically.

2 Related Work

Type-based MWE classification aims to extract multiword expression types in text from observations of the token distribution. It aims to pick up on word combinations which occur with comparatively high frequencies when compared to the frequencies of the individual words (Evert and Krenn, 2001; Smadja, 19993). The lexical and syntactic fixedness property can also be utilized to automatically extract MWEs (Baldwin and Villavicencio, 2002).

The study of semantic compositionality of MWEs focuses on the degree to which the semantics of the parts of an MWE contribute towards the meaning of the whole. The aim is a binary classification of the MWEs as idiosyncratically decomposable (*e.g. spill the beans*) or non-decomposable (*e.g. kick the bucket*). Several approaches have been proposed. Lin (1999) uses the substitution test[2] and mutual information (MI) to determine the compositionality of the phrase. An obvious change of the MI value of the phrase in the substitution test is taken as the evidence of the MWEs being non-compositional. Bannard et al. (2003) assume that compositional MWEs occur in similar lexical context as their component parts. The co-occurrence vector representations of verb particle construction (VPC) and the component words are utilized to determine the compositionality of the MWE.

There have also been a few token-based classification approaches, aimed at classifying individual instances of a potential idiom as literal or non-literal. Katz and Giesbrecht (2006) make use of latent semantic analysis (LSA) to explore the local linguistic context that can serve to identify multiword expressions that have non-compositional meaning. They measure the cosine vector similarity between the vectors associated with an MWE as a whole and the vectors associated with its constituent parts and interpret it as the degree to which the MWE is compositional. They report an av-

[1] By modeling lexical cohesion as a graph structure, we follow earlier approaches in information retrieval, notably by Salton and colleagues (Salton et al., 1994). The difference is that these works aim at representing similarity between larger text segments (e.g., paragraphs) in a so-called 'text' or 'paragraph relation map', whose vertices correspond to a text segment and whose edges represent the similarity between the segments (modeled as weighted term overlap).

[2] The substitution test aims to replace part of the idiom's component words with semantically similar words, and test how the co-occurrence frequency changes.

erage accuracy of 72%, but the data set used in their evaluation is small. Birke and Sarkar (2006) use literal and non-literal seed sets acquired without human supervision to perform bootstrapping learning. The new instances of potential idioms are always labeled according to the closest set. While their approach is unsupervised clustering, they do rely on some resources such as databases of idioms. Cook et al. (2007) and Fazly et al. (2009) rely crucially on the concept of *canonical form* (CForm). It is assumed that for each idiom there is a fixed form (or a small set of those) corresponding to the syntactic pattern(s) in which the idiom normally occurs. The canonical form allows for inflection variation of the heard verb but not for other variations (such as nominal inflection, choice of determiner etc.). It has been observed that if an expression is used idiomatically it typically occurs in its canonical form (Riehemann, 2001). Fazly and her colleagues exploit this behavior and propose an unsupervised method for token-based idiom classification in which an expression is classified as idiomatic if it occurs in canonical form and literal otherwise. The canonical forms are determined automatically using a statistical, frequency-based measure. They also developed statistical measures to measure the lexical and syntactic fixedness of a given expression, which is used to automatically recognize expression types, as well as their token identification in context. They report an average accuracy of 72% for their canonical form (CForm) classifier.

3 Cohesion Graph

In this section, we first give a formal definition of the cohesion graph that is used for modeling discourse connectivity, then we define the discourse connectivity. Finally, we introduced our graph-based classifier for distinguishing literal and non-literal use of MWEs.

3.1 Cohesion Graph Structure

A cohesion graph (CG) is an undirected complete graph [3] $G = (V, E)$, where

V: is a set of nodes $\{v_1, v_2, ..., v_n\}$, where each node $v_i = (t_i, id_i)$ represents a unique token in the discourse. t_i is the string form of the token, and id_i denotes the position of the token in the context.

[3] In the mathematical field of graph theory, a complete graph is a simple graph in which every pair of distinct vertices is connected by an edge. The complete graph on n vertices has $n(n-1)/2$ edges.

E: is a set of edges $\{e_{12}, e_{13}, ..., e_{(n)(n-1)}\}$, such that each edge e_{ij} connects a pair of nodes (v_i, v_j). n is the total number of tokens in the discourse that the graph models. The value of e_{ij} represents the semantic relatedness of the two tokens t_i, t_j that e_{ij} connects:

$$e_{ij} = h(t_i, t_j) \quad (5)$$

where h is a semantic relatedness assignment function. The explicit form of h will be discussed in the next section.

e_i is the average semantic relatedness of the token t_i in the discourse. It represents the average relatedness score of a certain token to its surrounding context:

$$e_i = \sum_{j=1, j\neq i}^{n} \lambda_{ij} \times e_{ij} \quad (6)$$

where λ_{ij} is the weight of the edge e_{ij}, with the constraint, $\sum_{j=1, j\neq i}^{n} \lambda_{ij} = 1$.

The edge weight function λ_{ij} allows us to weight the relatedness between two tokens, for example based on their distance in the text. The motivation for this is that the closer two tokens occur together, the more likely it is that their relatedness is not accidental. For instance, the idiom *break the ice* in Example 7 could be misclassified as literal due to there being a high relatedness score between *ice* and *snow*. The weight function is introduced so that relatedness with tokens that are closer to MWE component words counts more.

(7) The train was canceled because of the wind and **snow**. All the people in the small village train station felt upset. Suddenly, one guy broke the **ice** and proposed to play a game.

The weight function λ_{ij} is defined in terms of the inverse of the distance δ between the two token positions id_i and id_j:

$$\lambda_{ij} = \frac{\delta(id_i, id_j)}{\sum_j \delta(id_i, id_j)} \quad (8)$$

As the semantic relatedness among the MWE component words does not contain any information of how these component words are semantically involved in the context, we do not count the edges *between* the MWE component words (as e_{45} in Figure 1). We set all the weights for connecting MWE component words to be 0, $\delta(id_i^{mwe'}, id_j^{mwe}) = 0$.

$c(G)$: is defined as the discourse connectivity of the cohesion graph. It represents the semantic relatedness score of the discourse.

$$c(G) = \sum_{i=1}^{n} (\beta_i \times e_i) \qquad (9)$$

where n is the total number of tokens in the discourse, β_i is the weight of the average semantic relatedness of the token t_i with the constraint $\sum_i \beta_i = 1$. It represents the importance of the relatedness contribution of a specific token t_i in the discourse. For instance, the word *Monday* in Example 12 should be assigned less weight than the word *bilateral* as it is not part of the central theme(s) of the discourse. This is often the case for time expressions. β_i is defined as:

$$\beta_i = \frac{salience(t_i)}{\sum_j salience(t_j)} \qquad (10)$$

To model the salience of a token for the semantic context of the text we use a $tf.idf$-based weighting scheme. Since we represent word tokens rather than word types in the cohesion graph, we do not need to model the term frequency tf separately, instead we set $salience$ to the log value of the inverse document frequency idf:

$$salience(t_i) = log \frac{|D|}{|\{d : t_i \in d\}|} \qquad (11)$$

where D is the total number of documents in our data set and $|\{d : t_i \in d\}|$ is the number of documents in which t_i occurs. Terms which are related to the sub-topics of a document will typically only occur in a few texts in the collection, hence their *idf* (and often also their tf) is high and they will thus be given more weight in the graph. Terms which are not related to the central themes of a text, such as temporal expressions, will be given a lower weight. A complication arises for component words of the MWE: these occur in all of our examples and thus will receive a very low idf. This is an artifact of the data and not what we want as it means that the average connectivity of the graph virtually always increases if the MWE is excluded, causing the classifier to over-predict 'non-literal'. To counteract this effect, we set $|\{d : t_i \in d\}|$ of these words uniformly to 1.

(12) "Gujral will meet Sharif on **Monday** and discuss **bilateral** relations," the Press Trust of India added. The minister said Sharif and Gujral would be able to "break the ice" over Kashmir.

3.2 Graph-based Classifier

The cohesion graph based classifier compares the cohesion graph connectivity of the discourse including the MWE component words with the connectivity of the discourse excluding the MWE component words to check how well the MWE component words are semantically connected to the context. If the cohesion graph connectivity increases by including MWE component words, the MWE is thought to be semantically well related to its discourse. It is classified as literal (otherwise as non-literal). In other words, the cohesion graph based algorithm detects the strength of relatedness between the MWE component words and their context by calculating the discourse connectivity gain, and classifies instances as literal or non-literal based on this gain. This process is described as Formula 13 (if $\Delta c > 0$, it is literal; otherwise it is non-literal):

$$\Delta c = c(G) - c(G') \qquad (13)$$

where, $c(G)$ is the discourse connectivity of the context with MWE component words (as shown with the complete graph in Figure 1); $c(G')$ is the discourse connectivity of the context without MWE component words (as shown with the sub-graph $\{v_1, v_2, v_3\}$ in Figure 1).

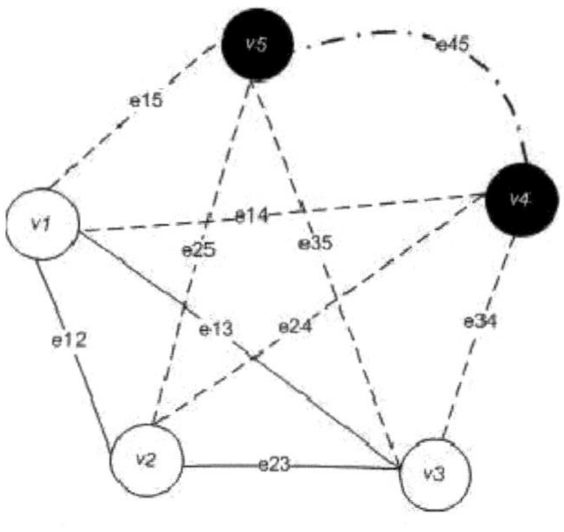

Figure 1: Cohesion Graph for identifying literal or non-literal usage of MWEs

4 Modeling Semantic Relatedness

In Section 3.1, we did not define how we model the semantic relatedness between two tokens ($h(t_i, t_j)$). Modeling semantic relatedness between two terms is currently an area of active research. There are two main approaches. Methods based on manually built lexical knowledge bases, such as WordNet, compute the shortest path between two concepts in the knowledge base and/or look at word overlap in the glosses (see Budanitsky and Hirst (2006) for an overview). Distributional approaches, on the other hand, rely on text corpora, and model relatedness by comparing the contexts in which two words occur, assuming that related words occur in similar context (e.g., Hindle (1990), Lin (1998a), Mohammad and Hirst (2006)). More recently, there has also been research on using Wikipedia and related resources for modeling semantic relatedness (Ponzetto and Strube, 2007; Zesch et al., 2008).

WordNet-based approaches are unsuitable for our purposes as they only model so-called "classical relations" like hypernymy, antonymy etc. For our task, we need to model a wide range of relations, e.g., between *ice* and *water*. Hence we opted for a distributional approach. We experimented with two different approaches, one (DV) based on syntactic co-occurrences in a large text corpus and the other (NGD) based on search engine page counts.

Dependency Vectors (DV) is a distributional approach which does not look simply at word co-occurrences in a fixed-size window but takes into account syntactic (dependency) relations between words (Padó and Lapata, 2007). Each target word is represented by a co-occurrence vector where dimension represents a chosen term and the vector contains the co-occurrence information between that word and the chosen terms in a corpus (we used the BNC in our experiments). A variety of distance measures can be used to compute the similarity of two vectors; here we use the cosine similarity which is defined as:

$$sim_{cos}(\overrightarrow{x}, \overrightarrow{y}) = \frac{\sum_{i=1}^{n} x_i y_i}{\sqrt{\sum_{i=1}^{n} x_i^2}\sqrt{\sum_{i=1}^{n} y_i^2}} \quad (14)$$

Normalized Google Distance (NGD) uses the page counts returned by a search engine as proxies for word co-occurrence and thereby quantifies the strength of a relationship between two words (see Cilibrasi and Vitanyi (2007)). The basic idea is that the more often two terms occur together relative to their overall occurrence the more closely they are related. NGD is defined as follows:

$$NGD(x, y) = \frac{max\{log\, f(x), log\, f(y)\} - log\, f(x, y)}{log\, M - min\{log\, f(x), log\, f(y)\}} \quad (15)$$

where x and y are the two words whose association strength is computed, $f(x)$ is the page count returned by the search engine for the term x (and likewise for $f(y)$ and y), $f(x, y)$ is the page count returned when querying for "x AND y" (i.e., the number of pages that contain both, x and y), and M is the number of web pages indexed by the search engine. When querying for a term we query for a disjunction of all its inflected forms.[4] As it is difficult to obtain a specific and reliable number for the number of pages indexed by a search engine, we approximated it by setting it to the number of hits obtained for the word *the*. The assumption is that the word *the* occurs in all English language web pages (Lapata and Keller, 2005).

Using web counts rather than bi-gram counts from a corpus as the basis for computing semantic relatedness has the advantage that the web is a significantly larger database than any compiled corpus, which makes it much more likely that we can find information about the concepts we are looking for (thus alleviating data sparseness). However, search engine counts are notoriously unreliable (Kilgariff, 2007; Matsuo et al., 2007) and while previous studies have shown that web counts can be used as reliable proxies for corpus-based counts for some applications (Zhu and Rosenfeld, 2001; Lapata and Keller, 2005) it is not clear that this also applies when modeling semantic relatedness. We thus carried out a number of experiments testing the reliability of page counts (Section 4.1) and comparing the NGD measure to a standard distributional approach (Section 4.2).

[4]The inflected forms were generated by applying the *morph* tools developed at the University of Sussex (Minnen et al., 2001) which are available at: `http://www.informatics.susx.ac.uk/research/groups/nlp/carroll/morph.html`

4.1 Search Engine Stability

We first carried out some experiments to test the stability of the page counts returned by two of the most widely-used search engines, Google and Yahoo. For both search engines, we found a number of problems.[5]

Total number of pages indexed The total number of the web pages indexed by a search engine varies across time and the numbers provided are somewhat unreliable. This is a potential problem for NGD because we need to fix the value of M in Formula 15. As an approximative solution, we set it to the number of hits obtained for the word *the*, assuming that it will occur in all English language pages (Lapata and Keller, 2005).

Page count variation The number of page hits for a given term also varies across time (see example (4.1) for two queries for *Jim* at different times $t1$ and $t2$). However, we found that the variance in the number of pages tends to be relatively stable over *short* time spans, hence we can address this problem by carrying out all queries in one quick session without much delay. However, this means we cannot store page counts in a database and reuse them at a later stage; for each new example which we want to classify at a later stage, we have to re-compute all relevant counts.

(16) Hits(Jim, t1) = 763,000,000
Hits(Jim, t2) = 757,000,000

Problems with conjunction and disjunction The search engines' AND and OR operators are problematic and can return counter-intuitive results (see Table 1). This is a potential problem for us because we have to query for conjunctions of terms and disjunctions of inflected forms. For the time being we ignored this problem as it is not straightforward to solve.

	OPT = AND	*OPT* = OR
car	3,590,000,000	
car *OPT* car	4,670,000,000	3,550,000,000
car *OPT* car *OPT* car	3,490,000,000	3,530,000,000

Table 1: Operator test for Yahoo

Problems with high-frequency terms We also found that both the Google and Yahoo API seem to have problems with high frequency words, with the Google SOAP API throwing an exception and the Yahoo API returning the same 10-digit number for every high frequency word. This might be a data overflow problem. We addressed this problem by excluding high frequency words.

When comparing Yahoo and Google we found that Yahoo's page counts tend to be more consistent than Google's. We therefore opted for Yahoo in our further experiments.

4.2 NGD vs. Co-occurrence Vectors

In principle, we believe that the web-based approach for computing relatedness is more suitable for our task since it gives us access to more data and allows us to also model relations based on (up-to-date) world knowledge. However, the question arises whether the stability problems observed in the previous section have a negative effect on the performance of the NGD measure. To test this, we conducted a small study in which we compared the relatedness scores obtained by NGD and the semantic vector space model to the human ratings compiled by Finkelstein et al. (2002).[6]

We used Spearman's correlation test (Spearman, 1904) to compare the ranked human ratings to the ranked ratings obtained by NGD and the vector space method. The (human) inter-annotator agreement varies a lot for different pairs of annotators (between 0.41 and 0.82 by Spearman's correlation test), suggesting that deciding on the semantic relatedness between arbitrary pairs of words is not an easy task even for humans. In general, the NGD-human agreement is comparable to the human-human agreement. The agreement between the NGD and average human agreement is higher than some human-human agreements. Furthermore, we found that NGD actually outperforms the dependency vector method on this data set.[7] Hence, we decided to use NGD in the following experiments.

5 Experiments

We tested our graph-based classifiers on a manually annotated data set, which we describe in Sec-

[5] See also the discussions in Jean Véronis blog: `http://aixtal.blogspot.com` and the comments in Kilgariff (2007).

[6] The data sets are available at: `http://www.cs.technion.ac.il/~gabr/resources/data/wordsim353/`

[7] There may be several reasons for this. Apart from the fact that NGD has access to a larger data set, it may also be that syntactic co-occurrence information is not ideal for modeling this type of relatedness; co-occurrence information in a fixed window might be more useful. Furthermore, we did not spend much time on finding an optimal parameter setting for the dependency vector method.

tion 5.1. We report on our experiments and results in Section 5.2.

5.1 Data

Throughout the experiments we used the data set from Sporleder and Li (2009). The data consist of 17 potentially idiomatic expressions from the English Gigaword corpus, which were extracted with five paragraphs of context and manually annotated as 'literal' or 'non-literal' (see Table 2). The inter-annotator agreement on a doubly annotated sample of the data was 97% and the kappa score 0.7 (Cohen, 1960).

expression	literal	non-lit.	all
back the wrong horse	0	25	25
bite off more than one can chew	2	142	144
bite one's tongue	16	150	166
blow one's own trumpet	0	9	9
bounce off the wall*	39	7	46
break the ice	20	521	541
drop the ball*	688	215	903
get one's feet wet	17	140	157
pass the buck	7	255	262
play with fire	34	532	566
pull the trigger*	11	4	15
rock the boat	8	470	478
set in stone	9	272	281
spill the beans	3	172	175
sweep under the carpet	0	9	9
swim against the tide	1	125	126
tear one's hair out	7	54	61
all	862	3102	3964

Table 2: Idiom statistics (* indicates expressions for which the literal usage is more common than the non-literal one)

5.2 The Influence of Context Size and Weighting Scheme

To gain some insights into the performance of the graph-based classifier, we experimented with different context sizes and weighting schemes. In addition to the basic cohesion graph approach with five paragraphs of context (CGA), we tested a variant which only uses the current paragraph as context (CGA$_{para}$) to determine how sensitive the classifier is to the context size. We also experimented with three weighting schemes. The basic classifier (CGA) uses uniform edge and node weights. CGA$_{ew}$ uses edge weights based on the inverse distance between the tokens. CGA$_{nw}$ uses node weights based on idf. Finally, CGA$_{ew+nw}$ uses both edge and node weights.

We also carried out a pruning experiment in which we removed nodes from the graph that are only weakly connected to the context (called *weak cohesion nodes*). We hypothesize that these do not contribute much to the overall connectivity but may add noise. Pruning can thus be seen as a more gentle version of node weighting, in which we only remove the top n outliers rather than re-weight all nodes. For comparison we also implemented a baseline (BASE), which always assigns the majority class ('non-literal').

Table 3 shows the results for the classifiers discussed above. In addition to accuracy, which is not very informative as the class distribution in our data set is quite skewed, we show the precision, recall, and F-score for the minority class (literal). All classifiers obtain a relatively high accuracy but vary in the precision, recall and F-Score values.

Method	LPrec.	LRec.	$LF_{\beta=1}$	*Acc.*
Base	–	–	–	0.78
CGA	0.50	0.69	0.58	0.79
CGA$_{para}$	0.42	0.67	0.51	0.71
CGA$_{prun}$	0.49	0.72	0.58	0.78
CGA$_{ew}$	0.51	0.63	0.57	0.79
CGA$_{nw}$	0.48	0.68	0.56	0.77
CGA$_{ew+nw}$	0.49	0.61	0.54	0.78

Table 3: Accuracy (Acc.), literal precision (LPrec.), recall (LRec.), and F-Score (LF$_{\beta=1}$) for the classifier

It can be seen that the basic cohesion graph classifier (CGA) outperforms the baseline on accuracy. Moreover, it is reasonably good at identifying literal usages among the majority of non-literal occurrences, as witnessed by an F-score of 58%. To obtain a better idea of the behavior of this classifier, we plotted the distribution of the MWE instances in the classifier's feature space, where the first dimension represents the discourse connectivity of the context with MWE component words ($c(G)$) and the second represents the discourse connectivity of the context without MWE component words ($c(G')$). The graph-based classifier, which calculates the connectivity gain (see Equation 13), is a simple linear classifier in which the line $y = x$ is chosen as the decision boundary. Examples above that line are classified as 'literal', examples below as 'non-literal'. Figure 2 shows the true distribution of literal and non-literal examples in our data set. It can be seen that most non-literal examples are indeed below the line while most literal ones are above it (though a certain number of literal examples can also be found below the line). So, in general we would expect our classifier to have a reasonable performance.

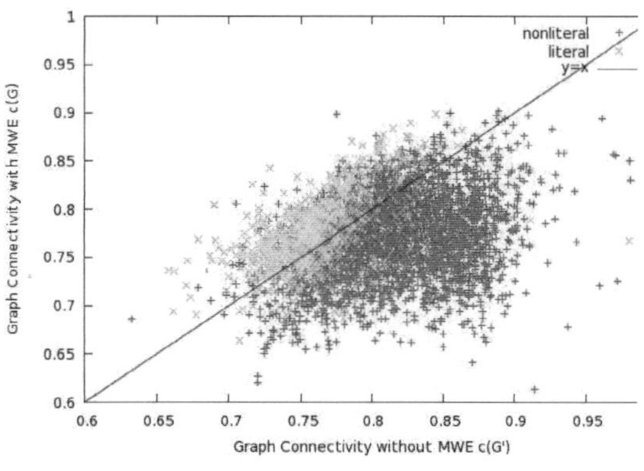

Figure 2: Decision boundaries of the cohesion graph

Returning to the results in Table 3, we find that a smaller context worsens the performance of the classifier (CGA_{para}). Pruning the 3 least connected nodes (CGA_{prun}) does not lead to a significant change in performance. Edge weighting (CGA_{ew}), node weighting (CGA_{nw}) and their combination (CGA_{ew+nw}), on the other hand, seem to have a somewhat negative influence on the literal recall and F-score. It seems that the weighting scheme scales down the influence of MWE component words. As a result, the product of the weight and the relatedness value for the idiom component words are lower than the average, which leads to the negative contribution of the idiom words to the cohesion graph (over predicting non-literal usage). We need to investigate more sophisticated weighting schemes to assign better weights to idiom component words in the future. The negative performance of the weighting scheme may be also due to the fact that we used a relatively small context of five paragraphs.[8] Both the idf and the distance weighting should probably be defined on larger contexts. For example, the distance between two tokens within a paragraph probably has not such a large effect on whether their relatedness score is reliable or accidental. Hence it might be better to model the edge weight as the distance in terms of paragraphs rather than words. The idf scores, too, might be more reliable if more context was used.

[8]Note that we used news texts which typically have very short paragraphs.

6 Conclusion

In this paper, we described an approach for token-based idiom classification. Our approach is based on the observation that literally used expressions typically exhibit strong cohesive ties with the surrounding discourse, while idiomatic expressions do not. Hence, idiomatic use of MWEs can be detected by the absence of such ties.

We propose a graph-based method which exploits this behavior to classify MWEs as literal or non-literal. The method compares how the MWE component words contribute the overall semantic connectivity of the graph. We provided a formalization of the graph and experimented with varying the context size and weighting scheme for nodes and edges. We found that the method generally works better for larger contexts; the weighting schemes proved somewhat unsuccessful, at least for our current context size. In the future, we plan to experiment with larger context sizes and more sophisticated weighting schemes.

Acknowledgments

This work was funded by the Cluster of Excellence "Multimodal Computing and Interaction".

References

T. Baldwin, A. Villavicencio. 2002. Extracting the unextractable: a case study on verb-particles. In *Proc. of CoNLL-02*.

T. Baldwin, E. M. Bender, D. Flickinger, A. Kim, S. Oepen. 2004. Road-testing the english resource grammar over the british national corpus. In *Proc. LREC-04*, 2047–2050.

C. Bannard, T. Baldwin, A. Lascarides. 2003. A statistical approach to the semantics of verb-particles. In *Proc. ACL 2003 Workshop on Multiword Expressions*.

J. Birke, A. Sarkar. 2006. A clustering approach for the nearly unsupervised recognition of nonliteral language. In *Proceedings of EACL-06*.

F. Bond, S. Shirai. 1997. Practical and efficient organization of a large valency dictionary. In *Workshop on Multilingual Information Processing Natural Language Processing Pacific Rim Symposium*.

A. Budanitsky, G. Hirst. 2006. Evaluating WordNet-based measures of semantic distance. *Computational Linguistics*, 32(1):13–47.

R. L. Cilibrasi, P. M. Vitanyi. 2007. The Google similarity distance. *IEEE Trans. Knowledge and Data Engineering*, 19(3):370–383.

J. Cohen. 1960. A coefficient of agreement for nominal scales. *Educational and Psychological Measurements*, 20:37–46.

P. Cook, A. Fazly, S. Stevenson. 2007. Pulling their weight: Exploiting syntactic forms for the automatic identification of idiomatic expressions in context. In *Proceedings of the ACL-07 Workshop on A Broader Perspective on Multiword Expressions*.

S. Evert, B. Krenn. 2001. Methods for the qualitative evaluation of lexical association measures. In *Proc. ACL-01*.

A. Fazly, P. Cook, S. Stevenson. 2009. Unsupervised type and token identification of idiomatic expressions. *Computational Linguistics*, 35(1):61–103.

L. Finkelstein, E. Gabrilovich, Y. Matias, E. Rivlin, Z. Solan, G. Wolfman, E. Ruppin. 2002. Placing search in context: The concept revisited. *ACM Transactions on Information Systems*, 20(1):116–131.

L. Gerber, J. Yang. 1997. Systran mt dictionary development. In *Proc. Fifth Machine Translation Summit*.

M. Halliday, R. Hasan. 1976. *Cohesion in English*. Longman House, New York.

D. Hindle. 1990. Noun classification from predicate-argument structures. In *Proceedings of ACL-90*, 268–275.

G. Hirst, D. St-Onge. 1998. Lexical chains as representations of context for the detection and correction of malapropisms. In C. Fellbaum, ed., *WordNet: An electronic lexical database*, 305–332. The MIT Press.

R. Jackendoff. 1997. *The Architecture of the Language Faculty*. MIT Press.

G. Katz, E. Giesbrecht. 2006. Automatic identification of non-compositional multi-word expressions using latent semantic analysis. In *Proceedings of the ACL/COLING-06 Workshop on Multiword Expressions: Identifying and Exploiting Underlying Properties*.

A. Kilgariff. 2007. Googleology is bad science. *Computational Linguistics*, 33(1):147–151.

M. Lapata, F. Keller. 2005. Web-based models for natural language processing. *ACM Transactions on Speech and Language Processing*, 2:1–31.

D. D. Lewis, W. B. Croft. 1990. Term clustering of syntactic phrase. In *Proceedings of SIGIR-90, 13th ACM International Conference on Research and Development in Information Retrieval*.

D. Lin. 1998a. Automatic retrieval and clustering of similar words. In *Proceedings of ACL-98*.

D. Lin. 1998b. Using collocation statistics in information extraction. In *Proc. MUC-7*.

D. Lin. 1999. Automatic identification of non-compositional phrases. In *Proceedings of ACL-99*, 317–324.

Y. Matsuo, H. Tomobe, T. Nishimura. 2007. Robust estimation of google counts for social network extraction. In *AAAI-07*.

G. Minnen, J. Carroll, D. Pearce. 2001. Applied morphological processing of English. *Natural Language Engineering*, 7(3):207–223.

S. Mohammad, G. Hirst. 2006. Distributional measures of concept-distance: A task-oriented evaluation. In *Proceedings of EMNLP-06*.

S. Padó, M. Lapata. 2007. Dependency-based construction of semantic space models. *Computational Linguistics*, 33(2):161–199.

S. S. L. Piao, P. Rayson, D. Archer, A. Wilson, T. McEnery. 2003. Extracting multiword expressions with a semantic tagger. In *Proc. of the ACL 2003 Workshop on Multiword Expressions*, 49–56.

S. P. Ponzetto, M. Strube. 2007. Knowledge derived from Wikipedia for computing semantic relatedness. *Journal of Artificial Intelligence Research*, 30:181–212.

S. Riehemann. 2001. *A Constructional Approach to Idioms and Word Formation*. Ph.D. thesis, Stanford University.

T. T. Rila Mandala, H. Tanaka. 2000. Query expansion using heterogeneous thesauri. *Inf. Process. Manage.*, 36(3).

I. A. Sag, T. Baldwin, F. Bond, A. Copestake, D. Flickinger. 2001. Multiword expressions: a pain in the neck for NLP. In *Lecture Notes in Computer Science*.

G. Salton, J. Allan, C. Buckley, A. Singhal. 1994. Automatic analysis, theme generation and summarization of machine-readable texts. *Science*, 264(3):1421–1426.

F. Smadja. 19993. Retrieving collocations from text: Xtract. *Computational Linguistics*, 19(1):143–177.

C. Spearman. 1904. The proof and measurement of association between two things. *Amer. J. Psychol*, 72–101.

C. Sporleder, L. Li. 2009. Unsupervised recognition of literal and non-literal use of idiomatic expressions. In *Proceedings of EACL-09*.

N. Wacholder, P. Song. 2003. Toward a task-based gold standard for evaluation of NP chunks and technical terms. In *Proc HLT-NAACL*.

T. Zesch, C. Müller, I. Gurevych. 2008. Using wiktionary for computing semantic relatedness. In *Proceedings of AAAI-08*, 861–867.

X. Zhu, R. Rosenfeld. 2001. Improving trigram language modeling with the world wide web. In *Proceedings of ICASSP-01*.

Quantitative analysis of treebanks using frequent subtree mining methods

Scott Martens
Centrum voor Computerlinguïstiek, KU Leuven
Blijde-Inkomststraat 13, bus 3315
3000 Leuven Belgium
scott@ccl.kuleuven.be

Abstract

The first task of statistical computational linguistics, or any other type of data-driven processing of language, is the extraction of counts and distributions of phenomena. This is much more difficult for the type of complex structured data found in treebanks and in corpora with sophisticated annotation than for tokenized texts. Recent developments in data mining, particularly in the extraction of frequent subtrees from treebanks, offer some solutions. We have applied a modified version of the *TreeMiner* algorithm to a small treebank and present some promising results.

1 Introduction

Statistical corpus linguistics and many natural language processing applications rely on extracting the frequencies and distributions of phenomena from natural language data sources. This is relatively simple when language data is treated as bags of tokens or as n-grams, but much more complicated for corpora annotated with complex feature schemes and for treebanks where syntactic dependencies are marked. A great deal of useful information is encoded in these more complex structured corpora, but access to it is very limited using the traditional algorithms and analytical tools of computational linguistics. Many of the most powerful techniques available to natural language processing have been built on the basis of *n-gram* and *bag of words* models, but we already know that these methods are inadequate to fully model the information in texts or we would have little use for treebanks or annotation schemes.

Suffix trees provide some improvement over n-grams and bag-of-words schemes by identifying all frequently occurring sequences regardless of length (Weiner, 1973; McCreight, 1976; Ravichandran and Hovy, 2002). While this has value in identifying some multi-word phenomena, any algorithm that models languages on the basis of frequent contiguous string discovery will have trouble modeling a number of pervasive phenomena in natural language. In particular:

- Long distance dependencies – i.e., dependencies between words that are too far apart to be accessible to n-gram models.
- Flexible word orders – languages usually have contexts where word order can vary.
- Languages with very rich morphologies that *must* be taken into account or where too much important information is lost through lemmatization.
- Correlations between different levels of abstraction in annotation, such as between the lemma of a verb and the semantic or syntactic class of its arguments.
- Extra-syntactic correlations that may involve *any* nearby word, such as semantic priming effects.

In treebanks and other annotated corpora that can be converted into rooted, directed graphs, many of these phenomena are accessible as *frequently recurring subtrees*. For example, consider the Dutch idiom "naar huis gaan", (*to go home*). The components of this phrase can appear in a variety of orders and with words inserted between the constituents:

1. Ik zou naar huis kunnen gaan. (I could go home.)
2. We gaan naar huis. (We're going home.)

In a treebank, these two sentences would share a common subtree that encompasses the phrase "naar huis gaan", as in Figure 1. Note that for this purpose, two subtrees are treated as identical if the

Proceedings of the 2009 Workshop on Graph-based Methods for Natural Language Processing, ACL-IJCNLP 2009, pages 84–92,
Suntec, Singapore, 7 August 2009.

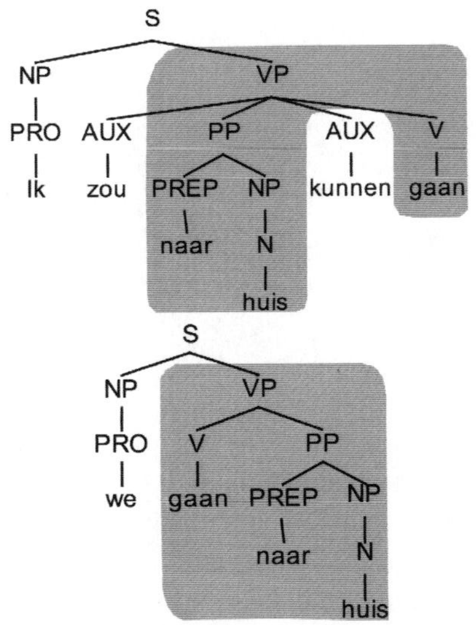

Figure 1: The two Dutch sentences *Ik zou naar huis kunnen gaan* and *We gaan naar huis*, parsed, and with the frequent section highlighted. Note that these two subtrees are identical except for the order of the nodes. (N.B.: This tree does not take the difference between the infinitive and conjugated forms into account.)

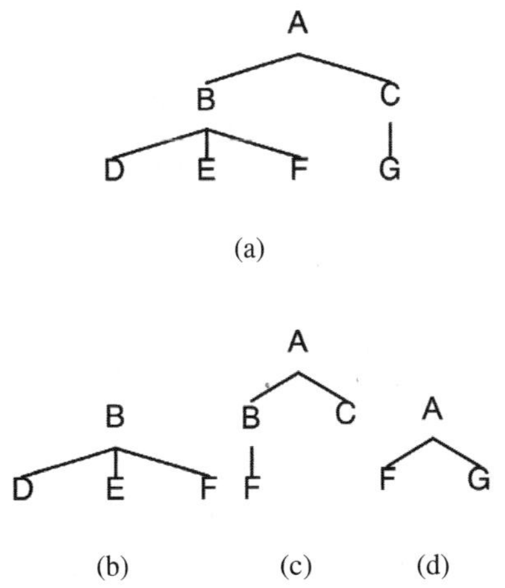

Figure 2: Tree (a) and different types of subtree: (b) a *bottom-up* subtree of (a), (c) an *induced* subtree of (a), and (d) an *embedded* subtree of (a).

only difference between them is the order of the children of some or all the nodes.

Most theories of syntax use trees to represent interlexical dependencies, and generally theories of morphology and phonology use either hierarchical tree structures to represent their formalisms, or use unstructured bags that can be trivially represented as trees. Most types of linguistic feature systems are at least in part hierarchical and representable in tree form. Because so many linguistic phenomena are manifest as frequent subtrees within hierarchical representations that are motivated by linguistic theories, efficient methods for extracting frequent subtrees from treebanks are therefore potentially very valuable to corpus and computational linguistics.

2 Previous and Related Work

Tree mining research is a subset of graph mining focused specifically on rooted, directed acyclic graphs. Although there is research into extracting frequent subtrees from free (unrooted and undirected) trees, free tree mining usually proceeds by deciding which node in any particular tree will be treated as a root, and then treating it as if it was a rooted and directed tree (Chi et al., 2003).

Research on frequent subtree discovery generally draws heavily on early work by Zaki (2002) and Asai et al. (2002) who roughly simultaneously began applying the *Apriori* algorithm to frequent tree discovery (Agrawal et al., 1993). For a summary of *Apriori*, which is widely used in data mining, and a short review of its extensive literature, see Kotsiantis and Kanellopoulos (2006). A broad summary of algorithms for frequent subtree mining can be found in Chi et al. (2004).

Research into frequent substructures in computational linguistics is quite limited. The *Data Oriented Processing* model (Bod et al., 2003) along with its extension into machine translation - the *Data Oriented Translation* model (Poutsma, 2000; Poutsma, 2003; Hearne and Way, 2003) - is the most developed approach to using frequent subtree statistics to do natural language processing. There is also growing work, largely stemming out of DOP research, into subtree alignment in bilingual parsed treebanks as an aid in the development of statistical and example-based machine translations systems (Hassan et al., 2006; Tinsley et al., 2007; Zhechev and Way, 2008).

3 Key concepts

Among the key concepts in tree mining is the difference between *bottom-up subtrees*, *induced subtrees* and *embedded subtrees*. A *bottom-up* subtree T' of a tree T is a subtree where, for every node in T', if its corresponding node in T has children, then all those children are also in T'. An *induced*

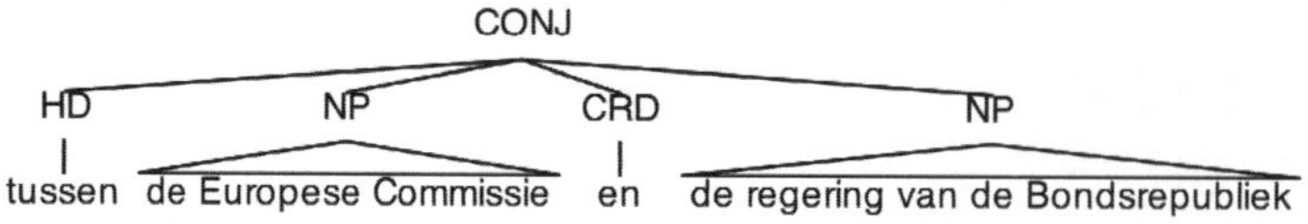

Figure 3: *"...between the European Commission and the government of the [German] Federal Republic..."* This structure is a subtree of one of the sentences in the Alpino corpus of Dutch where a node has two children with the same labels - two NPs. This often occurs with conjunctions and can prevent the algorithm from discovering some frequent subtrees.

subtree T' of T is a subtree where every node in T' is either the root of T' or its parent in T is also its parent in T'. An *embedded* subtree T' of T is a subtree where every node in T' is either the root of T' or its parent in T' is one of its ancestors in T. See Figure 2 for an example of these different types of subtrees.

Linear time solutions exist for finding all frequent *bottom-up* subtrees in a treebank because this problem can be transformed into finding all frequent substrings in a string, a problem for which fast solutions are well known (Luccio et al., 2001; Luccio et al., 2004).

Solutions for *induced* and *embedded* subtrees draw heavily on Zaki (2002) (the *TreeMiner* algorithm) and Asai et al. (2002) (the *FREQT* algorithm), both of whom propose *Apriori*-style approaches. This type of solution has the general property that runtime is proportionate to the size of the *output*: the sum of the number of times each frequent subtree appears in the treebank. This is not readily predictable, because the number and frequencies of subtrees is not formally determinable from the size of the treebank and can grow very rapidly.

3.1 Ordered and unordered trees

TreeMiner/FREQT approaches require all trees to be *ordered* so that the nodes of any frequent subtree will always appear in the same order every time it appears. The children of each non-leaf node are sorted into a lexicographic order, *but this only guarantees that frequent subtrees will always appear with the same ordering if no node has more than one non-leaf child node with the same label.* This is not uniformly true of natural language parse trees, as shown in Figure 3. Solutions exist that remove this limitation - notably Chi et al. (2003) - but they come at a significantly increased processing cost.

3.2 Closed trees

Given that this type of approach to subtree discovery has runtime bounds proportionate to the unpredictable size of the output, one way to keep subtree discovery within manageable bounds is to restrict the output. Many of the frequent trees present in treebanks are *redundant*, since they are identically distributed with other, larger trees, as in Figure 4.

If a corpus has a sequence of tokens $ABCDE$ that appears f times, then that corpus also contains at least f instances of the sequences A, B, C, D, E, AB, BC, CD, DE, ABC, BCD, CDE, $ABCD$, and $BCDE$. If any of these sequences appears *only* in the context of $ABCDE$, then they are *redundant*, because they have the same count and distribution as the longer sequence $ABCDE$.

If a set of sequences is *identically distributed* - appearing in all the same places - then the longest of those sequences is called a *closed sequence*. In more formal terms, a sequence S that appears f times in a corpus is called closed if and only if there is no prefix or suffix a such that aS or Sa also appears f times in the corpus. This definition extends easily to trees: A subtree T in a treebank is closed if and only if there is no node that can be added to it to produce a new subtree T' such that the frequency of T' is equal to the frequency of T. All subtrees in a corpus are either closed subtrees or are subtrees of closed subtrees that appear in exactly the same places in the treebank. The set of closed subtrees in a treebank is the smallest set of subtrees that encompasses all the distributions of subtrees in the treebank. Any subtree that is not in the list of closed subtrees is either a subtree of one of the closed subtrees that appears exactly as often and in all the same places, or does not appear in the treebank at all.

There are algorithms that extract *only* closed subtrees from treebanks - notably Chi et al. (2005a) - and thereby increase their speed dramatically without producing less

(a) The common subtree of the two parse trees in Figure 1: "naar huis gaan"

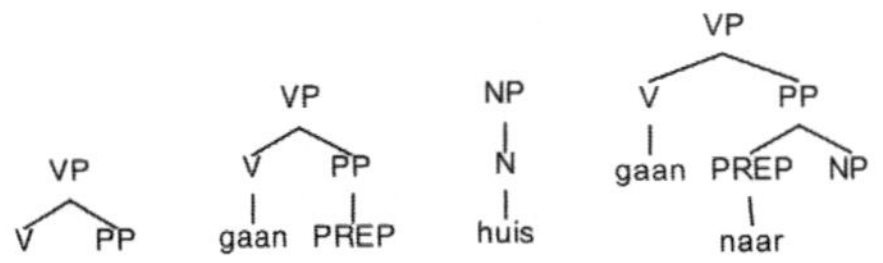

(b) Redundant subtrees of tree (a). There are many more such structures.

Figure 4: Closed and non-closed subtrees in *just* the two sentences in Figure 1. In a larger treebank, some of these might not be redundant.

information, since any non-closed subtree present in the treebank is a subtree of a closed one and shares its distribution.

4 Algorithm and data structures

The algorithm used in this research is an extension of the *TreeMiner* algorithm (Zaki, 2002), modified to extract only closed subtrees. It takes a minimum frequency threshold as a parameter and extracts only those subtrees which are closed and whose frequency is at least equal to the threshold. This algorithm suffers from the same shortcoming of Zaki's original algorithm in that it is only guaranteed to find all frequent subtrees among *ordered* trees where no node has two non-leaf children with the same label.

It has one novel property which it appears not to share with any other subtree extraction scheme to date: This algorithm outputs subtrees in order from the most frequent to the least. Given the difficulty of predicting in advance how large the output will be, and the large size of many natural language data sources, this can be a real boon. If output size or memory usage grow too large, or too much time has passed, the program can be stopped while still guaranteeing that it has not missed any more frequent subtree than the last one outputted.

This section can only very briefly describe the algorithm.

4.1 Definitions

A treebank is any collection of trees where each node bears a label and each node is uniquely addressable in such a way that the address a_n of a node n is always greater than the address a_p of its parent p. This is accomplished by representing all trees as *ordered depth-first canonical strings*. (See Chi et al. (2005b).)

Each appearance of a subtree within a treebank is characterized by the address of its root in the treebank and the address of its rightmost node. This data structure will be called a *Hit*. The list of all *Hits* corresponding to all the appearances of some subtree in the treebank will be called a *HitList*. So, for each subtree there is a corresponding *HitList* and vice-versa. *HitLists* are always constructed in sequential order, from first instance in the treebank to last, and can never contain duplicates.

We will define the function *queueKey* on *HitLists* to output an array of four numbers in a specific order, given a *HitList* as input:

1. The number of *Hits* in the *HitList*.
2. The distance from the address of the root of the first *Hit* to the *end* of the treebank.
3. The distance from the address of the rightmost node of the first *Hit* to the end of the treebank.
4. The number of nodes in the subtree associated with that *HitList*.

These keys are sortable and designed to ensure that *HitLists* from a single treebank can always be sorted into a fixed order such that, for two *HitLists* A and B, if $A > B$ then:

1. A has more *Hits* than B.
2. If A has the same number of *Hits* as B, then the root of the first *Hit* in A precedes the root of the first *Hit* in B.
3. If A's first root is identical to B's, then the address of the rightmost node of the first *Hit* in A precedes the address of the rightmost node of the first *Hit* in B.
4. If the first *Hit* in A is exactly the same the first *Hit* in B, then the subtree associated with A has more nodes than the subtree associated with B.

A *self-sorting queue* is any data structure that stores key-data pairs and stores the keys in order from greatest to least. The data structure used to implement a self-sorting queue in this research is an *AVL tree* (Adelson-Velskii and Landis, 1962), however, other structures could equally well have been used. The self-sorting queue will be used to maintain a sorted list of *HitLists*, sorted in the order of their *queueKeys* as described above.

4.2 Initialization

Fix a minimum frequency threshold t for the subtrees you wish to extract from the treebank. Start processing by initializing one *HitList* for each unique label in the treebank with the set of *Hits* that corresponds to each occurrence of that label. We will treat each as a *HitList* with an associated subtree containing only one node. This set is constructed in linear time by iterating over all the nodes in the treebank.

Of the initial *HitLists*, throw away all those with fewer than threshold frequency t *Hits* in them. The remaining *HitLists* are inserted into the self-sorting queue.

4.3 Extracting induced subtrees without checking for closure

Extracting *all* the subtrees above a fixed frequency - not just the closed subtrees - in order from the most frequent to the least, proceeds as follows:

1. **Initialize** as described in Section 4.2.
2. **Pop** the top *HitList* hl and its associated subtree s from the queue.
3. **Extend** hl:
   (a) **Visit** each *Hit* in hl and find all the nodes that can be added to the right side of s to produce new induced subtrees.
   (b) **Generate** new *HitLists* for all subtrees that extend s by one node to the right.
   (c) **Test** each new *HitList* to make sure it appears more than threshold frequency t times, and if it does, insert it into the queue.
   (d) **Output** s and hl.
4. **Repeat** until the queue is empty.

This is essentially identical to the *TreeMiner* and *FREQT* algorithms already published by Zaki (2002) and by Asai et al. (2002), except that it outputs frequent subtrees in order from the most frequent to the least.

4.4 Extracting only closed induced subtrees

By controlling the order in which *HitLists* reach the top of the queue, it is possible to efficiently prevent any subtree which is not a closed subtree or a prefix of a closed subtree from being extended, and to prevent any subtree that is not closed from being outputted.

Every subtree with a frequency of f is either a closed subtree, a prefix of a closed subtree that also has a frequency of f and can be constructed by adding more nodes to the right, or is a redundant non-closed subtree that need not be extended or stored. Consider a redundant, non-closed subtree x and a closed subtree or prefix of a closed subtree y which has the same frequency, and has the same set of addresses for the rightmost node of each of its appearances in the treebank. The sort order of the self-sorting queue (see Section 4.1) ensures that if a prefix of a closed subtree y is in the queue and some subtree of it x is also in the queue, then y is closer to the top of the queue than x is. Furthermore, it can be proven that the prefix of a closed subtree with the same distribution as any non-closed, redundant subtree will be generated, inserted into the queue, and removed from the top of the queue before x can reach the top.

So, to prevent x from being extended or stored, all that is necessary is to check to see there is some closed subtree or prefix of a closed subtree y such that:

- y has already been at the top of the queue.
- y has the same frequency as x.
- The set of rightmost nodes of every *Hit* in y's *HitList* is identical to the set of rightmost nodes of every *Hit* in x's *HitList*.
- x is a subtree of y

This can be checked by constructing a hash value for each *HitList* based on its frequency and some subset of the set of rightmost nodes of every *Hit*. In our experiments, we used only the first node of each HitList. If x's hash value matches some previously processed y's hash value, then check if x is a subtree of y and reject it if it is. The result is to only instantiate closed subtrees and their prefixes, and subtrees which are one node extensions of closed subtrees and their prefixes.

Like *TreeMiner*, worst case space and time bounds are proportionate to the number of subtrees instantiated and the number of times each appears in the corpus. This is smaller than the worst case bounds for *TreeMiner* because it does not instantiate all frequent subtrees. There is additional approximately constant time processing for each instantiated subtree to check for closure and to store it in the self-sorting queue. At the lowest frequency thresholds, this can take up the majority of runtime, but is generally negligible at high frequencies.

5 Results

We applied this algorithm to a parsed and hand-corrected 7137 sentence subset of the Alpino Treebank of Dutch.[1] The average sentence length in this small treebank is roughly 20 words, and the corresponding trees have an average of approximately 32 nodes for a total of 230,673 nodes. With the minimum frequency set to 2, this algorithm extracted 342,401 closed subtrees in about 2000 seconds on a conventional workstation running Linux[2]. The same implementation but without testing for closure - which makes this algorithm equivalent to *TreeMiner* - extracted some 4.2 million trees in roughly 11,000 seconds. Closed tree extraction contrasts quite favorably to extraction without closure, even over a small dataset.

Min. Freq. Threshold	Subtrees extracted	Runtime
2	342401	1952.33s
3	243484	1004.30s
4	176885	588.58s
5	134495	402.26s
8	72732	209.51s
10	53842	163.22s
15	30681	112.39s
20	20610	85.24s
30	11516	66.05s
40	7620	54.14s
50	5549	47.98s
60	4219	43.24s
70	3365	39.97s

Table 1: Runtime and closed trees extracted at different minimum frequency thresholds, using the 7137 sentence sample of the Alpino Treebank.

Runtime and the number of trees produced fall very dramatically as thresholds rise - so much so that setting the minimum frequency to 3 instead of 2 *halved* the runtime. This pattern is characteristic of a power law distribution like Zipf's law. (See Table 1 and Figure 5.) Given the pervasiveness of power law distributions in word frequencies, it should perhaps not be surprising to discover that frequent closed subtrees in treebanks are similarly distributed. This research may be the first effort to empirically support such a conclusion, although admittedly only very tentatively.

Sentences	Total nodes	Subtrees extracted	Runtime
2500	94528	37607	61.08s
5000	189170	98538	260.91s
10000	379980	264616	1495.19s
15000	573629	477750	3829.29s
20000	763502	704018	7998.57s

Table 2: Runtime and closed trees extracted from automatically parsed samples of the *Europarl* Dutch corpus, keeping the minimum frequency threshold constant at 5 for all sizes of treebank.

To test the impact of varying the size of the treebank, but keeping the minimum frequency threshold constant, we used a section of the Dutch portion of the *Europarl corpus* (Koehn, 2005) automatically parsed using the Alpino Dutch parser (van Noord, 2006) without any manual correction. Random samples of 2500, 5000, 10000, 15000 and 20000 sentences were selected, and all subtrees of frequency 5 or higher were extracted from each, as summarized in Table 2. As treebank size grows, the number of subtrees extracted at the same minimum frequency threshold, and the time and memory used extracting them, grows exponentially. This is in sharp contrast to algorithms that extract frequently recurring strings, which increase linearly in time and memory usage as the data grows.

However, if the minimum frequency threshold is kept constant as a proportion of the size of the treebank, then the number of trees extracted remains roughly constant and the time and memory used to extract them grows roughly linearly with the size of the treebank. Table 3 shows the result for different sized random samples of the parsed *Europarl* corpus.

Lastly, since this algorithm has known difficulties when presented with trees where more than one non-leaf child of a node can have the same

[1] `http://www.let.rug.nl/vannoord/trees/`

[2] A Dell Precision 490 workstation with an Intel Dual-Core Xeon processor and 8GB of memory. The algorithm was not implemented to use two processors.

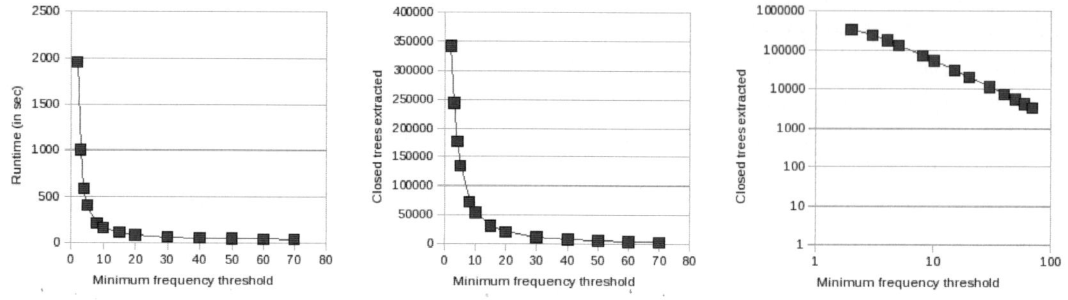

(a) Runtime by minimum frequency threshold.

(b) Subtrees extracted by minimum frequency threshold.

(c) Log-log plot of (b).

Figure 5: Runtime (a) and subtrees extracted (b) from the Alpino sample using different minimum frequency thresholds. Figure (c) is a log-log plot of (b). Figure (c) looks close to a straight line, which is characteristic of a power law distribution.

Sents	Total nodes	Min. Freq. Thres.	Subtrees extracted	Run time
2500	99323	5	42905	72.95s
5000	194736	10	42783	122.18s
10000	382022	20	41988	216.23s
15000	574632	30	43078	325.86s
20000	770240	40	44416	435.19s

Table 3: Runtime and closed trees extracted from automatically parsed samples of the *Europarl* Dutch corpus, with minimum frequency thresholds kept roughly constant as a proportion of the sample size.

label (see sections 3.1 and 4), we attempted to determine if this problem is marginal or pervasive. The 7137 sentence Alpino Treebank sample contains 3833 nodes with more than one non-leaf child node with identical labels or roughly 1.7% of all nodes. Furthermore, these nodes are present in 2666 sentences - some 37% of all sentences! This is a very large minority.

In order to estimate the effect this phenomenon has on the extraction of closed trees, we looked for outputted trees that are not closed by comparing the *HitLists* of all outputted trees to all other outputted trees with the same frequency. Table 4 shows the number of trees with identical distributions to other outputted trees - i.e. trees that appeared to be closed to this algorithm, but in fact are not. The number was surprisingly large, but distributed overwhelmingly at the very lowest frequencies.

Min. Freq. Threshold	Non-closed trees	as a % of all trees extracted
2	2874	0.84%
3	693	0.28%
4	225	0.13%
5	101	0.08%
8	18	0.02%
10	11	0.02%
15	6	0.02%
20	3	0.01%
30	0	0.00%

Table 4: Non-closed trees from the 7137 sentence sample of the Alpino Treebank, produced erroneously as closed trees because of repeated labels. There were no non-closed trees extracted at frequencies over 30.

6 Conclusions

The algorithm presented above opens up treebanks and annotated corpora to much more detailed quantitative analysis, and extends the tools available for data-driven natural language processing. This makes a number of new applications possible. We are developing treebank indexing for fast retrieval by tree similarity, in order to make full treebanks available for example-based parsing and machine translation in real time. This algorithm also has applications in constructing concordances of syntactic, morphological and semantic structures - types of information that are not traditionally amenable to indexing. Furthermore, statistical models of natural language data can take advantage of comprehensive subtree censuses to become fully syntax-aware, instead of relying on *bag of words* and *n-gram* models.

However, there are a number of drawbacks and caveats that must be highlighted.

Runtime, memory usage and output size are difficult to estimate in advance. This is mitigated in part by the order in which subtrees are outputted, making it possible to extract only the most frequent subset of subtrees given fixed time and space bounds. Empirically, it appears that resource requirements and output size can also be estimated by sampling, if minimum frequency thresholds can be kept constant as a proportion of total treebank size.

The formalisms used in most theories of syntax allow nodes to have multiple non-leaf children with the same labels. Although errors caused by non-unique labels are overwhelmingly present only among the lowest frequency subtrees, errors appear often enough to pose a non-negligible problem for this algorithm.

We are investigating the degree to which this can be mitigated by making different choices of linguistic formalism. Syntax trees that contain only binary trees - for example, those constructed using *Chomsky Normal Form* rules (Jurafsky and Martin, 2009) - cannot have identically labelled non-leaf children, but must suffer some loss of generality in their frequent subtrees because if it. Other theories can reduce the size of this source of error, notably dependency syntax which often uses fewer abstract labels (Tesnière, 1959; Mel'čuk, 1988; Sugayama and Hudson, 2006), but will most likely be poor sources of highly general rules as a consequence.

Furthermore, tree mining algorithms exist that eliminate this problem, but at some cost. We are investigating a hybrid solution to the non-unique label problem that identifies only those subtrees where more resource-intensive closure checking is necessary. This will guarantee the correct extraction of closed subtrees in all cases while minimizing the additional processing burden.

Among the open problems suggested by this research is the degree to which the empirical results obtained above are dependent on the language of the underlying data and the linguistic formalisms used to produce treebanks. Different linguistic theories use different abstractions and use their abstract categories differently. This has an immediate effect on the number of nodes in a treebank and on the topology of the trees. Some theories produce more compact trees than others. Some produce deep trees, others produce shallow trees. It is likely that the formalisms used in treebanks have a pervasive influence on the number and kind of frequent subtrees extracted. By doing quantitative research on the structures found in treebanks, it may become possible to make reliable operational choices about the linguistic formalisms used in treebanks on the basis of the kinds of structures one hopes to get out of them.

Acknowledgments

This research is supported by the AMASS++ Project[3] directly funded by the *Institute for the Promotion of Innovation by Science and Technology in Flanders (IWT)* (SBO IWT 060051).

References

Georgiy M. Adelson-Velskii and Yevgeniy M. Landis. 1962. An algorithm for the organization of information. *Proceedings of the USSR Academy of Sciences*, 146(2):263–266.

Rakesh Agrawal, Tomasz Imielinski and Arun Swami. 1993. Mining association rules between sets of items in large databases. *Proceedings of the 1993 ACM SIGMOD International Conference on Management of Data*, 207–216.

Tatsuya Asai, Kenji Abe, Shinji Kawasoe, Hiroki Arimura, Hiroshi Sakamoto and Setsuo Arikawa. 2002. Efficient substructure discovery from large semi-structured data. *Proceedings of the Second SIAM International Conference on Data Mining*, 158–174.

Rens Bod, Khalil Sima'an and Remko Scha, editors. 2003. *Data-Oriented Parsing*. CLSI Publicatons, Stanford, CA.

Yun Chi, Yirong Yang and Richard R. Muntz. 2003. Indexing and Mining Free Trees. *UCLA Computer Science Department Technical Report No. 030041.*

Yun Chi, Richard R. Muntz, Siegfried Nijssen and Joost N. Kok. 2004. Frequent Subtree Mining – An Overview. *Fundamenta Informaticae*, 66(1-2):161–198.

Yun Chi, Yi Xia, Yirong Yang and Richard R. Muntz. 2005a. Mining Closed and Maximal Frequent Subtrees from Databases of Labeled Rooted Trees. *IEEE Transactions on Knowledge and Data Engineering*, 17(2):190–202.

[3] `http://www.cs.kuleuven.be/~liir/projects/amass/`

Yun Chi, Yi Xia, Yirong Yang and Richard R. Muntz. 2005b. Canonical forms for labelled trees and their applications in frequent subtree mining. *IEEE Transactions on Knowledge and Data Engineering*, 8(2):203–234.

Hany Hassan, Mary Hearne, Khalil Sima'an and Andy Way. 2006. Syntactic Phrase-Based Statistical Machine Translation. *Proceedings of the IEEE 2006 Workshop on Spoken Language Translation*, 238–241.

Mary Hearne and Andy Way. 2003. Seeing the Wood for the Trees: Data-Oriented Translation. *Proceedings of the 9th Machine Translation Summit*, 165–172.

Daniel Jurafsky and James H. Martin. 2009. *Speech and Language Processing*. Pearson Prentice Hall, Upper Saddle River, NJ.

Philipp Koehn. 2005. Europarl: A Parallel Corpus for Statistical Machine Translation. *Proceedings of the 10th Machine Translation Summit*, 79–86.

Sotiris Kotsiantis and Dimitris Kanellopoulos. 2006. Association Rules Mining: A Recent Overview. *GESTS International Transactions on Computer Science and Engineering*, 32(1):71–82.

Fabrizio Luccio, Antonio Enriquez, Pablo Rieumont and Linda Pagli. 2001. Exact Rooted Subtree Matching in Sublinear Time. *Università Di Pisa Technical Report TR-01-14*.

Fabrizio Luccio, Antonio Enriquez, Pablo Rieumont and Linda Pagli. 2004. Bottom-up subtree isomorphism for unordered labeled trees. *Università Di Pisa Technical Report TR-04-13*.

Edward M. McCreight. 1976. A Space-Economical Suffix Tree Construction Algorithm. *Journal of the Association for Computing Machinery*, 23(2):262–272.

Igor A. Mel'čuk. 1988. *Dependency Syntax: Theory and Practice*. State University of New York Press, Albany, NY.

Arjen Poutsma. 2000. Data-Oriented Translation. *Proc. of the 18th International Conference on Computational Linguistics (COLING 2000)*, 635–641.

Arjen Poutsma. 2003. Machine Translation with Tree-DOP. *Data-Oriented Parsing*, 63–81.

Deepak Ravichandran and Eduard Hovy 2002. Learning surface text patterns for a question answering system. *Proceedings of the 40th Annual Meeting of the Association for Computational Linguistics (ACL-02)*, 41–47.

Kensei Sugayama and Richard Hudson, editors. 2006. *Word Grammar: New Perspectives on a Theory of Language Structure*. Continuum International Publishing, London.

Lucien Tesnière. 1959. *Eléments de la syntaxe structurale*. Editions Klincksieck, Paris.

John Tinsley, Mary Hearne and Andy Way. 2007. Exploiting Parallel Treebanks for use in Statistical Machine Translation. *Proceedings of Treebanks and Linguistic Theories (TLT '07), Bergen, Norway* 175–187.

Gertjan van Noord. 2006. At last parsing is now operational. *Verbum Ex Machina. Actes de la 13e conférence sur le traitement automatique des langues naturelles (TALN6)*, 20–42.

Peter Weiner. 1973 Linear pattern matching algorithm. *14th Annual IEEE Symposium on Switching and Automata Theory*, 1–11.

Mohammed J. Zaki. 2002. Efficiently mining frequent trees in a forest. *Proceedings of the 8th ACM SIGKDD International Conference on Knowledge Discovery and Data Mining*, 1021–1035.

Ventsislav Zhechev and Andy Way. 2008. Automatic Generation of Parallel Treebanks. *Proceedings of the 22nd International Conference on Computational Linguistics (COLING 2008)*, 1105–1112.

Author Index